Maximum Influence

The 12 Universal Laws of
Power Persuasion

Second Edition

Kurt W. Mortensen

AMACOM

American Management Association

New York • Atlanta • Brussels • Chicago • Mexico City • San Francisco
Shanghai • Tokyo • Toronto • Washington, D. C.

Bulk discounts available. For details visit:
www.amacombooks.org/go/specialsales
Or contact special sales:
Phone: 800-250-5308
E-mail: specialsls@amanet.org
View all the AMACOM titles at: www.amacombooks.org
American Management Association: www.amanet.org

This publication is designed to provide accurate and authoritative information in regard to the subject matter covered. It is sold with the understanding that the publisher is not engaged in rendering legal, accounting, or other professional service. If legal advice or other expert assistance is required, the services of a competent professional person should be sought.

Library of Congress Cataloging-in-Publication Data

Mortensen, Kurt W.
  Maximum influence : the 12 universal laws of power persuasion / Kurt W. Mortensen.
— Second edition.
     pages cm
  Includes bibliographical references and index.
  ISBN-13: 978-0-8144-3209-9
  ISBN-10: 0-8144-3209-3   5209 1062 8/13
  1. Persuasion (Psychology) 2. Influence (Psychology) 3. Success—Psychological
aspects. I. Title.
  BF637.P4M67 2013
  153.8'52—dc23
                                                              2012047022

About AMA

American Management Association (www.amanet.org) is a world leader in talent development, advancing the skills of individuals to drive business success. Our mission is to support the goals of individuals and organizations through a complete range of products and services, including classroom and virtual seminars, webcasts, webinars, podcasts, conferences, corporate and government solutions, business books and research. AMA's approach to improving performance combines experiential learning—learning through doing—with opportunities for ongoing professional growth at every step of one's career journey.

Printing number

10 9 8 7 6 5 4 3 2 1

Contents

Foreword

Napoleon Hill said, "Persuasion is the magic ingredient that will help you to forge ahead in your profession or business—and to achieve happy and lasting personal relationships." As we all know, persuasion is the skill of the ultraprosperous. It is how people gain power and influence. It is how people create staggering wealth—how businesses thrive, how books are published, how properties are purchased, and how websites sell millions of dollars worth of product. Persuasion is the lifeblood of powerful and effective day-to-day living. The art of persuasion is what makes the world turn.

I have known Kurt Mortensen for years. A master of persuasion himself, he exudes every quality and possesses every skill set forth in this book. Through this book, Kurt has provided the most complete, comprehensive work on persuasion and influence I have ever read. Nowhere in persuasion literature have I ever seen the art broken down into such thorough and easy-to-understand concepts, covering every aspect of persuasion imaginable. Never before has it been so easy to understand human behavior and how to use it to your advantage. Based on true-life examples and exhaustive psychological and sociological research, Kurt imparts of his wisdom, knowledge, and experience with insight, wit, and enthusiasm.

The powerful, time-tested, and proven techniques in the following pages will equip the reader with the tools necessary to make profound life changes. These very laws of persuasion have made me millions of dollars and have helped thousands of others apply them in both their business and personal lives to strengthen relationships, to create wealth, to transform careers, to influence lives for the better. Each one of the laws discussed will improve your success dramatically, even doubling and tripling your income. I only wish I had had this kind of information earlier in my career! It would have limited the number of lessons I had to learn at the school of hard knocks.

One of the number one skills you must learn in building your financial empires is persuasion. Reading this book will be a truly life-changing influence for anyone who applies the principles so thoroughly and carefully outlined. *Maximum Influence* is a must for the library of anyone who wants to be in control of all aspects of his or her life. Reading this book will not only make you a student of persuasion, but also a learned scholar.

Robert G. Allen
Author of *Nothing Down, Creating Wealth,*
Multiple Streams of Income, and
Coauthor of *The One-Minute Millionaire*

Acknowledgments

A *big* thanks to all the customers, clients, partners, and employees who helped make *Maximum Influence* and Advanced Influence a reality. I want to express my love and appreciation to my loving wife Denita. She is my light and the main reason for my success. I also want to thank my children, Brooke, Mitchell, Bailey, and Madison, for their love, laughter, and support throughout this project and throughout my life. Family is what makes life a joy and our dreams worth pursuing. I also want to express special thanks to my colleagues and students, who made this research possible.

Introduction

My Persuasion Journey began with a university education and a degree. I then went off to a graduate school to master the world of business. Upon graduation, I was thrust into a management situation where I had to manage salespeople, motivate customer service, and coordinate with other department managers.

Then the shocker hit. I had learned the important business topics in graduate school, but that learning didn't seem to matter to real human beings. Although what I had learned was valuable information and important for business, it did not prepare me for the human side of business. I had to learn how to deal with human emotions. I needed to know how to persuade other managers to help me, to influence and inspire others, and to increase sales. Sure I could read a balance sheet, understand accounting, and comprehend economics, but I had not mastered the priceless skill of persuasion that studies show is 85 percent of our success in business.[1] I soon found that some managers would resist a great idea just because it was not their idea. Some people would clash just because of their personalities. Coworkers would get upset with one other for the strangest things. Ah, the emotional side of business!

In short, I discovered that we all persuade and influence. We all have to work with other people for a living. I realized that, if I could not influence others or help them influence themselves, the workday would be long, and productivity would suffer. I also realized that the ability to persuade and influence was good time management: Getting others to want to do what you want them to do and to do it the first time.

Then my Persuasion Journey led me to become an entrepreneur, and these skills became ten times more critical. I had to learn how to market, sell, do Web promotion, get referrals, and convince others that I was their best choice. These experiences pushed me to research and master the world of persuasion, negotiation, and influence.

INFLUENCE: AN ABSOLUTE MUST FOR:

Sales professionals	Parents
Business managers	Negotiators
Marketers/advertisers	Leaders
Lawyers	Teachers
Entrepreneurs	Everyone (We *all* influence.)

Persuasion permeates every aspect of our lives. How can someone be an effective manager, entrepreneur, or sales person without persuasion skills? We have all seen the old style of management: Do it or you're fired. Sure, this results in short-term compliance, but it also results in long-term resentment and mistrust. It hurts people's ability to lead, and it definitely does not result in effective, long-term persuasion. So I dedicated my life to finding the powerful, honorable, win-win forms of persuasion, negotiation, and influence. These missing ingredients are contained in *Maximum Influence.* Learn them and use them, and you'll change your world and your income.

I appreciate all the feedback from leaders, salespeople, entrepreneurs, and marketers to update and revise the Laws of Persuasion. My goal has been to help persuaders discover that the old techniques no longer work. The 12 Laws of Persuasion stand true. In this second edition of *Maximum Influence*, I have updated the studies, fine-tuned the applications, and reveal additional cutting-edge persuasion and influence techniques.

Persuasion and influence have dramatically changed in the past 20 years. Social media have changed the way we communicate. Your consumers, your prospects, and your customers all have changed. According to *Advertising Age* magazine, they are bombarded with more than 5,000 persuasive messages a day. Roselli, Skelly, and Mackie point out that "even by conservative estimates, the average person is exposed to 300 to 400 persuasive media messages a day from the mass media alone."[2] In this digital age, people are better educated and more skeptical than ever. If you use the same outdated tactics you learned years ago, you'll lose your ability to influence. Have you ever had potential customers who you knew needed your product or service? They wanted your product or service, they could afford it, but they still didn't buy from you. What happened? It was a perfect fit for both parties. As you master persuasion and influence, you will understand your prospects' mindset and their decision-making process, and you can help them persuade themselves.

Through research, I have found that most people use only three or four persuasive techniques. This is like trying to chop down a tree with a pocketknife because that is the only tool you have. When you follow the steps I outline in the following chapters, you will be equipped with countless techniques, strategies, insights, and tools to influence anyone in any situation. You will find yourself starting to exude Maximum Influence.

To help you as you learn the techniques and strategies of Maximum Influence, let me outline what I call the Five P's of Success. The first *P* is your *psyche*, or mindset, the mental aspect of the game (self-persuasion). It's a critical skill for all successful people. You will not be able to achieve your goals until you can visualize them. The universe will not reward you physically until you believe in your goals mentally. All the best techniques and tools will not help you until you first believe in yourself. Unfortunately, most of the people we know tend to bring us down. When you tell them about your dreams and the things you want to accomplish in life, they can be very discouraging. They will give you the list of all the reasons you can't do it.

When you have the right mindset, you know where you're going and what you want to accomplish. Anything that people say is not going to matter. The right psyche involves knowing what you want and having a plan to get it. When your mindset is in its proper place, you will always follow your heart and find untapped persistence. This motivation is the driving force that determines why people are successful.

The second *P* is for *presence*. Have you ever noticed how some people can influence others effortlessly? Have you seen them enter a room and everyone notices? People instinctively like them and want to be influenced by them. They command attention and influence with everyone they meet. This is the power of presence. Presence is a function of confidence and charisma. A good presence attracts people to you. They *want* you to persuade them.

We have all met charismatic people. They are captivating and inspiring.

They instantly command our attention, and we tend to listen to every word out of their mouths. Presence is the ability to empower and influence to believe in you and trust you. In essence, presence is a source of empowerment, encouragement, and inspiration. You don't have to be born with charisma. Charisma is a skill that can be learned.

The next *P* is *personal development*. All top producers have a personal development program. There is a direct relationship between your personal development program and your income. Personal success expert Brian Tracy says, "If you can get yourself to read thirty minutes a day, you're going to double your income every year." I know from personal experience that this technique works! Millionaires have libraries in their homes. Studies consistently demonstrate that those who are learning and growing every day are more optimistic about life. They are more enthusiastic about where they're going and what they hope to accomplish. Those who aren't learning and growing every day become negative, pessimistic, and doubtful about themselves and their future. Turn your car into an income center by listening to educational and motivational material. When you're at home, turn off the TV and read a book.

There are two ways to learn in life: You can learn by trial and error, attempting to figure things out on your own. That route is expensive. Or you can learn from somebody else, who's already been there and done it. Somebody has already figured out everything you need to learn about life and has written a book, created a seminar (or webinar), or put it on audio. So invest in your future by investing in your personal development.

The fourth *P* is *passion*. More than anything, passion will allow you to recruit the hearts and minds of your audience. Do you have passion and heartfelt conviction for your product or service? We love people who are excited, animated, and full of passion. When you have passion for something, you're excited about it, you want to share it with the world. When you have passion "no" does not slow you down, and the fear of rejection becomes a nonissue. You're excited to convert as many people as possible to your cause. Passion alone can be effective in swaying opinion and getting people to support your product or service. Passion springs from a combination of belief, enthusiasm, and emotion. Find and share your passion for your product, service, or cause.

The fifth and final *P*—and the one that comprises most of this book—is *persuasion*. Spend a little time each day learning and mastering the world of persuasion and influence. The basic aim of Maximum Influence is to get what you want when you want it and, in the process, to win friends and help people want to do what you want them to do. Anyone can spit out a list of features and benefits or demonstrate their product. When you use Maximum Influence, you draw people to you and are able to attract more customers. We want you to get customers to beg for your product or service and to win customers for life. And that's exactly what Maximum Influence will do.

ADDITIONAL RESOURCES

For further information on any of the topics covered in this book, to take your Persuasion IQ Assessment, or for additional training or keynotes based on Maximum Influence, go to www.maximuminfluence.com.

CHAPTER 1

The Power of Persuasion

Key to Success

Study the art of persuasion. Practice it. Develop an understanding of its profound value across all aspects of life.   —DONALD TRUMP

Has this happened to you? You are talking to a potential client, a prospect, or a manager of another department. In your mind what you are proposing is a no-brainer, and it will take only a few minutes to influence the other person to do what you want done. It is a perfect fit and will solve the problem. The more you talk, the more they resist. What happened? Why weren't you able to persuade them?

Or even worse, have you even met someone who did not seem very smart but was making ten times more money than you? Someone who didn't seem very sharp but got your promotion. Didn't seem that sharp, but got all the business. Didn't seem that bright, but could persuade anyone to do anything? What do they have that you don't have? They have mastered the *power of persuasion*.

Do you realize that the best way to double your income is to double your persuasion skills? Think about it: Twice as many people will call you back and say yes. This vital success skill will permeate every aspect of your life. Have you ever wondered why two people with the same education, the same contacts, the same IQ, and the same experience get dramatically different results? Have you ever noticed how some people can persuade without effort? Have you seen people always get what they want because everyone around them wants to give it to them? This is the *power of persuasion.*

Have you ever tried to persuade to someone who wanted, needed, liked, and could afford your product or proposal? Yet they still said no. What if you had a special app on your phone that, when activated, would instantly influence them to your point of view? What would that app be worth to you? Persuasion is not as easy as having an app, but it is a skill that can easily be mastered.

Understanding the laws of persuasion, motivation, and influence will put you in life's driver's seat. Everything you want—or will want—in life comes from the power of influence. I am going to reveal the secrets of influence and the science of persuasion. You will be able to persuade and influence with complete accuracy. You will gain instant influence over people and inspire others to take action, all while getting exactly what you want from life. You will win people to your way of thinking and will empower yourself with an unshakable confidence. You will triple sales, become a power negotiator, improve as a manager, and increase your results in marketing. The bottom line is that, when you need to persuade someone, it is too late to learn.

As you develop what I call Maximum Influence, you will become magnetic; others will be drawn to you like metal filings, to a powerful magnet. You won't have to force them to do anything. Others are drawn to you and want you to persuade them. Financial, social, and personal success will come to you. Closed doors will swing wide open, and the world of opportunity will open up to you. The life-changing skills and techniques described in this book are based on proven scientific principles. These laws have been developed from countless hours of persuasion research, intercepts, and exhaustive studies of human nature. Now the *complete* list of persuasion tools will be revealed to you.

It is a common misconception that only individuals involved in sales, marketing, or leadership positions need to learn the laws of persuasion. This is simply not true! Sales professionals, business managers, parents, negotiators, lawyers, leaders, speakers, and advertisers all use these skills. Everyone needs persuasion skills, no matter their occupation. We all persuade for a living. What people don't realize is that everyone uses the techniques and tactics of persuasion every day. Mastering communication and understanding human nature are essential life lessons if you want to effectively persuade and influence people. You can't get anywhere in life unless you are able to work with other human beings. It is through your dealing with and influencing others that you achieve success.

This book reveals the 12 Laws of Persuasion and instructs you on how to use these cutting-edge persuasion strategies so that you can gain the influence you need *now*. You'll discover how to make people instinctively like and trust you, an ability that might otherwise take you years to acquire. No longer will you face the unexpected with fear or intimidation. Rather, you will confront it head-on with credibility, control, and confidence.

Central to understanding persuasion is the concept of neutrality. The Laws of Persuasion are neither good nor evil. They simply exist. Just as nuclear energy can be used to create electricity or an atomic bomb, persuasion can be used to create unity or to force compliance. Whether the outcome is good or bad depends on the person using the laws and on how that person applies the techniques of persuasion. Some people want to win at any cost, using any available tactics, including misusing the Laws of Persuasion. These individuals are willing to use guilt, violence, intimidation, bribery, or blackmail to get the desired result.

However, when used properly, persuasion is our best friend. Through persuasion, we create peace agreements, promote fund-raising efforts, and convince motorists to buckle up. Persuasion is the means by which the coach of an underdog team inspires players to win, how managers increase employee performance and morale, or how someone is convinced to purchase your product or service.

PERSUASION: THE ENGINE TO YOUR SUCCESS

Jay Conger wrote in the *Harvard Business Review*, "If there ever was a time for businesspeople to learn the fine art of persuasion, it is now. Gone are the command-and-control days of executives managing by decree."[1] The power of persuasion is of extraordinary and critical importance in today's business world. Nearly every human encounter includes an attempt to gain influence or to persuade others to our way of thinking. We all want to be able to persuade and influence so that others will listen to us and trust us. You don't see large corporations downsizing their sales forces. Sales professionals are assets to the company, not liabilities. Power Persuaders will always find employment, even in the slowest of economies. Great persuaders are always employed. Persuasive entrepreneurs will always get the business. Influential marketers are always in demand. In fact, did you know that more CEOs of major U.S. corporations come from sales and marketing backgrounds than from any other discipline?[2]

Some people define persuasion as being forceful, manipulative, or pushy. Such an assumption is dead wrong. Tactics like these might get instant results and maintain influence for the short term, but Maximum Influence is about getting short-term compliance while maintaining the long-term relationship. Lasting influence isn't derived from calculated maneuvers, deliberate tactics, or intimidation. Rather, proper implementation of the latest persuasion strategies will allow you to influence with integrity. People will naturally and automatically trust you, have confidence in you, and want to be persuaded by you. In short, they will want to do what you want them to do (and will like doing it).

WITH THE RIGHT TOOLS, YOU WILL SUCCEED

Maximum Influence supplies a complete toolbox of effective persuasion techniques. Most people use the same limited persuasion tools over and over, achieving only temporary or even undesired results. We need to open our eyes to the whole toolbox of persuasion and influence. We have all heard the saying: "If the only tool you have is a hammer, you tend to see every problem as a nail." But not every problem is a nail. You can do only so many things with a hammer, right? The art of persuasion must be customized to every group or individual, to every situation or event. It is time to get more persuasion tools. I am sure you could chop down a tree with a hammer, or you might even be able to change a tire with a pair of pliers. Why take ten hours with the wrong tool (the incorrect persuasive technique) when you can do it in two minutes with the right tool.

Modern-day Power Persuaders run into three major factors that make persuasion a greater challenge than it was in the past. First, people have access to more information than they did in any other time in history. With the explosion of the Internet, information is instantly available. We can now find out the cost of a car before we even enter the dealership. The second roadblock to persuasion is that today's consumers are increasingly doubtful and skeptical. Trust is at an all-time low. The number of persuasive arguments we see and hear every day is growing at an alarming rate, and it takes more and more effort to sort out the valid offers from the scams. The third barrier to persuasion is choice. Now, via the Internet, the consumer has access to the world market. In the past, if you had the only bookstore in town, that is where people had to shop. Now, a bookstore owner has to compete with hundreds of bookstores around the globe and with Amazon.com for the same business.

COMMON PERSUASION BLUNDERS

Are you still using the same old tools over and over again without seeing the desired results? Or, worse, are you making the same old mistakes over and over again? What are the top persuasion and influence blunders? Do you want to know what your prospects are complaining about? One of the fun things I get to do with my research is to interview your prospects after they have said no (or lied to you). I get to ask them why they resisted you. I gain access to the truth about why your prospects resisted your solution. Here are the top five blunders.

1. Constant Vomit

We can verbally vomit all the facts, figures, studies, and statistics in the world, but doing so will not convince your prospect or client. Our decisions are comprised of part emotion and part logic. The skill lies in knowing what percentage of each to use. A long list of features and benefits will actually overpersuade your prospects and give them a reason not be persuaded by you. Learn to ask questions instead of vomiting information. My studies show that great persuaders ask three times more questions than the average persuader, so that they can consult instead of vomiting a list of features and benefits. When you ask the right questions, you become the consultant.

2. Your Default Setting

Your default setting as a human is to persuade others in the way that you like to be persuaded. This approach works when you are persuading people who have your same style and personality, but it repels the rest of the human race. This tendency reduces your ability to persuade and influence. You must learn how to adapt and read other people and personalities. Great persuaders know how to persuade prospects in the way they want to be persuaded. This also involves learning how to help others persuade themselves. Which approach do you think will have better long-term results: you persuading them or you helping them to persuade themselves?

3. Everyone Trusts Me

Wrong. The reality is that most people do not trust you. Even though you are a good, trustworthy person, people do not necessarily trust you. You may think and feel that you have developed trust, but there is no trust on their end. Here's the deal when it comes to trust: In the past, people were more trusting. At one time the attitude was: "I trust you. Give me a reason not to." Now, it is the opposite: "I don't trust you. Give me a reason to trust you."

4. I Am a People Person

Of course, some stereotypical persuaders are friendly, outgoing, and extroverted. Research reveals, however, that some of the best persuaders are actually introverts. How can you persuade if you are always talking? Great persuaders listen more than they talk. In fact, great persuaders use their listening and people skills to get prospects/customers to tell them everything they need to know to persuade them.

5. I Need More Closing Skills

Sure, it's nice to have closing skills in your persuasion toolbox. But shouldn't you spend more time opening up your prospects before you even think about closing a deal with them? In fact, great persuaders don't even need closing techniques because their customers are ready to purchase even before the end of the conversation. The only time you really need a closing skill is when you have blown your presentation by not following the proper persuasion process. Using closing skills when your prospect does not like or trust you is like trying to get a kiss after a bad date.

EFFECTIVE PERSUASION REQUIRES ADAPTATION

Have you ever tried an approach that has worked in the past, and it bombed miserably? Maybe you tried a technique that works for your colleague, but it backfired on you. Becoming a Power Persuader requires more than mimicking other persuaders. In fact, most great persuaders usually aren't good teachers. Persuasion has become second nature to them. They tell you to read a script that works for them every time, but it doesn't work for you. Not only must you fully understand the wide variety of available persuasive techniques, but you must also be ready to use the techniques that are best suited for the situation. Acquiring this level of skill demands a commitment to watch, analyze, study, and apply the concepts of Maximum Influence.

Human nature varies from person to person. Human actions and thoughts keep us on our toes because each of us has different emotions, attitudes, beliefs, personalities, and traits. A beginner's tendency is to find one persuasive technique that works and to stick with it. Then you become a one-hit wonder. Unfortunately, you cannot use the same persuasion tool on everyone. Depending on the situation and your techniques, people will either agree with you, refuse to listen, or be indifferent to your efforts. The Power Persuader has many tools that you can adapt and customize to suit any situation or personality. In Chapter 15, I will spend more time on how to analyze, adapt to, and read your audience.

EFFECTIVE PERSUASION HAS LASTING IMPACT

Do you want short-term temporary results or permanent long-term results? Effective persuasion has lasting impact, but it requires dedicated study and long-term commitment on the part of the persuader. The Hierarchy of Persuasion (Figure 1-1) sheds light on how the world uses different levels of persuasion, ranging from the short-term to the long-term levels.

The qualities listed at the base of the illustration are the easiest to use. However, they achieve only temporary results because they do not address a person's genuine wants or desires. Persuasion based on the qualities listed at the top of the illustration is effective whether pressure is perceived or not. Such a method creates lasting results because it taps into and involves a person's true interests. Determining whether you want short- or long-term results dictates which area on the illustration should be the focus of your efforts.

Figure 1-1. The Hierarchy of Persuasion.

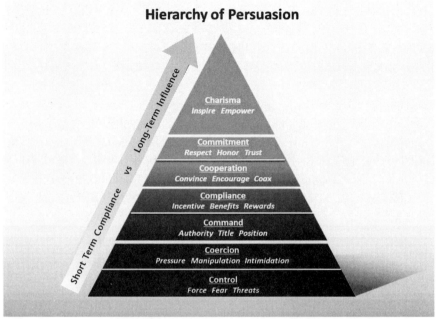

Imagine the CEO of a large corporation calling one of his vice presidents to a meeting. At the meeting, the vice president is informed that he must raise $20,000 in employee contributions for a charity the company is going to sponsor. The CEO is not concerned with the means the vice president uses as long as they result in a check for $20,000. Raising such a sum requires getting around $100 from each employee—a daunting challenge!

The vice president considers the various ways he could accomplish this task. Using *control* to approach the employees would be both quick and easy. He could use fear or threats to obtain the money. This do-it-or-else mentality would get immediate results. The long-term impact, however, would likely involve rebellion, revenge, or resentment. What about *coercion*? Surely the employees would provide the requested donation if they felt it would negatively affect their next job evaluation or raise. Would this tactic get immediate results? Sure. Again, however, the long-term effects would be resentment, rebellion, and revenge. The vice president decides control and coercion do not provide the best outcomes. He could *command* them to donate—use his authority or position in the company to make them donate. But he decides that command is too much like coercion.

Next he considers *compliance*. If he offered incentives, benefits, or rewards, it would be a win-win situation, right? Suppose each employee who donates $100 gets an extra couple of days of paid vacation. The problem is that, once the incentive is gone, compliance also disappears. The vice president might get the $100 this time, but what about the next time he asks for a donation? This method is still only a temporary fix because the employees will be conditioned to expect a reward for their compliance.

The vice president then considers *cooperation*. He could spend time with the employees explaining why this charity is so important and how it would be a great honor for them to participate. He could convince, encourage, or "sell" with logic, emotion, and information to get the employees to donate to this worthy cause. Now, armed with the tools of effective persuasion, he's onto an approach that will have lasting, positive results. As long as the employees feel he is telling the truth and acting in their best interest, they will be open to his proposal.

However, the vice president considers an even higher form of persuasion: *commitment*. If he has a great reputation and relationship with his employees, there will be mutual respect, honor, and trust. These conditions will enable the employees to comfortably give $100. They know the vice president is a person of honor who would never ask them to do anything that would not be in their best interest. They can commit to him because they feel he is committed to them.

Commitment is part of having Maximum Influence because its impact is not only short term; it is also permanent and far-reaching. Your reputation as someone possessing integrity, honor, trust, and respect will continuously inspire commitment from everyone you seek to persuade.

After we master the laws of persuasion, we can achieve the highest level, which is *charisma*. Charisma is the ability to empower and influence others into believing in you and wanting to be influenced by you. You inspire them. You help them see themselves in the future carrying out your vision. They are lifted and inspired by your optimism and expectations. In essence, you're a source of empowerment, encouragement, and inspiration. (For more information on Charisma, visit www.lawsofcharisma.com.)

THE FABLE OF THE SUN AND THE WIND

This book focuses on using Maximum Influence in positive ways. The following fable is an excellent example of properly implemented persuasion.

The sun and the wind were always arguing about which of them was stronger. The wind believed he was stronger because of his destructive power in tornados and hurricanes. He wanted the sun to admit that he was stronger, but the sun held fast to his own opinion and could not be convinced. One day the sun decided he wanted the matter settled once and for all, so he invited the wind to compete with him in a contest. The sun chose the contest carefully. He pointed out an elderly gentleman taking a walk and challenged the wind to use his power to blow the man's jacket off. The wind felt this would be an easy contest to win and began to blow. To his surprise, each gust of wind only made the man cling more tightly to his jacket. The wind blew harder, and the man held on tighter. The harder the wind blew, the more the man resisted. The powerful blows of wind even knocked the man down, but he would not let go of his jacket. Finally, the wind gave up and challenged the sun to succeed in getting the man to take off his jacket. The sun smiled and shone radiantly on the man. The man felt the warmth of the sun, and sweat broke out on his forehead. The sun continued pouring out warmth and sunshine on the man, and, at last, the man took off his jacket. The sun had won the contest.

This story is an example of Maximum Influence at its best. The tools outlined in this book are powerful. They should not be considered a means of gaining a desired result at any cost. Misuse of the laws will only come back to haunt you in the long run. Rather, you should use these tools to get your desired outcome only when it is a win-win situation for all involved. If your attempt to persuade is a win-win, others will be eager to do what you want them to do. As you perform the exercises and techniques outlined in this book, you will notice powerful changes in your ability to persuade and influence others.

THE FORMULA: 12 LAWS OF MAXIMUM INFLUENCE

Getting people to do what you want is not an accident or coincidence. You must use techniques based on the proven Laws of Persuasion to achieve such results. As you master these techniques, you'll experience predictable control and influence over others.

Professional negotiators, sales professionals, and upper management around the world use these 12 laws. They are the same principles that help thousands of people gain control of their lives and their financial futures.

Mastery of all the 12 laws is crucial for Maximum Influence. I promise that if you read this book and act on your newly acquired knowledge, before long you will find yourself in a completely different position than you are in today. You will act instead of being acted on. You will speak and be heard. You will lead and be followed.

In this updated version of *Maximum Influence*, I have added case studies and additional examples and application. They are taken from corporate consulting, consumer intercepts, and coaching clients. I express my appreciation to them for letting me share their examples and insights.

Additional Resources: Test Your Persuasion IQ (maximuminfluence.com)

CHAPTER 2

Subconscious Triggers

The Automatic Yes

Thinking is the hardest work there is, which is probably the reason why so few engage in it.   —HENRY FORD

Has this ever happened to you? I made a commitment to myself earlier in the month to eat healthier, and I was doing pretty well. I was late for a meeting, I was starving, and I had time only for fast food. I thought it through and decided that having fast food would be OK as long it was a grilled chicken sandwich that was light on the mayo. I could add a diet drink and skip the French fries or replace them with a healthy salad. I would keep my commitment to be healthy, and I would be on time for my meeting. Then, at the drive-through order window, the young lady asked what I wanted. Without hesitating, I replied, "I want a double bacon cheeseburger with large fries and a regular drink." Whoa! Where did that come from? That is not what I decided to do. What happened? It all occurred in a fraction of a second. Welcome to the world of *subconscious triggers*.

As a species whose thinking ability supposedly separates us from the animals, we really don't spend much of our life thinking or reasoning. Most of the time our minds get stuck on cruise control; thinking takes up too much time and requires too much energy. Imagine having to analyze every decision we make. That process would overwhelm us, and it wouldn't leave us much time to accomplish anything else. Most of us have an automatic way interpreting our world. When this subconscious mode is operating, our minds are perfectly primed to automatically respond to persuasion triggers.

What might be some of the subconscious triggers I experienced when I went to that fast-food restaurant? One could be the smell of cooking beef in the air. Maybe another was a commercial I saw the day before. Another might be a picture of that double bacon cheeseburger. Maybe someone recommended that same burger last week. Did I hear someone else order the same thing? These subconscious triggers are powerful and will affect your ability to persuade and influence. These subconscious triggers are the foundation of the Laws of Persuasion.

THE AUTOMATIC TRIGGERS OF PERSUASION

The Laws of Persuasion operate below our conscious thought radar. When these laws are employed properly, your audience doesn't even realize you're using them. On the other hand, if you blunder your way through a persuasion situation, your audience will be totally aware of what you're doing. It's like seeing a police car on the side of the road—it jars us back to reality. A skilled persuader will use the Laws of Persuasion so that the message is delivered below the radar.

Understanding the Laws of Persuasion involves understanding human nature, which empowers you to improve your persuasive abilities. Influence magnifies your effectiveness in relationships, improves sales enhances your leadership ability, and helps you sell yourself and your ideas. In short, it maximizes your effectiveness.

THINKING ABOUT NOT THINKING

In his book *Triggers*, best-selling author Joseph Sugarman reveals that 95 percent of a consumer's purchase is associated with a subconscious decision.

In other words, most buying is done for reasons a person hasn't fully formulated.

Whether we realize it or not, we love shortcuts to thinking. When we buy an item, we don't always take the time to research the product or read the latest consumer guide's ratings on the product. Instead, we may rely on the salesperson's advice. We might just buy the most popular brand, or the cheapest, or rely on a friend's opinion. Although we would never admit it, we sometimes even buy an item just because of its color, smell, or packaging. Certainly we know this is not the best way to make decisions, but we all do it anyway, even when we know we might make a mistake or feel regretful afterward. If we meticulously considered every single decision, we would be so constantly overwhelmed that our brain would shut down, and we'd never get anything done.

This tendency means that inclinations like, "It just feels right," "I like this product," or "I don't trust this person" are all based on subconscious triggers. Such thoughts and emotional reactions occur in the unconscious mind, without our awareness. What's more, our conscious awareness of reality is the result of the neurons in our brain processing all the information around us in unconscious ways.[4]

The reason for this type of behavior is the amygdala. Joseph Ledoux of New York University says the amygdala allows emotions to dominate and control our thinking. The amygdala has control over the cortex in the brain. What does that mean? The cortex is responsible for memory, perceptual awareness, thought, and consciousness. The amygdala stores the memories that we associate with emotional events. As a result, subconscious triggers are constantly occurring and triggering feelings and emotions, usually without our awareness. Neuroscientist Antonio Demasio said it best: "We are not thinking machines that feel, we are feeling machines that think."

Why do we let these feelings guide our decision making? First, sometimes the amount of incoming information is so overwhelming we don't even attempt to digest any of it. Sometimes our decisions simply aren't important enough to warrant the effort of researching all the available information. Consciously and subconsciously, from the bombardment of information we receive, we selectively choose what to acknowledge and what to ignore.

SOME OF YOUR SUBCONSCIOUS TRIGGERS

➤ An aroma that reminds you of a past sweetheart

➤ Music that increases your adrenaline level

➤ A color that makes you calm

➤ Trusting someone you have just met for the first time

➤ Gestures that subconsciously make you uneasy

➤ The tone of someone's voice that is an instant turn-on (or turnoff)

➤ Not connecting with someone because he or she acts like someone you don't like

Most persuasion involves both conscious (logical) and subconscious (emotional) paths. The key is knowing when to use either method and when to combine them. You might think you are an analytical person who uses the logical path of persuasion, but whether you are an emotional or logical person, you use both paths during the persuasion process. Think of an iceberg. The logical side of persuasion is the part showing above the water surface. The emotional or subconscious side is the submerged part of the iceberg. The successful application of all the laws and techniques taught in this book will help you to quickly identify which ones will be the most effective in a given situation.

We all tend to think that persuasion does not affect us. You might think it works on other people but not on you. Yet mindless persuasion or subconscious triggers are working on us constantly. The Monkey Business Illusion was a famous study that was called the invisible gorilla study and that you can find on youtube.com. The video shows two basketball teams, one in white and the other in black. They begin to pass the basketball to the other members of the team. Your job is to count how many times the white team passes the ball. Your brain focuses on the passing. Most people get the answer correct, but they don't see the black gorilla that walks out right in the middle of the game. This gorilla even looks at the camera and beats its chest, yet most people never see it. Our brain selectively see/hears what it wants.[5]

THE 12 LAWS OF PERSUASION

This book explores and categorizes the 12 Laws of Persuasion. These laws form the basis of the art and science of persuasion and influence. Adherence to these laws can help you understand and gain control of any situation requiring persuasion. Our minds are programmed with automatic persuasion triggers. Most of us experience persuasive situations without realizing or thinking about them. Power Persuaders know what these triggers are and how to use them to their advantage. Understanding the Laws of Persuasion help us become aware of how we are influenced without having conscious knowledge of it.

Learning to influence and persuade takes time, skill, and experience. What most people don't realize is that we already instinctively use many of these laws in our daily communications. The Laws of Persuasion that we unknowingly use every day are the very same ones that Power Persuaders use deliberately, consciously, and consistently. Power Persuaders make persuasion a habit. For example, recall how conscientious you were when you first started driving. Now, after years of practice, driving a car doesn't require as much thought or focus. Power Persuaders understand the laws of persuasion, have practiced them constantly, and can therefore apply the techniques without even thinking about them. For them, the application of persuasion has become second nature. Learn, implement, and make the 12 Laws of Persuasion a part of your life.

THE 12 UNIVERSAL LAWS OF POWER PERSUASION

Figure 2-1 maps out the 12 Laws of Persuasion. Each law can be used at any time, although they will always have a higher impact when used at the right time and in the correct way. The first key is to understand the foundational principles of Maximum Influence. The more of these elements that exist during the influence process, the faster and easier persuasion will be. They will cause your prospects to be more open, lower their resistance, and prepare them to be persuaded.

Foundational Principles of Maximum Influence

➤ When your prospects have a definite *need* or *want* for your product or service, they are much easier to influence. They are qualified and interested in your solution. Back to the old saying: "What's in it for me? (WIIFM)?"

Figure 2-1. The 12 Laws of Persuasion.

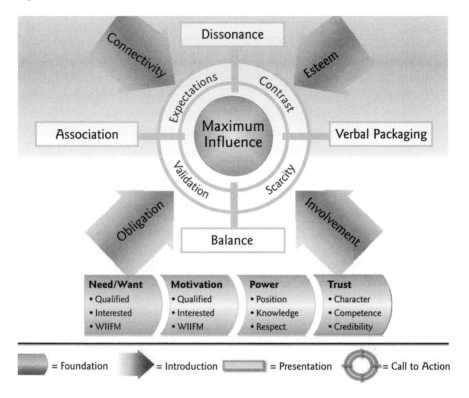

➤ *Motivation* creates prospects who are ready to move out of their comfort zone. They are prepared to be influenced by you and driven to use your product or service. Can you tap into their inspiration or desperation?

➤ Your foundation to persuade and influence is also strengthened when you possess various forms of *power*. If you have positional power, you are the prospects' supervisor or boss, and that enhances your ability to persuade. You might have more knowledge than your prospect or have built respect power over time.

➤ Then there is the key element of *trust*. When your prospect trusts you, the doors of persuasion swing open. You are credible and competent, and they are willing to be influenced by you.

The rest of the illustration covers the laws that I will reveal during this book.

- ➤ Four Laws of Persuasion not only work well during your introduction but are also critical during the whole persuasion process: Connectivity, Involvement, Esteem, and Obligation.
- ➤ During your persuasive presentation, the important laws are Dissonance, Verbal Packaging, Association, and Balance.
- ➤ When you are ready for your call to action, the laws that will seal the deal are Expectations, Contrast, Social Validation, and Scarcity.

Master the implementation and timing of these laws, and you will become a Power Persuader.

Additional Resources: Maximum Influence Newsletter (maximuminfluence .com)

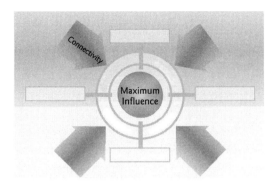

CHAPTER 3

The Law of Connectivity

Contagious Cooperation

The most important single ingredient in the formula of success is knowing how to get along with people. —THEODORE ROOSEVELT

I was traveling and speaking with a famous personal development speaker (who will remain anonymous). It had been a very long day by the time we arrived at our next destination very late at night. We were checking into our hotel for our speaking engagement the next day. He asked the young lady for an upgrade, and she replied that no upgrades were available.

He said, "Do you know who I am?"

"No," she answered.

"Do you know how often I frequent your hotel?"

"Sorry, sir, I don't," she politely responded.

He started to raise his voice and get angry. When she would not give him a complimentary upgrade, his anger escalated as he asked to see her manager. She quickly told him, "I am the manager." He went to his room disgruntled, and he did not get his upgrade. I approached the desk and said, "I am sorry for that. Nobody should treat you like that."

She said, "That's OK. It's part of the job."

We chatted for a bit, and I made sure there was a connection. At the end of our conversation, she said, "Thank you for your patience. Would you like a complimentary upgrade?"

We have all had the experience of feeling an instant connection or bond with someone after just a few seconds of being in their presence. This is the Law of Connectivity. On the flip side, we have all met someone who rubbed us the wrong way or repelled us. We instantly did not want to be around them. This reaction is caused by a lack of connectivity and usually takes only a few seconds to manifest itself. This disconnect closes the door to persuasion.

The Law of Connectivity states that the more someone feels connected to, similar to, liked by, or attracted to you, the more persuasive you become. When you create an instant bond or connection, people will feel more comfortable and open around you. They will feel as though they have known you for a long time and that they can easily relate to you. When we feel connected with people, we feel comfortable and understood; they can relate to us, and a sense of trust ensues. This connectivity is critical on the phone, during a presentation, or in social media.

Note: Really connecting with others requires an attitude of sincerity, practice, and a true interest in the other person. Whatever you do, never assume they like you.

Connectivity involves four main factors in: attraction, similarity, people skills, and rapport.

ATTRACTION: THE HALO EFFECT

Some might say that this section is *not* politically correct or that it is not fair or too judgmental, The reality is that everyone judges. Some perceptions or triggers you can fix; others you cannot. Focus on the things you can improve, and don't worry about the rest.

Attraction operates by making one of your positive characteristics affect other people's overall perception of you. As a result of what is called the Halo Effect, people automatically associate traits of kindness, trust, and intelligence with attractiveness. We naturally try to please people we like and find attractive. If your audience likes you, they will forgive you for your "wrongs" and remember your "rights." In fact, studies show that physically attractive people are more able to persuade others. They are also perceived as friendlier and more talented, and they usually have higher incomes.[1] But the term *attractive* means more than just looking beautiful or handsome; it also involves having the ability to attract and draw people to you. Your physical attractiveness will influence attitude changes,[2] enhance your expertise, and increase agreement.[3]

The effect of attractiveness transcends all situations. For example, the judicial system, which is supposed to be based upon evidence, has documented cases where attractiveness made a dramatic difference. In one Pennsylvania study, researchers rated the attractiveness of 74 male defendants at the start of their criminal trials. Later, the researchers reviewed the court records for the decisions in these cases and found that the handsome men had received significantly lighter sentences. In fact, the researchers found that the attractive defendants were twice as likely to avoid jail time as unattractive defendants. In the same study, a defendant who was better looking than his victim was assessed an average fine of $5,623. Yet when the victim was the more attractive of the two, the average compensation was twice that much.[4] What's more, both female and male jurors showed the same bias.

Have you ever noticed that some children seem to be able to get away with anything? Some research has shown that attractive children who misbehave are considered "less naughty" by adults than less attractive children. In elementary school, teachers often presume the more attractive children are more intelligent than the less attractive ones.[5] The Halo Effect also affects political elections. One study found that attractive political candidates received more than two and a half times as many votes as unattractive candidates.[6]

In various studies, attractive men and women, when compared to those who were considered to be less attractive, were judged to be happier, smarter, friendlier, and more likable. They were also considered to have better jobs, be better marital partners, and be able to get more dates. The Halo Effect causes us to see such people more positively, giving them increased persuasive power. Because of the way we view them, we want to be like them, and we hope for them to like us in return.[7]

Note: I am not talking about drop-dead gorgeous or incredibly handsome. Apparently, when your looks are perfect or well above the norm, it can have the opposite affect.

When we come into contact with someone of the opposite sex, the attractiveness concept is magnified. Attractive females can persuade men more easily than unattractive ones, and attractive males can persuade females more easily than unattractive males can. We see obvious examples of this all around us. At conventions and trade shows, large corporations fill their space with sexy and attractive females. They have been called booth babes. (Relax, there are also booth dudes.) In one study, men who saw a new car ad that included a seductive female model rated the car as faster, more appealing, more expensive looking, and better designed than did men who viewed the same ad without the model.[8] Additionally, female students who are perceived to be more attractive by their professors often receive substantially higher grades than unattractive females. Store managers commonly assign an attractive female sales associate to the young man who walks in the door. Most store managers (although they won't admit it) hire attractive salespeople to attract more customers.

Some people we meet have attractive personalities; some have ugly personalities. A study was done on how an attractive personality affects the ability to influence. Participants were asked to rate the attractiveness of a group of photographs with a full range of different-looking people. Some people in the photographs were given positive personality characteristics, and others were given negative characteristics. The positive traits were descriptors like *extraverted*, *agreeable*, *conscientious*, *open*, and *stable*. The pictures with positive descriptors (regardless of looks) were gauged to be more attractive than those without the positive traits.[9]

Another study proves the same point. Yearbook pictures were shown to both men and woman. The pictures then were assigned various negative and positive personality traits. Again, the photos with positive personality traits were rated as more attractive, and negative personality traits were less attractive. This occurred with pictures of both "attractive" and unattractive students. This happened for both men and woman, although the women tended to be a bit more sensitive to negative personality information than the men. It also influenced how the people were judged to be a dating partner.[10]

Our clothes can influence attractiveness. Researchers conducted a now famous experiment on how easy it would be to encourage people to ignore a "Don't Walk" sign at a city intersection. When a well-dressed individual ignored the sign and walked into the street, 14 percent of the people who had been waiting for the light to change followed him. When the same person repeated the experiment the next day, now dressed in sloppy clothes, only 4 percent of the people followed him. A similar effect has been found in hiring situations. In one study, the good grooming of applicants in a simulated employment interview accounted for more favorable hiring decisions than did their job qualifications. This happened even though the interviewers claimed that appearance played only a minor role in their choices.[11]

When I travel, how I am treated is directly related to how I am dressed. I can persuade the airline attendant to give me better seats, a better flight, or the help I need much more easily and faster when I am in a suit than when I am wearing casual attire. When I have on jeans and a T-shirt, I am viewed as less attractive, and, as a result, I get less cooperation.

Physical shape and accessories are also factors. Attractiveness lies in the simple things that many people overlook, such as being in good physical shape, watching your weight, paying attention to your accessories (i.e., jewelry, glasses, earrings, etc.), and having well-groomed hair. Keep track of hair and clothing styles. Styles can change dramatically, and, if you ignore fashion, your persuasive ability may be put in jeopardy. When in doubt, look to national newscasters as conservative role models for style.

Also, have you ever noticed that height often seems to have some bearing on one's position? Even though it is not fair, taller people tend to get better jobs and have higher salaries.

Similarity: Similar Is Familiar

Similarity theory states that familiar objects are more liked than less familiar ones. The same holds true with people: We like people who are similar to us. The theory seems to hold true whether the commonality is in the area of opinions, personality traits, background, or lifestyle.

Studies show that we tend to like and are more connected to those who are like us and with whom we can relate. If you watch people at a party, you will see them instantly gravitate toward people who are similar or familiar to one another. Once, while walking in a foreign country and taking in the unfamiliar sights and sounds, I ran into someone from the United States. We could have been from opposites sides of the country with nothing in common, but we had an instantaneous bond because we had something in common in an unfamiliar place.

Similarity theory is true even in the judicial system. If jurors feel that they share some common ground with you and, better yet, like you—even subconsciously—for that similarity, then you will have a markedly better chance of winning your case. Anytime others can see something about ourselves that they will identify with, our persuasive powers increase. In one study, demonstrators were more inclined to sign petitions of those similarly dressed, and often they didn't even bother to read the petition before signing![12] Numerous studies conclude that an audience is most responsive to individuals who dress and act similarly to them.

Do you remember all the cliques in junior high, high school, or even college? People associate and interact with those they view as similar to themselves. Cliques are often based on such commonalities as gender, age, educational background, professional interests, hobbies, sports teams, and ethnic background. In one study, researchers examined the social networks of prison inmates.[13] Their cliques were typically centered on commonalities of race, geographical origin, and the types of crime committed. One group of three men stood out to the researchers because they shared a tight companionship yet seemed to have no common backgrounds. Just as the study was coming to a close, the three men escaped together, demonstrating that we also build alliances based on common goals.

Researchers McCroskey, Richmond, and Daly say there are four parts to similarity: attitude, morality, background, and appearance.[14] Of the four similarity factors, attitudes and morals are always the most important.[15] Power Persuaders are always looking for similarities or common beliefs to form common foundations with their prospects. We want to be persuaded by those who are like us and with whom we can relate.

Real-world examples of this are found in advertisements. We want to see people we can identify with, and the advertising executives accommodate us. When we see a commercial, we think, "Hey, he's just like me! He's also broke!" Or, "That couple has a messy, cluttered house too." We see ads showing the average Joe or Jill because they create that feeling of similarity.

Your audience will connect with you when they perceive the similarity. D. J. O'Keefe found two important points regarding similarity and persuasion. First, the similarity must be relevant to your subject or issue. Second, to allow you to persuade someone, the similarities must involve positive rather than negative qualities.[16] The bottom line is that we are interpersonally connected to others when they possess similar values and beliefs.[17]

PEOPLE SKILLS: WINNING INSTANT ACCEPTANCE

Are you able to get along with different personalities? Are you sure? Getting along is a skill we need to work on everyday. It is one of the most overrated of all critical life skills; that is, most people say they have it, but they don't. An interesting fact is that 90 percent of all people rate their people skills as above average.[18]

The ability to connect and work well with people tops the list for common skills and habits of highly successful people. Studies show that 91 percent of those surveyed assert that people skills are important in business.[19] Studies also show that as much as 85 percent of your success in life depends on your people skills and on the ability to get others to like you. In fact, the Carnegie Institute of Technology found that only 15 percent of employment and management success is due to technical training or intelligence, whereas the other 85 percent is due to personality factors, that is, the ability to deal with people successfully. A Harvard University study also found that, for every person who lost a job for failure to do work, two people lost their jobs for failure to deal successfully with people.

In an era when technology is taking over our lives, it is tempting to think that personality and the ability to deal with people are no longer important qualities. On the contrary, we crave personal interaction now more than ever. Most people still want to get to know you and like you before the doors of persuasion and influence are unlocked. We prefer to say yes to the requests of people we know and like.

People skills are crucial because they have a huge impact on our success. First impressions are made within only four minutes of an initial interaction with a stranger,[20] so we don't have time to *not* have good people skills. Whole books have been written on people skills; you can never stop developing yours.

RAPPORT: THE INSTANT CONNECTION

Rapport is the secret ingredient that makes us feel a harmonious link with someone else. It is equivalent to being on the same wavelength with the other person. Rapport is the key that makes mutual trust materialize.

Have you ever met a perfect stranger and just hit it off? Finding plenty to talk about, you felt as if you might have met before. The connection just felt right. You could talk about practically anything, and you lost track of time. You developed such a strong bond with that person that you knew what he or she was going to say. Everything just clicked between the two of you, and you felt a strong connection with this person. You felt your ideas were in sync, and you enjoyed your time with each other. This is rapport.

Mastering four skills will help you to develop rapport faster: humor, body language, touch and mirroring.

Humor

Humor can be a powerful tool in creating rapport. Humor makes the persuader seem friendly and accepting. Humor helps gain attention, helps you create rapport, and makes your message more memorable. It can relieve tension, enhance relationships, and motivate people. The appropriate use of humor increases trust among your audience.[21]

Humor can also distract your audience from negative arguments or grab their attention if they are not listening. Humor diverts attention away from the negative context of a message, thereby interfering with the ability of listeners to carefully scrutinize it or engage in counterarguments. If listeners are laughing at the jokes, they may pay less attention to the content of a message. Humor can soften up or disarm listeners. Humor connects you with your audience and increases their attention to your message.[22]

Humor must be used cautiously, however. If used inappropriately, it can be offensive and may cause your audience to turn against you. Humor should be used only as a pleasant but moderate distraction. As a rule of thumb, if you are generally not good at telling jokes, don't attempt to do so. If you try it, be sure that you have good material. Dull or ineffective humor is not only ineffective but irritating. Modify your humor so that it is appropriate for your audience.

Smile

Another aspect of humor is the smile. A smile is free, generates a great first impression, and shows happiness, acceptance, and confidence. Your smile shows that you are pleased to be where you are or happy to meet this person. As a result, they become more interested in meeting you. Smiling also conveys a feeling of acceptance, which allows your listener to place more trust in you. It has been shown that sales representatives who smiled during the sales process increased their success rate by 20 percent. However, as with traditional humor, use a smile appropriately.

Body Language: Attracts or Distracts

Whether we realize it or not, we are constantly reading others and being read by them. Even without uttering any words, the language of the body speaks volumes. Often, interpreting body language is a subconscious feeling. We may not consciously think through all the details of why someone has just folded his arms across his chest and narrowed his eyes at us. Yet somehow this body language registers subliminally and makes us feel uneasy. The subconscious instantly interprets these actions to indicate resistance, suspicion, or spite, even if we have not made a conscious study of the opposing person or her background.

Using body language to its fullest involves not only mastering your own use of outward gestures to create and maintain rapport, but also acquiring the ability to read the body language of others. When you can effectively read body language, you can identify the emotions and discomfort of others. You can see tension and disagreement. You can feel rejection and suspicion.

At the same time, your body language adds to or detracts from your message. In other words, your subconscious gestures and expressions can either help or hurt your ability to persuade others. You can create rapport by understanding and adopting the right body postures for your prospect.

Everything about you communicates something. The words you use, your facial expressions, what you do with your hands, your tone of voice, and your level of eye contact all determine whether people accept or reject you and your message.

Albert Mehrabian says we are perceived in three ways:

1. 55 percent: Visually (body language)
2. 38 percent: Vocally (tone of voice)
3. 7 percent: Verbally (spoken words)[23]

Other research estimates that as much as 93 percent of your message's impact depends on nonverbal elements.[24] This includes facial expressions, body movement, vocal cues, and proxemics (the study of spatial separation between individuals).

Studies also show the wrong gestures can create impressions that the speaker lacks confidence.[25] Nonverbal behaviors affect impressions of a speaker's sociability and attractiveness.[26] There is a direct correlation between our ability to read body language and our relationships. In one study, college students were tested to see whether they could accurately identify the meanings behind certain facial expressions and tones of voice. The research consistently showed that the students who made the most errors in interpreting the meanings were those who had troubled relationships and/or heightened feelings of depression.[27]

Eyes

As Ralph Waldo Emerson said, "The eyes of men converse as much as their tongues." The more common phrase we hear is, "The eyes are the windows to the soul." Through our eyes, we can gauge the truthfulness, attitude, and feelings of a speaker. Not making the proper amount of eye contact can have devastating results. Our pupils are one of the most sensitive and complicated parts of our body. They react to light, but they also respond to our emotions, revealing a variety of feelings. Note the following example:

> **Pennzoil Oil took the Texaco Oil Company to court over Texaco's allegedly interfering with a contract that Pennzoil already had with Getty Oil. Throughout the trial, Pennzoil's counsel was accused of trying to sway the jury by encouraging their witnesses to make eye contact and to joke with the jurors. To show that they were serious and did not consider the circumstances a joking matter, Texaco's counsel told witnesses not to joke at all and to avoid eye contact with the jurors. Unfortunately, the advice proved to be unwise and cost Texaco dearly in the end. Pennzoil was granted more than $2.5 billion in damages. Why? Afterward, jurors expressed distrust toward the witnesses who had avoided eye contact, even going so far as to call them "arrogant" and "indifferent."**

Making eye contact can also convey love or passion. In a number of studies on eye contact and attraction, researchers found that simply looking into one another's eyes can create passionate feelings. In one particular case, two members of the opposite sex who were complete strangers were found to have amorous feelings toward each other after merely gazing into one another's eyes.[28] In another study, beggars were interviewed about their tactics for getting donations. Several of the beggars stated that one of the very first things they tried to do was establish eye contact. They claimed that making eye contact made it harder for people to pretend they hadn't seen them, to ignore them, or to just keep walking.[29] Other studies have shown that public speakers who make more eye contact, use pleasant facial expressions, and incorporate appropriate gestures into their speeches have more persuasive power than speakers who do not.[30]

WHAT YOU NEED TO KNOW ABOUT THE EYES

Sunglasses: Hiding the eyes and arousing distrust

Avoidance of eye contact: Lack of confidence

Less than 50 percent eye contact: Insincerity and distance

Increased eye contact: Starting to accept you or your idea

Rapid blinking: Resistance to what has been done or said

Extended eye contact: Anger, love, or frustration

Pupils dilate: Interested and receptive

Touching to Influence and Persuade

Touch is another powerful part of body language, important enough to devote a whole section to it. Touch can be a very effective psychological technique. Subconsciously, most of us like to be touched; touching makes us feel appreciated and builds rapport. However, we need to be aware of and careful with a small percentage of the population who dislikes being touched in any way. In most instances, however, touch can help put people at ease and make them more receptive to you and your ideas. Touch increases influence. When you are able to touch your prospects, they usually become more agreeable; touching enhances their mood and increases the chances that they will agree and do what you are asking.

Touch can create a positive perception. It carries with it favorable interpretations of immediacy, similarity, relaxation, and informality.[31] In one research study, librarians did one of two things to university students: Either they did not touch the person at all during the exchange, or they made light, physical contact by placing a hand over the student's palm. Invariably, those students who were touched during the interaction rated the library service more favorably than those who were not touched at all.[32] Waiters and waitresses who touched customers on the arm when asking whether everything was okay received larger tips and were evaluated more favorably than those who didn't touch their customers. Touch also induces customers to spend more time shopping in stores. In one study, physical contact on the part of salespeople induced customers to buy more and to evaluate the store more favorably.[33]

In another example, touch was found to increase the number of people who volunteered to score papers, sign petitions, and return money that had been left in a telephone booth. Syracuse professor Jacob Hornik discovered that lightly touching bookstore customers on the upper arm caused them to shop longer (22.11 minutes versus 13.56 minutes), to purchase more ($15.03 versus $12.23), and to evaluate the store more positively than customers who had not been touched. Hornik also found that supermarket customers who had been touched were more likely to taste and purchase food samples than nontouched customers.[34] Touch also made bus drivers more likely to give away a free ride when they were being touched while the potential rider was making the request.[35]

We know that certain areas of the body can be freely touched while other areas are off-limits. Safe areas of contact include the shoulders, forearms and hands, and sometimes the upper back. This all depends on the situation, the culture, and the relationship between the two parties prior to the touch.

Handshake as a Form of Touch

Did you know many experts think the handshake originated in Medieval Europe? It was a way for knights to show they did not have any hidden weapons or intent to harm you.[36] The way we shake hands also tells people a lot about us. In business, it is customary to shake hands with someone when we first meet them or when we are sealing a deal. A handshake can make or break that first impression. It can help or hurt rapport. Your handshake communicates strength, weakness, indifference, or even warmth.[37] Weak or limp handshakes, on the other hand, portray just that: weakness, incompetence, or maybe even disinterest. Be sure your handshakes are always firm and appropriately energetic. A firm handshake demonstrates your persuasive ability and interpersonal skills.[38]

What factors are you being judged on? Desirable handshakes have been described in the following way:

- ➤ Firm shake
- ➤ Complete grip
- ➤ Good duration
- ➤ Eye contact[39]

Mirroring and Matching

John Grinder and Richard Bandler, founders of neurolinguistic programming (NLP), developed the concept of *mirror and matching*, that is, of aligning your movements and energy with those of your prospects. The goal is to mirror or reflect their actions, not to imitate them. If people think you are imitating them, they may feel as though you're mocking them, and they may become offended. They will see you as phony and no longer trust you. Instead of directly imitating, just mirror or match the overall tone and demeanor of your prospect. You can safely mirror their language, posture, gestures, and mood. Mirror and matching is a natural human response.

Duke University found that it was an automatic and unconscious response to mimic or mirror others' mannerisms.[40] In fact, they found mirroring mannerisms (touching the face, tapping a foot, etc.) helped negotiators have higher success rates. It was also reported that the person being mirrored showed higher levels of rapport and liking.[41] The bottom line is that mirroring your prospect increases trust. It also increases the amount of information shared during a negotiation, produces better negotiation outcomes, and gets a bigger piece of the pie for the negotiator.[42]

When you mirror your prospects, you build rapport with them. Because of your similar demeanors, your prospects will feel a subconscious connection with you. People are inclined to follow and be influenced by those they perceive as similar to themselves. If they shift in their posture, you should eventually do so too. If they cross their legs, you should cross your legs as well. If they smile, you smile too. When you do this, your prospects will subconsciously feel that you have much more in common with them than is actually the case.

We unconsciously mirror others without even realizing it. Mirroring is just a natural thing that we do. Have you ever noticed at social gatherings how people tend to match each other in their body language and their attitudes? For example, when two people greet each other, they typically tend to use the same posture and behave with the same demeanor. When you are a Power Persuader, you will use mirroring skillfully and conscientiously.

Mirroring Language

You will be amazed at the effectiveness of using vocabulary, or so-called lingo, that is similar to that of your prospect. Pick up on and use some of the words or phrases that your prospect uses. You may also find it helpful to mirror his or her rate of speech. If he speaks in a slower and more relaxed tone, you can do the same. If he speaks quickly, feel free to do the same.

Matching Voice

Matching voice is different from matching language in that it refers to the actual tone or inflection of your prospect's voice. Be very careful, however, that you do not come across as mocking. The mirrored voice you use should never be so different or foreign from your own voice that you arouse suspicion. Just minor and subtle adjustments in tone are all that are necessary to get the desired results.

Matching Energy Level

Some people always seem to be relaxed and mellow, whereas others seem to be constantly active or vivacious. Seeking to mirror your prospect's energy level is another subtle way you get in sync with your prospect. This technique is also effective when giving a group presentation: Match the overall energy level present in the room, or adopt the level of energy emanating from the group.

Breaking the Mirror

Certainly, you sometimes may not want to mirror someone. For example, a lawyer will often seek to create anxiety or uneasiness in a witness. To accomplish this, the lawyer needs to avoid mirroring. When the witness is slumped in the seat looking at the ground, the lawyer may hover or stand rigidly and look intensely at the witness's face. Have you ever noticed or felt the uneasiness while someone stood in the middle of a conversation where everyone was seated? Breaking the mirror breaks the synchronization that makes everyone feel calm and comfortable. If you need to break the mirror, simply stop mirroring and sit, speak, or gesture differently from the person you're dealing with. You can create even further distance by altering your demeanor abruptly or suddenly.

Most persuaders don't know how to maintain their rapport throughout the persuasive process. People in sales break the ice, find similarities, build rapport for the first five minutes, and then launch into their presentation. All of a sudden, they get serious and change their demeanor. What is the prospect going to think? The salesperson has now changed. Which version is the real person? The salesperson and prospect were getting along, having fun. All of a sudden, without warning, the salesperson becomes serious and dives into a sales pitch. The discontinuity breaks rapport and seems incongruent to the prospect. You both know why you are there and what the ultimate goal will be, so continue to build on that rapport.

BACKFIRE

The Law of Connectivity will backfire if you are perceived as fake or incongruent. Connectivity takes time, research, and practice to master. You need to learn how to read your prospects and your customers. Learn how to determine whether your prospects are relaxed, nervous, confident, or indifferent.

CASE STUDY

A large hospital conglomerate was concerned with profits, and one of the biggest anchors on increasing profits was lawsuits. Many of their best doctors were getting sued, and management did not know what to do. Even if the claim was not their fault, the doctors were named in the lawsuit. Why would people sue doctors who didn't make a mistake? Why would their best, most conscientious doctors be the victim of so many lawsuits? Using the Law of Connectivity, what would you suggest?

The number one reason doctors are sued is that their patients did not like them. In medical care (and in any other business), profitability can be determined by how much people like you. The ability to adapt to every personality, understand emotions, and explain risks is critical not only to doctors but to everyone involved in persuasion. The conscientious analytical doctor may have done it by the book and without emotions—but never really connected in the bedside manner. This causes a disconnect and makes it easier for people to sue their doctors. The lawsuit problem was solved with people skill training and implementing connectivity.

. . . .

Additional Resources: Reading Nonverbals Report (maximuminfluence.com)

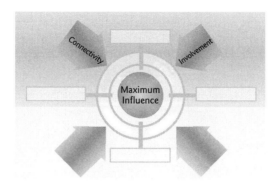

CHAPTER 4

The Law of Involvement

Create and Maintain Interest

Without involvement, there is no commitment. Mark it down, asterisk it, circle it, underline it. No involvement, no commitment. —STEPHEN COVEY

Hopefully you have been to Hershey, Pennsylvania, home of world famous Hershey's Chocolate Company. I am a big fan of chocolate and decided to take the tour of Hershey's simulated chocolate factory. This is a Disneyland type of ride with all the smells you would expect from a chocolate tour. You can see them make chocolate and how they create all the Hershey magic. Do you know how much the tour costs? It is free. Why would Hershey spend millions of dollars on a free tour? Well, after the tour and right before you enter the largest chocolate shop in the world, you are given a free Hershey Kiss. You see countless sweets and all things chocolate ready for purchase. Hershey makes more money on chocolate sales after a free tour than it could on the tour itself. When you can get others involved, get them to participate; they are easier to persuade.

The Law of Involvement suggests that the more you engage someone's five senses, involve them mentally and physically, and create the right atmosphere for persuasion, the more effective and persuasive you'll be. Listening can be a very passive act; you can listen to an entire presentation and not feel or do a thing. As a persuader, you need to move your audience one step closer to taking action. As a Power Persuader, your goal is to decrease the distance someone has to go to reach your objective. Your task is to make it as easy and as simple as possible. You need to decrease the mental, social, or physical distance that they need to travel to be persuaded.

For example, getting people to take a sample of a product is easier than getting them to buy. Getting them to test-drive a car is easier than convincing them to buy a car. Getting them to agree to a five-minute meeting to discuss participation in a larger project is easier than asking them to participate in a three-hour project.

When you get people to start something, they are more likely follow through and complete your desired outcome. The more involved they become, the less psychological distance there is between the start and the finish. The desired outcome becomes more and more realistic instead of just an idea you are proposing. If you put on your shoes to go to the store, get your coat, and find your keys, each step increases the chances that you will continue in that direction. On the other hand, if you sit down and turn on the TV or get on the Internet, your goal of going to the store is less likely to be reached. This is also true on the Web. As the number of pages or steps you ask someone to click on or go through increases, compliance and sales decrease.

You can use involvement by:

1. Increasing participation.
2. Creating the right atmosphere.
3. Maintaining attention.
4. Using the art of questioning.
5. Telling mesmerizing stories.
6. Engaging the five senses.

INCREASING PARTICIPATION

You can create involvement through increased participation. The more individuals take an active role and get involved, the more open to persuasion they become. When they take an active part in something, they feel connected to and have stronger feelings for the issue at hand. They have a personal stake in what they are doing.

One of the keys to successful participation is making your problem their problem. This technique creates ownership and a willingness to help on the part of your prospects. Obviously, asking for help is much milder than telling someone what to do or think. You will have more success involving your prospects in the solution if you give them the option of participating. Feeling that it was their choice and their solution, your prospects will take ownership: They have persuaded themselves. It becomes their own problem and their own solution. By nature, people will support what they help create.

Store and mall owners understand participation. They attempt to get you participating by making eye contact with you, by arranging their stores to force you to spend more time in them, or by saying hello as you pass. When you shop for goods in a foreign country, the store owner knows that if he can get you inside the store and mentally or physically involved, there is a greater chance of persuasion and a purchase. The storekeeper will make eye contact and do everything possible to get you into the store. If you don't go into the store, the owner might follow you for blocks, showing you the store's products and trying to get you to buy.

The amount of time you spend in a store is directly related to how much you will buy: the more time spent, the more money spent. For example, in an electronics store, nonbuyers shopped for an average of about 5 minutes and 6 seconds, whereas buyers averaged 9 minutes and 29 seconds in the store. In a toy store, the longest any nonbuyer stayed was 10 minutes, while buyers spent just over 17 minutes. In some cases, buyers stayed up to four times longer than nonbuyers.[1]

Stores make many other arrangements to persuade people to get interested and involved. For example, hallways and walking paths at malls are made of hard marble or tiles. But the floors of individual stores are soft and carpeted, encouraging you to stay longer. Have you ever noticed that it is easy to get disoriented in an unfamiliar mall? Malls purposely design their structures with hexagonal floor plans, which are the most difficult to navigate: They have complicated hallways and confusing angles. You can get lost; you can walk forever and still not know exactly where you are. This is also the reason why department stores are at the opposite ends of the mall. Department stores are draws. For people to get from one to another, they will have to walk past every other store in the mall. Grocery stores place their milk at the back of the store so that customers have to walk through the rest of the store to grab a carton. All of these techniques increase the time that customers spend in the store. And, as we know, increased time in a store means increased sales.

Casinos

Casinos are examples of extreme involvement. Everything in a casino is designed to get you mentally, emotionally, and physically involved. A casino is a subconscious-trigger war zone. There are no clocks to let you know what time it is and how long you have been gaming. Rarely does a dealer wear a watch. There are also no windows to help you tell the time, and the air and temperature are regulated so that you never think about going outside. The carpets are loud and obnoxious to look at, so you look at all the blinking lights on the machines, watch the wheels spinning, and see everyone having fun and gambling. It looks and sounds as though everyone is winning but you. There are plenty of distractions while you are playing: free drinks, the winner in the next row, or the revealing outfit of the cocktail waitress.

The lighting in a casino tends to be low and inviting. It has a friendly, homelike feel and increases our comfort level. The music is just below our radar. This music is soft, is easy to listen to, and has been known to put people in a slight trance. We feel obligated to continue gambling (even though we lost money) by the free meals, the casino points, the comped rooms, and the free show tickets. We keep spending and losing money, but who cares because we are earning points to redeem at a later date? So even though we lose money, at least we feel as though we earned something.

Walking down the strip at Las Vegas, I found it very easy to enter a large and famous casino (via escalator). However, getting out was quite the adventure and harder to navigate. Have you noticed that you never need to leave a casino because the food and lodging are all under one roof? The casino has been designed to be very easy to get into and very difficult to leave. The patterns and layout maximize your time spent in the casino. If you need to find anything (i.e., a restroom, restaurant, parking, check in, cashier), you must walk farther into the casino past the many stores and additional gambling places. Then guess what? You have to walk by everything again on the way out; there are more chances you will stop and buy or play.

Role-Playing

One way to get your audience involved is to use role-playing, which helps people see themselves doing the task. The task becomes more realistic and usually appears easier than they thought. This technique has proven to be effective in getting people to actually convince themselves of something. Role-playing is the single most powerful way to induce attitude change through a vicarious experience. In essence, you are getting people to create arguments against their own beliefs.

Do you want to know just how powerful role-playing is? One experiment used role-playing to convince people to stop smoking. The subjects role-played having x-rays, receiving news of lung cancer, and coughing with emphysema. When compared with a control group of smokers who were educated about cancer, those who role-played were more likely to quit than those who passively learned about lung cancer.[2]

During World War II, the U.S. government had to ration traditional meats such as beef, chicken, and pork. However, Americans tend to be very picky about the meats they eat and often do not accept other types. The Committee on Food Habits was charged with overcoming the shortages of popular foods. How could they overcome the aversion to eating other types of meat?

Psychologist Kurt Lewin devised a program to persuade Americans to eat intestinal meats. Yes, our favorite—intestinal meats (not hot dogs). He set up an experiment with two groups. One group was lectured on the benefits of eating intestinal meats. Members of the committee emphasized to them how making the switch would help the war effort. Then they heard fervent testimonials and were given recipes. The second group was led in a group discussion about how they could persuade other people to eat intestinal meat. This group covered the same main topics as the other group, role-playing and discussing the question, "How would they persuade and convince others to eat intestinal meats?" Of that group, 32 percent went on to serve their families intestinal meats, compared to 3 percent of the first group.[3] Often when you attempt to persuade an audience and they know you are attempting to persuade them, they will resist you. Coming across as the consultant, getting them involved, is much more persuasive. In fact, they will persuade themselves.

Asking for Advice

Another way to get people to participate with you is to ask their opinions or advice. Simple phrases can immediately spark the interest of your listener: "I need your help." "What is your opinion?" "What do you think about . . . ?" "How could I do this?" "How would you do this?" "Do you think I am doing it right?" "Do you have any ideas?" Seeking advice boosts their esteem, and their brain automatically starts work toward a solution.

Watch how another person brightens up when you ask for his or her advice. For example, suppose you ask your colleague, "Frank, how about helping me with this proposal?" He will probably tell you he is busy and has his plate full for the next 12 months. But suppose you say something like this:

> **Frank, I have a challenge with this proposal that I can't solve. I don't know what I am doing wrong and can't seem to get anywhere. I am not sure if I am doing it right or what to do next. Do you have ideas about how I could rework this paperwork? Could you take a quick look?**

You will see a marked difference in response between the first request and the second.

People have an innate desire to feel wanted and needed (see Law of Esteem). When you fulfill this need, you open the door to persuasion and action, a fact that has been proved beyond a doubt by records kept on industrial workers. Workers who have no voice whatsoever in management, who cannot make suggestions, or who are not allowed to express their ideas simply do not do as much work as workers who are encouraged to contribute. The same is true in families. As family relations expert Ruth Barbee has said: "It is surprising how willingly a child will accept the final authority of the parents, even if the decision goes against him, provided he has had a chance to voice his opinions, and make his suggestions, before the final decision is reached."[4]

Visualization

Another participation technique is to use visualization. No one can follow through on an act or message without first thinking or mentally seeing that accomplishing it is possible. You can mentally achieve participation by helping your audience visualize and see in their minds how your product or service will help them. Real estate agents attempt to help their clients visualize living with their family in a home. When showing the home, the agents want the people to envision it as their own. They have the children pick out their own room. They ask the parents to decide where they could put the piano. They might even introduce the neighbors.

A group of researchers went door-to-door selling cable TV subscriptions. When they included the phrase "imagine how cable TV will provide you with broader entertainment," they immediately achieved more success. Forty-seven percent of those who were told to imagine cable TV bought a subscription, whereas only 20 percent of the control group purchased. The mind is activated when you help your prospect visualize your product or service.[5]

Here is a great example of visualization. Imagine seeing a homeless person with a sign that says, "I am hungry." That will get some response. Now imagine if the sign read, "What if your parents were hungry?"

In many persuasive situations, your audience may pretend not be interested at all in your message, service, or product. How do you pull them in? Often, when we see a persuasive situation, we like to remain anonymous. We don't want to feel any pressure, so we watch from a distance. If someone at the clothing store asks whether we want help, we say, "No, just looking." We avoid the involvement because deep down we know that becoming involved will decrease our resistance.

Every night before dusk in Key West in the Florida Keys, people gather at Sunset Pier to watch the sunset and enjoy the view. It is a great time of the day to unwind and enjoy nature's beauty. It is also the perfect opportunity for vendors and street performers to hawk their wares—jugglers, sword swallowers, magic tricks, the works. One night, as I watched people walk by, many of them wanted to watch but felt timid unless a crowd had already gathered around the performers. The performers knew that, if they didn't get a crowd, they wouldn't make any money. When people remain anonymous, they feel little pressure to donate. I saw a performer who was doing a magic act call over to someone who was trying to remain anonymous. Soon, the performer got the man involved in his act. This attracted more people to watch and also got a donation from the gentleman, who was no longer anonymous.

If someone around you or in your audience is avoiding or rejecting your message, try to get him or her involved. Get that person, as a volunteer from your audience, to willingly participate, and you will completely change his or her perspective. Pet store owners are famous for this. They see children come in just to look around. The parents don't want to have a dog in the house, but their son or daughter still wants to look. The owner waits patiently to see the child's eyes light up, as the child falls in love with a new puppy. The child holds and hugs the puppy, and the dad knows he is in for a struggle. The owner is wise and does not want to fight the father. He just says, "It looks like she's fallen in love with this puppy. I understand your apprehension about having a new puppy. Tell you what—just take the puppy home for the weekend and if it doesn't work out, bring him back." The rest is history. Who can't fall in love with a puppy after a weekend? The owner has successfully gotten a reluctant customer involved.

Many studies show the relationship between visualization and success in sports. In a well-known study, Russian scientists wanted to know the relationship between physical and mental training and which is more important. They tested four groups of athletes. This is what they found:

1. Group 1 received 100 percent physical training with no mental training.
2. Group 2 received 75 percent physical training with 25 percent mental training.
3. Group 3 received 50 percent physical training with 50 percent mental training.
4. Group 4 received 25 percent physical training with 75 percent mental training.

The fourth group had the best results, revealing that visualization has measurable results in sports. The same is true for persuasion. If your prospects can't see themselves doing it, they won't do it.

Physical Movement

Making your audience physically move can also affect the way your message is received. Involvement can be something as simple as getting people to say yes, to raise their hands, or even just to nod their heads yes. The more movement and involvement you can create, the greater your ability is to persuade. Great persuaders look for times when they can get affirmation from their audience. They engineer their persuasive message to get as many verbal, mental, or physical yesses as they can throughout their presentation.

There is good evidence to support this practice. One study brought in a large group of students to do "market research on high-tech headphones." The students were told that the researchers wanted to test how well the headphones worked while they were in motion. (Students were dancing up and down and moving their heads to the beat of music.) Following the songs, the researchers played a commercial about how the university's tuition should be raised. One group of students had been told to move their heads up and down throughout the music and the speaking. Another group was told to move their heads from side to side. A last group was told to make no movements at all.

After "testing the headsets," the students were asked to fill out a questionnaire about not only the headsets but also the university's tuition. Those nodding their heads up and down (in a yes motion) overall rated a jump in tuition as favorable. Those shaking their heads side to side (no motion) overall wanted the tuition to be lowered. Those who had not moved their heads didn't really seem to be persuaded one way or the other.[6] In a similar study at the University of Missouri, the researchers found that TV advertisements were more persuasive when the visual display had repetitive vertical movements, that is, up-and-down yes movements, such as a bouncing ball.[7]

The Power of Yes

Use questions that will create yesses. As you create your marketing and persuasive presentations, you must engineer the number of times you get your audience to raise their hands, say yes, or nod their heads. How many verbal yeses are you getting? One easy and effective way to get more affirmative responses is to engineer questions that will receive a positive answer. For example, when a word ends in -n't, it will usually bring a yes response. Consider the following phrases:

Wouldn't it?	Shouldn't it?
Isn't it?	Won't you?
Couldn't it?	Can't you?
Doesn't it?	Wasn't it?

Obviously, this technique won't work if they don't like or trust you.

Contact

Obviously, this technique won't work if they don't like or trust you.

Engaging customers with human contact also works well for retail stores. Human beings are naturally drawn to other human activity.[8] The sight of other humans in motion attracts people—and increases sales. Studies show that the more contact employees make with customers, the greater the average sale is.[9] In fact, any contact initiated by a store employee increases the likelihood that a shopper will buy something.[10] A shopper who talks to a salesperson and tries something on is twice as likely to buy as a shopper who does neither. Talking with an employee has a way of drawing customers in closer and actively involving them.

CREATING THE RIGHT ATMOSPHERE

Another way to boost participation is with atmosphere. Atmosphere is really just a state of mind that you can create. Think about the following locations and the atmosphere they purposefully create:

Hardware stores	Themed restaurants
Bookstores	Amusement parks
Malls	Hospitals
Casinos	Law offices

Each establishment is vastly different, but, when you walk in, you know immediately the atmosphere or feeling that it evokes. In this way, the atmosphere moves you. Antique stores purposefully create an atmosphere of chaos. They appear to be unorganized with everything strewn around or disheveled. This is done so that customers believe they have stumbled upon a great find, a piece of buried treasure. What about large sporting good stores, each with an athletic theme. Customers who are successfully seduced by the excitement and energy of the athletic atmosphere will want to make themselves just a little worthier of it. This means buying a new pair of running shoes.

Rushed Versus Relaxed

Atmosphere can also include the tension in the air. Are customers rushing or relaxed? What type of climate are you trying to create? Do you want a quick, fast decision, or do you want your customers to feel comfortable enough to stay for a while? An interesting study on what happens when you create an atmosphere of being rushed can be seen in the following example:

Princeton University psychologists John Darley and Daniel Batson wanted to see how seminary students would respond if they were in a situation replicating the biblical account of the Good Samaritan.[11] As the story goes, a band of thieves beat a traveler, robbed him, and left him by the roadside to die. A devout priest and a reputable Levite passed by. Neither of the men stopped to help the dying man. Finally, a Samaritan stopped to help him. The Samaritan bound up his wounds, took him to an inn, and even paid the innkeeper to care for him until he returned.

Darley and Batson asked seminarians on a one-on-one basis to prepare and present a short speech on an assigned biblical topic. The test was set up so that, on their way to the location where they would deliver their speech, each student would cross a man slumped over, coughing and groaning. Which students would actually stop and help? Before preparing their speeches, the students filled out a questionnaire asking why they had chosen to study theology. They stated on their questionnaires that they had chosen to study theology so that they could help people. Then a variety of speech topics were assigned, including the story of the Good Samaritan. As the students were leaving to deliver their speeches, some were told, "You'd better hurry. They were expecting you about three minutes ago." Others were told, "They won't be ready for a few minutes, but you may as well head over now."

Now, most people would assume that seminarians, assigned to speak on the Good Samaritan, would be very likely to stop and help the ailing man on their way. Interestingly, neither their intended profession or their desire to help people seemed to make much difference. In fact, Darley and Batson stated, "Indeed, on several occasions, a seminary student going to give his talk on the parable of the Good Samaritan literally stepped over the victim as he hurried on his way." The element that seemed to be most influential was whether the student was in a rush. Of the students who were told they were already a little late, only 10 percent stopped to help. Of the students who were told they had a little bit more time, 63 percent stopped to help.[12]

We can learn from this example that we can create atmospheres in which people are so involved that they ignore other factors they normally would not overlook. On the flip side, if participants are too relaxed, they become difficult to persuade.

Hands-On Experience

Another good way to get people involved is to get your product into their hands. If they can begin to use it, chances are they will continue to use it. That is why car dealers encourage test drives. You will even see car dealerships give their loyal customers a newer model to drive for a few days. How can you go back to your old car after driving around in a new car? By that point, neighbors and coworkers have already seen you in the car and have commented about your new vehicle. You're thoroughly involved, and the new car is yours. You want people to experience your product for free. Free trials can be seen in food courts, at beauty counters, in software sales, and at vacation resorts.

Many TV advertisers offer a free one-month trial before you have to pay for their product. After the month is up, most consumers will keep the product, even if they didn't use it. The trial period has created a sense of ownership in the product, and consumers don't like to relinquish ownership. This is also why so many companies use introductory offers. Credit card issuers are known for tempting customers with introductory deals that give very low interest rates. One study showed that offering samples increased sales by 500 percent.[13]

To get your product into your prospects' hands, get them to open the box and play with the object, give them the feeling of ownership, make them feel as if they already bought it, and suggest how the product can be used. There are many other examples of the Law of Involvement: the listening stations in the music stores, the comfortable chairs in which you can kick back and read in the bookstores, booths set up at the malls for you to try out and test products and equipment, software you can demo, frequent-user programs, coupons, contests, and the variety of services offering free estimates.

The 3M Company certainly discovered the value of putting products into customers' hands. At their outset, Post-it® Notes were not very successful. 3M was going to discontinue the whole product line until the brand manager sent a case of Post-it Notes to 499 of the Fortune 500 Companies.

Because of their trial run, the Fortune 500 companies loved the effectiveness of the notes, and the rest is history.[14]

Think about it. Post-it notes were a new, cutting-edge product. Nobody knew they needed sticky notes because they had never used or needed them in the past. Verbally explaining what a Post-it Note is and what it does would have been difficult. Just letting customers use the notes enabled them to see that they needed it, and they bought the product.

Usually we are inclined to favor our own ideas over those of others, right? Knowing that people do not typically resist their own ideas can be key when you are trying to influence others. Always seek to get your prospects to think your ideas are their own. An example of this strategy in action is when companies have customers fill out a sales agreement. Cancellations are amazingly low when customers have filled out their agreements on their own. It's a double whammy: Not only are your prospects agreeing to what you want, but they are also putting it in writing!

MAINTAINING ATTENTION

It is common sense: You have to keep your audience's attention in order to persuade them. If you lose them, you lose your chance for them to understand and accept your proposal. We know from our own personal experience that we tend to let our minds drift when we are listening to other people. We cannot focus on one item for too long unless we are forced to do so. Power Persuaders can make a person want to pay attention and stay focused. You may lose your audience's attention from time to time, but it is your job to get back to their full attention. You can help your prospect lose track of time.

Some studies estimate that the average adult attention span is about 15–20 minutes.[15] What's more, studies indicate that attention spans have been decreasing steadily over the past decade. The blame tends to be put on the media, on the lack of circumstances that require concentration, and the current generation always wanting to be entertained or tuning out. Whatever the reason, after our attention span has lapsed, we become bored and no longer listen. You have to be creative to maintain the mental involvement that is required to persuade someone. One way to keep the mind harnessed is to give your audience enough time to process what you are telling them. You can tell by the look in their eyes if you have lost them. Recall the seminars or college classes during which you have been completely lost. When the professor asks questions, you don't raise your hand because you have no idea what is going on. Give your listeners enough time to absorb what you're saying, but obviously not so long that they become bored and detached.

WAYS TO HELP PEOPLE PAY ATTENTION

- ➤ Ask questions.
- ➤ Use engaging visual aids.
- ➤ Create group exercises.
- ➤ Show video clips.
- ➤ Use appropriate humor.
- ➤ Make startling statements.
- ➤ Provide relevant examples.
- ➤ Change mediums.
- ➤ Give them shortcuts or tips.
- ➤ Keep your body moving.
- ➤ Avoid excessive detail.
- ➤ Make sure your transitions flow.

You can see that these techniques are used to seize the attention of your listeners when their minds have started wandering. Use these techniques, and you will be able to bring back your audience's attention.

Movement is another common technique for grabbing attention. It causes us to be alert. Stores utilizing movement-oriented end-caps (displays at the end of the aisle) always have more shoppers in the store than those using end-caps without movement. You will see movement at the grocery store as the coupon flies toward you when it detects your movement. You will also see people dancing on the street in strange costumes and waving large signs drawing your attention toward the store. You can use this strategy to your advantage during a presentation. When your movements are purposeful and well timed, your audience will be more tuned in to your message.

When all else fails and you are losing your audience, maybe you should try a little caffeine. Caffeine can arouse and increase attention, and it can therefore help in the world of persuasion. A study was done where participants drank orange juice laced with caffeine before reading a persuasive communication. The study found that those who had the caffeine in their orange juice had greater processing and were more influenced by the persuasive communication.[16]

USING THE ART OF QUESTIONING

Of all the tools in your persuasion toolbox, questioning is probably the one that Power Persuaders use the most.. Questions are used in the persuasion process to create mental involvement, to guide the conversation, and to find out what your prospect needs. Questioning is a very diverse and useful tool. An important study observed hundreds of negotiators in action in an attempt to discover what it takes to be a top negotiator. Their key finding was that skilled negotiators ask more than twice as many questions as average negotiators.[17]

Much like movement, questions elicit an automatic response from our brains. We are taught to answer questions. We automatically think of a response when asked a question. Even if we don't verbalize the answer, we think about it. Most people want to be cooperative. We don't want to be considered rude by not answering the question. Questions stimulate a thinking response.

How do you form a good question? First, design your questions ahead of time. The structure of your questions dictates how your listener will answer them. When asked to estimate a person's height, people will answer differently depending on whether the question is "How tall is he?" versus "How short is he?" In one study, when asking how tall versus how short a basketball player was, researchers received dramatically different results. The how-tall question received an average guess of 79 inches, whereas the how-short question received the guess of 69 inches.[18] Words have a definite effect on how people respond. "How fast was the car going?" suggests a high speed, but "At what speed was the car traveling?" suggests a moderate speed. "How far was the intersection?" suggests that the intersection was far away.

One questioning technique is the use of leading questions. Stanford professor Elizabeth Loftus researched how leading questions influenced eyewitness testimonies. In one project, her subjects watched a multiple-car accident. One group was asked, "About how fast were the cars going when they smashed into each other?" The second group was asked, "How fast were the cars going when they hit?" The third group was asked, "How fast were they going when they contacted?" The first group estimated that the cars were going about 40.8 miles an hour, the second group estimated 34 miles an hour, and the third group estimated 31.8 miles an hour.[19] The same question, worded three ways, led to three different answers.

Leading questions not only alter the way we interpret facts, but they also influence what we remember. In another study conducted by Loftus, subjects who were asked, "Did you see *the* broken headlight?" were three times more likely to answer yes than subjects who were asked, "Did you see *a* broken headlight?"[20]

When you are probing for information, ask open-ended questions. Responding to a question that can be answered with a simple yes or no is just too easy. For example, instead of saying, "Do you wish you had decided differently?" ask, "How did you feel after you made that decision?" Then the person's answer can be used to lead to your more detailed questions without seeming too intrusive: "Why did you make that decision?" or "What do you wish you could change about your decision?"

A good rule of thumb is to start with the easiest questions first. Draw your audience into the conversation, and help them feel relaxed and comfortable. People are encouraged by answers they know are right. Begin the conversation by starting with a general topic instead of a specific subject. You need to get the wheels in your listeners' minds rolling before you ask them to answer the more specific questions.

A Two-Way Street

Questioning can measure your prospects' level of receptivity. How receptive your audience is correlates with how many questions they ask or how many statements they make. So what do you do if there are no questions? A lack of questions could be due to several reasons: The audience needs time to think about what you have just said. They could be afraid to ask because of what others might think. Or they just might not be able to think of a good question to ask. Maybe you went on too long or stepped on a sensitive issue. Perhaps the audience has already made up their minds, or maybe they don't speak English.

The best questions draw a person into a conversation. So it is to your advantage to direct questions at your prospects that will reel them in:

➤ What do you think about . . . ?
➤ Have you ever thought about . . . ?
➤ How do you feel about . . . ?
➤ When did you start . . . ?
➤ Where did you find . . . ?

Be prepared to field questions that the audience will ask and want answers for. Brainstorm ahead of time for possible questions, scenarios, and answers. There will always be someone who asks the tough questions. If you are the expert, you are expected to know the answers. Obviously, if you don't know the answer, you should not make one up. If the question is way out of line, you can say you don't know the answer. But what do you do when your audience expects you to know the answer and you don't? How do you save yourself from losing credibility?

One way is to throw the question back to the audience and ask for the audience's help or opinions. Another strategy is asking the person to repeat the question, giving you more time to think of a response. To make sure you understand the question, you could also restate the question and ask whether that is correct. You can request that the person asking the question consult with you later: "Get with me at the break so we can talk about that." It is always better to tell one person you don't know than admitting it to the whole audience. Alternatively, you can ask questioners whether they have any of their own insights into the subject.

Handling Objections

When you get people involved in the process, you will get some objections. How you handle objections will correlate with how mentally involved people become with your message. The better you become at handling objections, the more persuasive you will become.

When you become a Power Persuader, you will learn to love objections. You will come to understand that voicing objections indicates interest and shows that the listeners are paying attention to what you are saying. The key to persuasion is anticipating all objections before you hear them. Fielding questions and handling objections can make or break you as a persuader. These skills will help you in every aspect of your life.

TIPS ON HOW TO HANDLE OBJECTIONS

1. *First find out whether the objection is something you can solve.* Suppose you are negotiating a large office furniture order, and the objection comes up about not being able to afford your furniture. You then find out your prospect just declared bankruptcy. Obviously nothing you can do or say will resolve such an objection.

2. *Let your prospect state the objection:* Hear out the prospect completely, without interruption. Wait until he is finished before you say anything. Hold your response until the other person is receptive to what you are about to say. This is the first time your prospect has voiced the objection and will not listen until he has said what is on his mind.

3. *Always ask your prospect to restate or repeat the key points.* With every replay, the objection becomes clearer in both your minds. Letting the prospect speak, particularly if she is upset, drains emotion from the objection. Allowing the concerns to be repeated also gives you time to think about a response and helps you determine the intent in bringing up the objection in the first place.

4. *Always compliment your prospect on her objection.* As a Power Persuader, you should appreciate a good objection; it dictates the direction in which you should take your presentation. You don't have to prove you are right 100 percent of the time. Skillful persuaders will always find some point of agreement.

5. *Stay calm.* Scientific tests have proven that calmly stated facts are more effective in getting people to change their minds than threats and force.

6. *Don't be arrogant or condescending.* Show empathy with your prospect's objection. Let him know that others have felt this way. Talk in the third person; use a disinterested party to prove your point. This is why we often use testimonials—to let someone else do the persuading for us.

7. *Give the person room to save face.* People will often change their minds and agree with you later. Unless your prospect has made a strong stand, leave the door open for him to later agree with you and save face at the same time. It could be that he didn't have all the facts, that he misunderstood, or that you didn't explain everything correctly.

Note: If you are dealing with a stubborn person who absolutely will not change his mind about anything, don't panic. This person is probably just closed-minded and always says no to everything. He might not have a clear idea about what you are proposing, he may have been hurt in the past, he may be afraid of being judged, or he may feel his ideas are not appreciated. Don't take it personally; it will happen from time to time. Keep the door open to revisit the issue at another time.

TELLING MESMERIZING STORIES

Stories are powerful tools for persuaders. Compelling storytelling automatically creates attention and involvement with your audience. We have all been in an audience and not paying attention to the speaker, off in our own world. All of a sudden we perk up and start to listen because the speaker begins to tell a story. We sit up, listen attentively, take note of what is being said, and want to know what happens next. Whenever you sense your audience is starting to wander, have a relevant story ready for the telling. As human beings, we are drawn to anything that gives us answers, and stories give us answers. Stories give people the room and ability to think and persuade themselves. Studies also show that stories statistically will connect with more people than facts, numbers, examples, or testimonials.[21]

Note the word *relevant*. You can capture attention by telling a story, but you will lose long-term persuasiveness if the story does not relate to you or your topic. When your stories work well to underscore your main points, your presentation will hold greater impact. Remember, facts presented alone will not persuade as powerfully as they will when coupled with stories that strike a chord within your listeners. By tapping into inspiration, hope, and a person's innermost feelings, you will move your prospects with your story.

THINGS THAT STORIES CAN DO

- ► Grab attention and create mental involvement
- ► Simplify complex ideas
- ► Create memorable hooks
- ► Trigger emotions

> ➤ Tap into existing beliefs
> ➤ Persuade without detection
> ➤ Bypass existing resistance to you or to your ideas
> ➤ Demonstrate who you are

Stories answer questions in the audience's mind about who you are and what you represent. If you don't answer these questions for your listeners, they will make up the answers themselves. Your audience members can tell from a story whether you are funny, honest, or even whether you want to be with them. Remember, building rapport is a key ingredient for persuasion. Because you usually don't have time to build trust based on personal experience, the best you can do is tell your prospects a story that simulates an experience of your trustworthiness. Hearing your story is as close as they can get to the firsthand experience of watching you in action.

Your goal is to have the listeners arrive at your conclusions of their own free will. Your story needs to take them on a step-by-step tour of your message. A persuasive story simplifies your concepts so that your audience can understand what you are talking about and what you want them to do. We love stories that give us answers to our problems. We accept the answers a story gives more than if someone were to just provide the answers.

Courtroom lawyers often create reenactments of events. They make the stories so rich in sensory detail that the jury literally sees, hears, and feels the event as it unfolded. The trial lawyer's goal is to make the description so vivid that the jurors feel the client's distress as their own and are moved by it. The more concrete and specific your descriptive details, the more persuasive your storytelling will be. Using specific details pulls the listener into the story, making it real, making it believable.

Pack your stories with authenticity, emotion, and humor. Make sure they are straightforward and that the timeline or character development is not confusing. A confusing story will not convince. Use your body, voice, props, or music if necessary to intensify your message because they reach all the senses. Engaging the senses of your listeners will make your story more effective. When you can get your listeners to see, hear, smell, feel, and taste the elements of your story, their imaginations will drive them to the point of experiencing without actually being there.

As you learn to incorporate the senses in your stories, you will find that their effects can persuade faster than your words. For example, smells and tastes can be very powerful. Both can evoke strong emotional memories and even physiological reactions in your listeners. Invite your audience to imagine the smell of freshly baked chocolate chip cookies, and you will see noses flare and faces relax with the feeling associated with that special aroma. Such sensations will fill their minds with feeling. You want the experience to come alive in their minds as if it were happening to them. Paint the picture in such a way that it becomes so real that your audience feels a part of it. People will participate in your stories when you let them.

The Zeigarnik Effect

Being left hanging drives us crazy! We want to know the end of the story—the missing piece. We want our tasks to be completed so that we can check them off our list. This reaction is known as the Zeigarnik effect, named after Bluma Zeigarnik, a Russian psychologist. This effect is the tendency we have to remember uncompleted thoughts, ideas, or tasks more than completed ones.

The story goes that the Bluma Zeigarnik was sitting in a café in Vienna when she observed that a waiter could remember everything someone had ordered but that, once the food was delivered, the waiter forgot everything. This led her to realize that it is easier to remember everything about an uncompleted task but that, once the task is completed, the memory immediately fades. That uncompleted task will hold onto our memory, improve the recall, and help us remember. We experience intrusive and almost nagging thoughts about a goal or an objective that was left incomplete. It is built into our psyche to want to finish what we start.[22]

We see the Zeigarnik effect on the television news and other programs. Right before a commercial break, the newscasters announce an interesting tidbit that will come later in the hour. This piques your interest, and, rather than flipping the channel, you stay tuned. Movies and dramas on television also leave you in suspense. By leaving something uncompleted right before the commercial break, the programs draw our attention, keep us involved, and motivate us to continue watching. We don't feel satisfaction until we receive finality, closure, or resolution of the message, our goals, or any aspect of our life. Incomplete tasks trigger thoughts, and the thoughts of the incomplete task trigger more memory retention. More memory retention triggers anxiety that triggers more thoughts of the uncompleted business.[23]

You also see the Zeigarnik effect in the courtroom. People feel more confident and impressed with information that they discover for themselves over time. Persuaders must therefore slowly disperse information, rather than dumping large volumes of it all at once. A good lawyer does not disclose everything known about the case or the plaintiff during the opening statement. As the trial progresses, the jury can fill in the blanks for themselves with the additional information they gradually receive. This works much better than dumping all the information on them at the beginning. Limiting the amount of information holds the jurors' attention longer and gives the message more validity. The jury discovers the answers for themselves and is more likely to arrive at the desired conclusion.

ENGAGING THE SENSES

Our five senses help us create generalizations about our world. You should engage as many senses as possible when trying to persuade an audience. When we learn, 75 percent comes to us visually, 13 percent comes through hearing, and 12 percent comes through smell, taste, and touch.[24]

However, keep in mind that we gravitate toward three dominant senses: sight, hearing, and feeling, or, visual, auditory, and kinesthetic sensations. Most people tend to favor one of these perceptions over the others. As a Power Persuader, you need to identify and use your prospect's dominant perspective of the world. Granted, we generally make use of all three senses, but the point is to find the dominant perception. As you determine the dominant mode, consider the size of your audience. If you are speaking to one person, for example, you would want to pinpoint the one dominant perception in that person. If you have an audience of one hundred, on the other hand, you need to use all three styles.

For example, if you were to ask an auditory person who was a eyewitness to a robbery, she might describe the situation as follows: "I was walking down First Avenue listening to the singing birds when I heard a scream for help. The yelling got louder, there was another scream, and the thief ran off." A visual person might describe the same situation this way: "I was walking down First Avenue watching the birds play in the air. I observed this large man coming around the corner. He looked mean and attacked the smaller man. I saw him take his wallet and run from the scene." The kinesthetic person might use this description: "I was walking down First Avenue, and I felt a lump in my throat, feeling that something bad was going to happen. There was a scream, there was tension, and I knew that a man was getting robbed. I felt helpless to do anything."

The most common sense is sight, or visual perception. One study showed that those who used visual presentation tools (slides, overheads, etc.) were 43 percent more persuasive than subjects who didn't. Also, those using a computer to present their visual aids were considered more professional, interesting, and effective.[25] Visually oriented people understand the world according to how it looks to them. They notice the details, like an object's shape, color, size, and texture. They say things like, "I see what you mean," "From your point of view . . . ," "How does that look to you?" "I can't picture it," and "Do you see what I mean?" They tend to use words like *see, show, view, look, watch,* and *observe.*"

Auditory people perceive everything according to sound and rhythm. Phrases you would commonly hear would be, "I hear you," "That sounds good to me," "Can you hear what I'm saying?" "It doesn't ring a bell," and "Let's talk about it." They use words such as *hear, listen, sounds, silence, harmony, say, speak, discuss,* and *verbalize.*

Kinesthetic people go with what they touch or feel, not only in a tactile way, but also internally. They are very into feelings and emotions. A kinesthetic person would say things like, "That feels right to me," "I will be in touch with you," "Do you feel that?" "I understand how you feel," and "I can sense it." They use words such as *feel, touch, hold, connect, reach, tension, sense, lift,* and *understand.*

On average, 40 percent of the population tends to be visual, 20 percent tends to be auditory and the other 40 percent tends to be kinesthetic. Visual people want images, visual aids, pictures, and props. Auditory people need it written down; they love a great story and the use of the spoken word. Kinesthetic people need it to feel right, touch the props, and perform tasks or exercises.

One last word on visual, auditory, and kinesthetic sensations: A general way to tell which type describes a person is to watch the movement of their eyes when they have to think about a question. Ask them a question, watch their eyes, and make sure the question is difficult enough that they have to ponder for a moment. Generally, although not 100 percent of the time, if they look up when they think, they are visual. When they look to either side, they are usually auditory. When they look down, they are kinesthetic. I am simplifying a complicated science, but, if you try it, you will be amazed at the accuracy of this technique.

Keep your audience mentally and physically involved, and watch your ability to persuade increase. Your job is to keep it simple, keep them involved, and turn those large steps into baby steps. It is very difficult to persuade someone who is:

- Bored.
- Confused.
- Not listening.
- Too comfortable.
- Too hot or cold.
- Overwhelmed.

BACKFIRE

The Law of Involvement will never work if those in your audience don't like you or don't trust you. The law will also be useless if your product or service has no perceived value or if the prospects don't have a need or want for it. Learn to reduce the distance from introduction to the call-to-action.

CASE STUDY

Walking into a local gym, I passed the front counter and made eye contact with the owner of the nutritional/smoothie store. The store offered professional advice, fresh smoothies, and pills and powders for everything. I noticed that my smile was not returned, so I asked him "How's business?" "Not good," he replied. He had plenty of foot traffic to do a good business, but sales were not soaring. I said, make me a smoothie and I will give you a strategy that will increase your sales by 50 percent. He agreed and made me a great smoothie. What would you recommend using the Law of Involvement?

Remember that the goal with involvement is to make it as easy as possible for your potential prospect to do business with you or consider doing business with you. The first thing I recommended was to offer monthly accounts. Think about it. You have just worked out, a smoothie sounds good, but your wallet is in the car. The store was losing sales because, to make a purchase, potential customers had that extra step. They had to had to go out to the car and come back. The next step would be to give out free samples to show people what they were missing or free consults to prove their worth.

. . . .

Additional Resources: Increase Involvement Report (maximuminfluence.com)

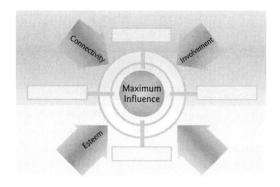

CHAPTER 5

The Law of Esteem

How Praise Releases Energy

I can live for two months on a good compliment.   —MARK TWAIN

I went to the local mall to try on suits. I had been thinking about buying a suit, but I was indifferent about making a purchase that day. A well dressed gentleman approached me and asked, "What type of suit are you looking for?"

I answered, "Probably blue."

"What size are you?" he asked.

I replied, "I'm not sure."

"Let's find out," he suggested. He measured my waist and then my chest and then my chest again. He looked at me with a twinkle in his eye and asked, "Do you work out?"

I responded, "Why yes, I do."

He nodded. "I thought so. You'll need a suit that has an athletic cut."

Smiling, I felt the rush of self-confidence. I knew he was attempting to sell me a suit, and he was doing it. I took the bait, and he reeled me in. His technique was so simple, yet so powerful. Yes, I went home that day with a new suit (it was on sale).

The Law of Esteem identifies that all humans need and want praise, recognition, and acceptance. Acceptance and praise are two of our deepest cravings; we can never get enough. William James once said, "The deepest principle of human nature is the craving to be appreciated." You can give simple praise to children and watch them soar to the top of the world. We know how a simple thank-you can make our day. Human beings have a psychological need to be respected and accepted. We need affection to satisfy the need to belong, we want praise so that we can feel admired, and we want recognition to satisfy our need for personal worth.

In the persuasion process, people will act and behave in a certain way in order to validate compliments. If you present your request in a manner that compliments or builds up your audience, they will be much more inclined not only to follow through but to do so eagerly. Compliments have the power to change behavior because they make the recipient feel needed and valued. The individual now has a reputation to live up to or an opportunity to prove the validity of the compliment. Further, it's hard to not get along and comply with people who admire you, agree with you, and do nice things for you. On the flip side, the doors of persuasion swing close when you bruise egos. This includes stepping on someone's toes, making them look bad, destroying their ideas, or topping their stories.

To use the Law of Esteem effectively, you must clearly understand the relationship between an inflated ego and a healthy self-esteem.

SELF-ESTEEM

Self-esteem (how much you like yourself) is the elusive aspiration of most people. It is confidence or self-satisfaction in oneself. Where does self-esteem come from? The people who are truly happy and comfortable with themselves are the ones who are able to live with and achieve what *they* want, not what they think *others* want. When people truly function in this manner, they are more pleasant to be around. They tend to be more generous, upbeat, and open-minded. They fulfill their own needs but are careful to consider the needs of others.

People who possess self-esteem are strong and secure; that is, they can admit when they are wrong. They are not unraveled by criticism. Their self-confidence permeates into all aspects of their lives: their jobs, their education, their relationships, and their income. After an in-depth study, the National Institute for Student Motivation even rated self-confidence as more influential in academic achievement than IQ.[1] Other studies have shown that self-esteem even impacts income levels.[2] A persuader must have a healthy self-esteem. A study has revealed that high-self-esteem people are more liked.[3]

Unfortunately, several studies show that Americans overall do not enjoy high self-esteem. Two out of three Americans suffer from varying levels of low self-esteem. In one survey of child development, 80 percent of children entering third grade said they felt good about themselves. By fifth grade, the number had dropped to 20 percent. By the last year of high school, only 5 percent of the seniors said that they felt good about themselves. To some degree, we all suffer from low self-esteem in different areas of our lives, whether it's our IQ, our looks, our education, or how we look in a swimsuit. The short list of symptoms attributable to low self-esteem includes:

- The inability to trust others
- Aggressive behavior
- Gossiping
- Resentment of others
- Criticism of others
- The inability to take criticism
- Defensiveness
- The inability to accept compliments

Our culture suffers so greatly from low self-worth for two main reasons. First, media and advertising continuously show us how we should look, what we should drive, and how we should smell. The message is that we are never good enough with what or who we are. We see images of grooming, fashion, popularity, and attractiveness to which we can never measure up. These images constantly remind us that we need to improve ourselves and that there is always someone better than us. Second, we judge and measure ourselves not against our own norm but against some other individual's norm. But because we think, believe, and assume that we should measure up to some other person's norm, we feel miserable and second-rate, concluding that something is wrong with us. In other words, the natural human tendency is to compare our weaknesses to other people's strengths.

Esteem is definitely among the very top of the list of all the human needs. When you're in a persuasive situation and not sure what to do, helping your prospect feel important is a fail-proof place to start. The studies show that low-self-esteem people are always looking for cues that indicate rejection.[4] Don't give them any such cues.

THE INFLATED EGO

Each of us has an ego, and at times a very fragile one. We all yearn to feel important. The ego demands respect, wants approval, and seeks accomplishment. Deep inside every man and woman is a desire to feel important and have the approval of others. This ego of ours can cause us to act illogically and destructively, or it can cause us to act nobly and bravely. When our ego is starved, we seek nourishment for it in any way we can get it. Feed the hungry ego, and it will be more persuadable. This hunger is universal; our egos must be fed daily. We need an affirmation every day that our worth as a human being is still intact and that we are appreciated and noticed. After analyzing many surveys, Researcher J. C. Staehle found that the principal causes of dissatisfied workers stemmed from the actions of their supervisors.[5] Those actions included the following, listed in the order of their importance:

- ➤ Failing to give employees credit for suggestions
- ➤ Failing to correct grievances
- ➤ Failing to encourage employees
- ➤ Criticizing employees in front of other people
- ➤ Failing to ask employees their opinions
- ➤ Failing to inform employees of their progress
- ➤ Practicing favoritism

All of these actions are related to a bruised ego. This is unfortunate because studies show that employees are most effective when they are recognized for their efforts. Psychologists at the University of Michigan found that the foreman of a construction crew who is interested in the people working under him gets more work out of them than the bossy type who tries to force them to work harder.[6]

When you find yourself in a persuasive situation, you must seek to enhance your prospect's esteem in some way. Too often we present ourselves in a manner that evokes feelings of threat, competition, jealousy, and mistrust. When enhancing someone's ego, be sure your praise is sincere and genuine. When we solicit someone's cooperation, everyone wins. For example, what happens when a sales associate tells a woman she looks great in the dress? The woman changes back into her original outfit and heads straight for the register! She feels great, and the associate gets her sale. Or how about when someone in shipping says she can really tell you've been working out? You do your "Can you tell?" expression, and then the next thing you know, you're helping her carry boxes. You get to bask in the glory of hearing someone say that you look strong, and then you're extended the opportunity to demonstrate your power and might.

We can all learn from General James Oglethorpe's example. The general wanted King George II of England's permission to establish a colony in the New World. Yet none of his arguments or presentations, no matter how carefully crafted, won the king over. At last, the general had a brilliant idea. He proposed that the colonies be named after the king. Suddenly, the general had not only permission but abundant financial means and even people to help populate the new colony of Georgia.

A particular set of ego rules should be employed when you are dealing with a superior. The Peter Principle states that people are promoted to the level of their incompetence or, in other words, to a position that is beyond their talents or skills. Many times when people get power, they have personal feelings of incompetence. They feel that somebody else could be smarter or that another manager might have a better idea. That creates an ego that can quickly get defensive. Many times these people will try to cover up their lack of self-confidence and go out of their way to make a mistake look like your fault. They put so much pressure and stress on themselves to be right, to be smart, or to look competent that they create high barriers to persuasion.

When trying to impress your boss, approach the conversation differently from how you would handle an employee. Always make those above you feel comfortably superior. In your desire to please or impress them, do not go too far in displaying your talents. Otherwise, by inspiring fear and insecurity, you might accomplish the opposite of what you hoped for. Outshining the master can be a blow to the ego. The master always wants to appear more brilliant than the student. One president of the United States (who will remain unnamed) thought his golf game was pretty good because, while he was president, he always won. Funny thing happened after he left office: He started to lose. Think about it.

Challenge to the Ego

Here's another very effective technique. Anytime someone challenges your abilities, especially your abilities to do your business, what's your immediate and instinctive reaction? To prove the challenger wrong! Try politely expressing your concerns about the proposal and then watch the results. For example, if you told a supervisor, "I'm not sure you're able to get those reps of yours producing, so I may hire a consultant." Don't worry, that manager will be on it, pronto! Or look what happens when you say, "You probably don't have the ability to pull this off." That person will make sure to prove you wrong! When employing this technique, however, be careful to avoid damaging the ego. When you cause damage instead of producing a challenge, you will create an air of indifference from your prospect.

Another challenge to someone's ego is commonly used by sports coaches. When a player is not putting out 100 percent at a practice, is late for meetings, or keeps making the same mistake, the coach has a perfect ego-based solution. He brings the team together and explains exactly what is going on with the player. He then has the whole team, except for the guilty player, run laps. This punishment is a challenge to the player's ego. Such a situation has to happen only once to be persuasive for every member of the team.

Pushing too hard, backing someone into a corner, or bruising an ego could have the opposite results. I was working as a general manager for a corporation and the biggest challenge I had was customer service. One woman in particular was on the list to be let go. She was insulting the customers, yelling at other employees, and usually late. It was time to have that talk to see whether she should be terminated or was salvageable. I set an appointment for her to come to my office. When she arrived, I stood up, greeted her at the door, smiled, and thanked her for coming. She was about to sit down in the visitor's chair when I told her, "No, don't sit there. Please sit in my chair."

She gave me a puzzled look and obliged. I sat in the other chair and spoke. "You know what's going on better than I do. If you were me, if you were the manager, how would you solve these challenges?" An amazing thing happened as she detailed solutions that were almost identical to the ones I had come up with. The magic was that there was no push-back, no bruised ego. The ideas were her own. Instead of resistance, there was instant compliance. She never became a model employee, but she became a contributing member of the team.

Many messages can challenge our egos. A teacher might tell the student, "I'd like you to do these advanced assignments." A sales representative who isn't able to close might make a subtle attack on the prospect's ego by remarking, "I guess you don't have the authority to make that decision." You should see the egos take action!

RESPOND INSTEAD OF REACT

In persuasion, we are faced with the difficult task of building the egos of our listeners while placing our own egos on hold. To effectively persuade, you have to let go of your ego and focus on your objective. You don't have time to mend your bruised ego. Check your ego at the door, and remember your overriding purpose. Focus on persuasion, not on yourself.

Ingratiation: Make Others Feel Important

Ingratiation is gaining favor by means of a deliberate effort, such as compliments, flattery, and agreeableness. Ingratiation can also involve a special recognition of someone, such as, "We don't usually do this, but in your case I'm going to make an exception." Or, "I am personally going to take care of this matter and see that you get what you want." Many people consider ingratiation sucking up or brown-nosing, but it is an effective technique for making others more persuadable. This strategy works because the Law of Esteem increases likability and promotes an increase in self-esteem

Research has demonstrated these conclusions about using ingratiation. In one study, "ingratiators were perceived as more competent, motivated, and qualified for leadership positions by their supervisors.[7] In another study, subordinates who used ingratiation developed an increased job satisfaction for themselves, their coworkers, and their supervisor.[8] In yet another study, ingratiators enjoyed a 5 percent edge over noningratiators in earning more favorable job evaluations.[9] Ingratiation works even when it is perceived as a deliberate effort to win someone over. Our esteem is so starved that we accept any flattery or praise we can get.

INTERESTING INGRATIATION FACTS

- ➤ It is better to use one great effective ingratiation method than lots of smaller ones; in other words, less is more.[10]

- ➤ Ingratiation will always work better when we are using same-level or downward influence (coworker, employee).[11]

- ➤ Using apology and self-deprecation is more successful when you are persuading up or when there is a large difference in status.[12] Favors or compliments will have little effect.[13]

- ➤ When you act ingratiatingly toward someone who knows you have an ulterior motive, the effort will likely fail and decrease the other's liking toward you.[14]

THE LEVERAGE OF PRAISE

Sincere praise and compliments can have a powerful effect on people. Praise boosts one's self-esteem. When you genuinely give praise, it releases energy in the other person. You have seen it and experienced it yourself. When you receive sincere compliments or praise, you smile, your spirits soar, and you have a new aura. When our own esteem is low or our ego is bruised, we tend not to praise others.

Praise Others Daily

We crave and yearn for a boost to our esteem. We all wear an imaginary badge that says, "Please make me feel important." It is criminal to withhold our praise when we see someone, especially children, do great and honorable things. Yet then, when they do something wrong, we jump down their throats. We would never think of physically harming others or depriving them of food and water, yet often without reservation we hurt people emotionally or deprive them of love and appreciation. George Bernard Shaw said, "The worst sin toward our fellow creatures is not to hate them, but to be indifferent to them." We should make it a habit to give genuine praise to someone every day. Don't wait for a reason or for something big to happen. Be generous with your praise. Praise makes others more open to persuasion.

How to Give Sincere Praise

Always be sincere. Even the most cunning flatterer is ultimately detected and discovered. Complimenting someone sincerely for something small is better than complimenting someone insincerely for something big. If, instead of being constantly self-focused, we are attentive to others, we will always find building moments where we can deliver honest and sincere praise.

Be careful if you have not been using consistent praise with someone in the past, or your praise can backfire. A man attended a seminar on influence and interpersonal relationships. His AHA moment during the training came when he realized he rarely remembered to praise his wife and tell her how much he appreciated her. At times he even took her for granted. On the way home, he bought some beautiful roses and a large box of chocolates to show his appreciation. He came into the house and approached his wife. She turned around and almost instantly started to cry. He was surprised and asked what was wrong? She said that she had had a terrible day and that everything went wrong. "The car broke down, little Jimmy got in trouble at school, the dog ran away, and now you come home drunk."

Often it is more effective to praise the specific act rather than the person. This way, your praise is attached to something distinct and concrete. It is less likely to be interpreted as flattery or favoritism when you praise is for something specific. General compliments may have temporary effect. However, they can incite jealousy from others and create even more insecurity in recipients who are often not really sure what they did to deserve a compliment. Then they feel pressure to live up to the standard you have set, even though they're not sure how or why it was set. They may even subconsciously fear that you will retract the praise because they don't know how to keep it. Things really backfire when they feel mistrustful toward you. Have you ever witnessed coworkers gathering to complain after a pep rally with the boss? Instead of feeling inspired and motivated, everyone gripes about how the boss was full of it. Of course, during the meeting, everyone played along because that was their job and they had to listen. When a boss asks you to do something, you do it because you have to. When someone has influence or is a leader, you do it because you want to. In other words, praise something they can't refute or think you are just saying because you are trying to be nice.

As a manager or supervisor, your responsibility to praise and recognize your employees is paramount. Regularly communicate the organization's changing objectives and priorities, and show employees that you feel they are important enough to be aligned with your goals. Invite new ideas from workers, stressing that there are always better ways to do any task. Trust workers by delegating responsibilities that give growth opportunities. Check with employees to determine what extra time or tools they need to fulfill these requests. Be fair to everyone. Playing favorites undermines morale. Praise each employee for any job well done. Doing so verbally is okay, but putting it in writing is even better. Want to know another plus? Sincere praise costs your organization absolutely nothing!

An interesting study was done with praise and hairdressers. Two female hairdressers would offer either no compliments, one compliment, or two compliments after washing and cutting their customers' hair (male and female). They would say either nothing or "Your hair looks terrific" or "Any hairstyle would look good on you." The researchers took a look at the amount of tips the hairdressers got. The difference between no compliments and one compliment was almost 4 percent. The interesting part of the study was that there was no significant increase in tips when the hairdressers added a second compliment.[15]

Effects of Praise

You know people are more likely to be persuaded to say yes when you make them feel good about themselves, their work, or their accomplishments. People will do almost anything for you when you treat them with respect and dignity and show them that their feelings are important.

The following example shows the immense strength of praise. At a small college in Virginia, students in a psychology course decided to see whether they could use compliments to change how the women on campus dressed. For a while, they complimented all the female students who wore blue. The percentage of the females wearing blue rose from 25 percent to 38 percent. The students then switched to complimenting any woman who wore red. This caused the appearance of red on campus to double, from 11 percent to 22 percent. These results indicate that when you favorably comment on behavior, that behavior will increase.

Praise can also cause people to change their minds. In another study, student essays were randomly given low or high marks (grades are a form of praise). When surveyed, the students who had gotten As tended to lean even more favorably in the direction of the positions they had advocated in their essays. Students who had received failing marks, however, weren't as willing to stand behind their previous positions.

When we show people that they are important, we can persuade them to do many things. For example, Andrew Carnegie devised a plan to sell his steel to the Pennsylvania Railroad. When he built a new steel mill in Pittsburgh, he named it the J. Edgar Thompson Steel Works, after the president of the Pennsylvania Railroad. Thompson was so flattered by the honor that he purchased steel exclusively from Carnegie.

BACKFIRE

Compliments need to be sincere, positive, and specific. Make sure the recipients know you mean it. Don't let your own ego or low self-esteem get in the way. Keep your ego in check, and focus on your prospect's esteem.

CASE STUDY

I was consulting with a group of auto technicians about increasing referrals and enhancing their marketing. An interesting scenario unfolded. One of the technicians explained that he customarily gave away basic automotive help. For example, if a female would drive up with an interesting noise, the technician would open the hood and fix it. Within, say, 90 seconds, the noise was gone. He would tell her that there would be no charge and that he would love her business in the future. He estimated that 80 percent of the time the females returned to his garage (Law of Obligation). When the prospect was a male, something different happened. Although the situations were identical, the males did not return most of the time. He estimated the males returned only 30 percent of the time. What was going on? Why the violation of reciprocity? Using the Law of Esteem, how would you fix this?

It came down to a bruised ego. The male saw that it was an easy fix, and he felt he should have known how to do it. He felt stupid. So I had the technician change the way he communicated, so as not to bruise the customer's ego. After doing the quick fix, he would say, "I got lucky. That's always a tough one to spot." Or, "It took me 20 years as a auto technician to figure that one out." Then the technician would say, "There's no charge. I would love your business in the future." That simple change helped his return rate shoot up dramatically.

. . . .

Additional Resources: Power of Praise Report (maximuminfluence.com)

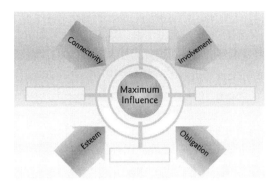

CHAPTER 6

The Law of Obligation

How to Get Anyone to Do a Favor for You

Nothing is more costly than something given free of charge.

—JAPANESE SAYING

Every month, a gentleman used to walk into my office, unsolicited, to try to get our business. He was selling office supplies and other items that we could get anywhere. I appreciated his tenacity, but we were under contract with another company. He would graciously give us a dozen cookies when he left. They were great cookies and always welcome during a business day afternoon. He would come by every month, accept our rejection, and leave us those tasty cookies. We soon started calling him the Cookie Man. Months passed, our contract expired, and we eventually bought supplies from the Cookie Man. The key to obligation is knowing that the results might not be instant but that the sense of reciprocity will put you higher on the list for a presentation or consideration for future business.

Obligation has been used as a persuasive technique since the beginning of time. We see companies offering free downloads, free estimates, or gifts in the hope of opening the door to persuasion. You probably have attended a party at the house of a friend who is promoting a product or business. Out of friendship, you attend, eat their refreshments, enjoy their hospitality, take their free gift, and feel an obligation to buy or do something. So what do you do? You order the cheapest item in the catalog to rid yourself of the obligation or indebtedness.

Or maybe this has happened to you. You are buying a car and playing hardball with the sales rep. You've negotiated back and forth and are getting nowhere. You are ready to walk away when he says that he will talk to his manager one last time. As he gets up, he says, "You know, I'm thirsty. I'm going to get myself a bottle of water. Would you like one?" "Sure!" you say, oblivious to his tactic. He comes back with the water and a better deal from his manager. It's not the deal you wanted, but you feel it's the best you're going to get. So you accept it. As you think about it later, you see that one of the reasons you bought the car was because of a subconscious trigger. That bottle of water served as an obligation trigger. You feel indebted to the car salesperson because of this small courtesy. He created the obligation with a $1 bottle of water. You return the favor and get out of his debt by buying a $20,000 car.

DEFINITION OF THE LAW OF OBLIGATION

The Law of Obligation, also known as pregiving or reciprocity, states that, when others do something for us, we feel a strong need, or urge, to return the favor. Returning the favor rids us of the obligation created by the first good deed. The adage "one good turn deserves another" is a part of social conditioning in every culture. And, even beyond that, the maxim serves as an ethical code that does not necessarily need to be taught but is nevertheless understood. For example, when someone smiles or gives us a compliment, we feel a great need to return the smile or compliment. Even when these gestures are unsolicited, we feel a sense of urgency to repay the person who has created the mental or psychological debt. In some cases, our need to subconsciously repay this debt is so overwhelming that we end up dramatically exceeding the original favor. The reciprocity trigger created by the car salesperson's water is a classic example of this principle. Most of us keep a mental scorecard of these favors.

People often consciously trigger feelings of indebtedness and obligation in others by carrying out an uninvited favor. Even if we don't want or ask for the gift, invitation, time, smile, or compliment, we still feel the need to return the favor when we receive it. Merely being indebted, even in the slightest sense of the word, can create enough psychological discomfort (and sometimes even public embarrassment) that we go to extraordinary lengths to remove the burdensome debt we feel. This is when we often disproportionately reward the original giver.

When my family moved to a new area, we gave a small Christmas gift to all our neighbors. I don't think the gifts cost more than $5 each. We were new on the block and wanted to get to know our neighbors. About 30 minutes after hand-delivering the gifts to our new neighbors, the doorbell rang. There stood one of our neighbors with a large box of truffles; this box had to have contained at least $50 worth of chocolates. He said, "Welcome to the neighborhood, and happy holidays." With that, he was off and on his way. He couldn't cope with the sudden subconscious debt he felt toward my family; so, to rid himself of his feelings of obligation, he gave back ten times more than he'd originally received. This is why many people buy extra holiday presents to have on hand just in case someone delivers a gift they did not count on.

The Law of Obligation also applies when we wish we could ask for favors, but we know we are not in a position to repay them or perhaps even ask for them in the first place.[1] The psychological and emotional burden created by such circumstances is often great enough that we would rather lose the benefits of the favor by not asking for it at all than experience the embarrassment and likely burden that might come from asking. For example, a woman who receives expensive gifts from a man may complain that, although she is flattered by and likes getting the gifts, she feels an uncomfortable sense of obligation to repay her suitor. Studies have shown that the converse is also true: When individuals break the reciprocity rule by showering favors on someone without giving them a chance to repay, there is an equal amount of discomfort.[2]

The drive to alleviate feelings of obligation is so powerful that it can make us bend toward people we don't even know. Accepting gifts or favors without attempting to return them is universally viewed as selfish, greedy, and heartless. It is often strictly due to this internal and external pressure that people conform to the rule of reciprocity. One university professor chose names at random from a telephone directory and then sent these complete strangers his Christmas cards. Holiday cards addressed to him came pouring back, all from people who did not know him and, for that matter, who had never even heard of him.[3] I had a student raise his hand at a seminar and say "I know that professor, and he is still getting Christmas cards from strangers more than 20 years later." Can you believe people have sent out Christmas cards all these years to someone they didn't even know!

The Law of Obligation can be used to eliminate animosity or suspicion. In one study, Cornell University researcher Dennis Regan had two individuals try to sell raffle tickets to unsuspecting workers. One individual made a conscientious effort to befriend the workers before attempting to sell any tickets. The other individual made a point of being rude and obnoxious around the workers. While on a break, the individual who had previously been rude to his prospects bought them drinks before trying to get them to buy tickets. The results of the study showed that the rude individual actually sold twice as many raffle tickets, even though the other had been much nicer and more likable.[4]

THE LAW OF OBLIGATION AND MARKETING

We often see this method at work when companies give out complimentary calendars, business pens, T-shirts, or mugs. This specialty advertising is an $18.5-billion industry.[5] It not only creates obligation but also keeps your name in front of your future customer. Studies show that 52 percent of people given a promotional product said they were more likely to do business with the person who gave it to them.

The same principle applies when you go to the grocery store and see those alluring sample tables. It is hard to take a free sample and then walk away without at least pretending to be interested in the product. Some individuals, as a means of appeasing their indebtedness, have learned to take the sample and walk off without making eye contact. Studies show that 70 percent will try the sample when asked and that 37 percent of those will buy the product.[6] However, some have taken so many samples that they no longer feel an obligation to buy or even pretend they're interested in the products anymore. Still, the technique works so well that it has been expanded to furniture and audio/video stores, which offer free pizza, hot dogs, and soft drinks to get you into the store and create instant obligation.

Pregiving is effective because it makes us feel as though we have to return the favor. M. S. Greenburg said this feeling of discomfort is created because the favor threatens our independence.[7] The more indebted we feel, the more motivated we are to eliminate the debt. An interesting report from the Disabled American Veterans organization revealed that their usual 18 percent donation response rate nearly doubled when the mailing included a small, free gift.[8]

A men's clothing store offers free pressing for suits bought in their store. This creates a sense of obligation among their customers, who, when they next decide to buy another suit, are more likely to buy it from the store that offered the freebie. Offering a free inspection or free estimate will also create obligation. Remember, this does not guarantee people will do business with you. But they will be more willing to listen, and this puts you higher on their list.

An interesting side effect to obligation is what it does to the giver. Those who help you or give you something feel more positive and have higher self-esteem.[9] The other bonus is that the giver also feels more committed to the recipient.[10] This means you should always let them reciprocate.

GIVE A GIFT, EXPECT A GIFT IN RETURN

Before a negotiation starts, offer some sort of gift. Note, however, that offering the gift before and not during the negotiation is of prime importance, or your token will come across as bribery. Your gift will almost always be accepted, even if only out of social custom and courtesy. Whether your recipient likes or wants your gift or not, the psychological need to reciprocate will take root, increasing the likelihood that your request will be met affirmatively. Of course, even when giving the gift before you make your request, be sure your motives come across as a sincere effort to help the recipient rather than yourself.

With regard to tipping, we know that reciprocity and giving have a direct effect on the size of the tip. A study was done in New York City on reciprocity and tipping. When a waiter or waitress gave chocolates to a customer with the bill, the tip increased an average of 3 percent. The tip increased even more when the waiter or waitress gave each person a chocolate, started to walk away, and then spontaneously offered them a second piece of chocolate.[11]

EXAMPLES OF THE LAW OF OBLIGATION

- ► Taking a potential client out to dinner or to play golf
- ► Offering free tire rotation or fluid fill-up between services
- ► Someone washing your car windows at a stoplight whether you want them to or not
- ► Generating money at "free" car washes by asking for a donation after the service is rendered
- ► A carpet cleaner offering to clean your couch for free
- ► Volunteering to help with a meeting
- ► Treating another manager to lunch
- ► Taking time to listen about another person's current challenge

Reciprocal Concessions

The research shows that the more you let someone persuade you or you give into their concessions, the more frequently the other party will reciprocate. Researchers have found that when others persuade you to change your mind, they will be inclined to do the same if you approach them. Conversely, if you resist someone's persuasion attempts and do not change your mind, then that person will likely reciprocate in a similar fashion, resisting your attempts. Consider how you can use this effect to your advantage. Just approach a person with whom you wish to deal in the future and say something like, "You know, I got to thinking about what you said, and you're right." Such a concession is especially important in negotiations. Giving up on one of your concessions makes it easier for them to be persuaded to give up one of theirs.

CONCESSION FACTS

- ► When someone makes a concession during the influence or negotiation process, you feel more obligated to make a concession, and doing so creates a greater bond.[12]
- ► The number of concessions you make during a negotiation is in direct correlation to the number of concessions your opponent will make.[13]
- ► Make people work for their concessions. Take time to think about it. If you give in too easily, you might be perceived as weak.[14]

A study was done with psychology students at a university. They were placed into small groups and put into a bargaining situation. They were randomly paired and told that one person would be the seller. They were buying a used appliance that could be purchased for $125 new or $35 used. The better the deal they negotiated, the more money they would earn. The biggest factor in reaching an agreement was concessions. The ones who reciprocated the most concessions reached the agreement the most often and the quickest.[15]

APPLYING THE LAW OF OBLIGATION

WAYS TO INCREASE THE POWER OF OBLIGATION

Is your gift/freebie *valuable*?

- ➤ Is it useful to your prospect?
- ➤ Does the prospect need it, or will he or she enjoy it?
- ➤ Does it have a high perceived value?

Is your gift/freebie *targeted*?

- ➤ Does your gift reach a specific demographic?
- ➤ Does it solve a problem, give you credibility, or prove your worth?
- ➤ Does it have your contact information? Will it always remind the prospect of you and keep you at top of the list?

Is your gift/freebie *timed*?

- ➤ Do you have a plan to keep on giving? (Obligation diminishes over time.)[16]
- ➤ Can you pregive (the sooner the better)?
- ➤ Can you make multiple deposits to their obligation bank account?
- ➤ Your giving must be perceived as altruistic. If the giver does this begrudgingly, the receiver is less likely to return the favor.[17]

This is a very simple law to implement. All you need to do is create a need or obligation in the mind of the other person. Ask yourself what you can do, give, or say that would create that indebtedness in your prospect's mind. As you think of the perfect persuasive situation, include one or more of the following items to help you create a greater sense of obligation. Any one, or any combination of several, of these will create a need to reciprocate in your prospect.

Examples of Reciprocity

Samples	Survey or analysis
Free product	No-cost assessment
Booklet	Travel bonus
Planning kit	Useful gift
Catalog	Food/treats
Industry report	Sports game (football, golf, etc.)
Exclusive information	Entertainment (movies, shows, etc.)
Audio/video	Concessions
Personal consult	Service
Free estimate	Favors
Inspection	Compliments
Vacation time	Invitations
Lunch or dinner	Personal attention

BACKFIRE

The Law of Obligation can backfire if you use it the wrong way or when you give a gift with an expectation. People are so skeptical now that they are suspicious of those who give them gifts. They will catch on to your tactics, quickly declining any gifts you might offer or even refusing to be around you. Your gifts will be perceived as setups. They will instinctively know that it's only a matter of time before you will be back asking for that favor to be returned. "When pre-giving is perceived as a bribe or a pressure tactic, it actually decreases compliance."[18] The obligation you create must be perceived as an unselfish act.

CASE STUDY

A local juice and coffee shop wanted to increase their business. Their goal was to get customers to linger longer and consume more beverages. The morning was always good, but they wanted the afternoon business to create more profit. They hoped to attract more business customers and entrepreneurs. They thought about charging for wi-fi, photocopies, or even a conference room in order to get more traffic. What would you recommend, using the Law of Obligation, to increase their business?

The key is *free*. They wanted to charge for additional services, but none of those services was their specialty or had the highest profit margin. They initially resisted offering free services, but they found that free wi-fi increased their sales and business traffic. Logically, it makes sense to charge for wi-fi, but, when it was given away, it increased product sales and overall income. They were concerned with people taking advantage, which will happen, but who cares when it increases profits? During this time, they gave out free samples and goodies (reciprocity), which also helped their long-term sales and profitability.

. . . .

Additional Resources: How Prospects Think Video (maximuminfluence.com)

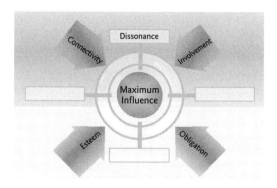

CHAPTER 7

The Law of Dissonance

Internal Pressure Is the Secret

There is only one way . . . to get anybody to do anything. And that is by making the other person want to do it.　　　　　—DALE CARNEGIE

My college students once conducted a research study on dissonance. They were looking to find a way to create inner pressure in other students. They did some research and found an interesting study about washing hands. The study found that 97 percent of females and 92 percent of males claim to always wash their hands after taking care of business. But in reality, only 75 percent of females and 58 percent of males actually wash their hands.[1] The students camped out in the university library restroom stalls waiting for someone who did not wash their hands. When they caught a culprit, they would follow him or her into the hallway between the restroom and library and call out in a loud voice, "Hey, wait! You forgot to wash your hands!" This event created what is called dissonance: the discrepancy between what you believe (or say you believe) and what you actually do. Dissonance is a critical persuasion tool.

The results from this experiment were fascinating. Very few people admitted they were wrong, made a mistake, or committed an error in judgment. Most of the students did not acknowledge that they did not wash their hands, but many made interesting comments:

- ➤ "No, you're mistaken. I did wash my hands."
- ➤ "Call security. This pervert was watching me in the bathroom."
- ➤ My professor said that the germs are so strong that it doesn't matter anymore."
- ➤ "I was just about to use my hand sanitizer."
- ➤ "You're supposed to wash your hands only before your eat."

It was rare to hear...

- ➤ "OK, I'll take care of that."

Cognitive dissonance is a psychological discomfort that happens when someone's actions or decisions are not congruent with their values, beliefs, or past commitments. The majority of people believed they should wash their hands. When they behaved contrary to their beliefs (i.e., did not wash their hands), they felt dissonance and sought ways to reduce that dissonance and justify why it was OK, rather than admit they were wrong.

Creating dissonance will increase your ability to persuade. When someone senses you are going to try to persuade them, say, to buy something—even though they need it, want it, like it, and can afford it—they will resist you. Dissonance will help people persuade themselves. Help them create their own internal pressure, and they will want to do what you want them to do.

Note: Careful! When you push too hard or back someone into a corner (as in this experiment), the approach could backfire on you.

THE THEORY OF COGNITIVE DISSONANCE

Leon Festinger formulated the cognitive dissonance theory at Stanford University. He asserted, "When attitudes or beliefs conflict with our actions,

we are uncomfortable and motivated to try to change." Festinger's theory sets the foundation for the Law of Dissonance.

The Law of Dissonance states that people will naturally act in a manner that is consistent with their cognitions and commitments. Cognition is a mental process that uses thoughts, beliefs, experiences, and past perceptions. Basically that means when people behave in a manner that is inconsistent with these cognitions (beliefs, thoughts or values), they find themselves in a state of discomfort. In this uncomfortable state, they will be motivated to adjust their behaviors or beliefs to regain mental and emotional balance. When our beliefs, attitudes, and actions mesh, we feel congruent. When they don't, we feel dissonance at some level—that is, we feel awkward, uncomfortable, upset, or nervous. To eliminate or reduce that tension, we will do everything possible to adjust our beliefs or rationalize our behavior, even if it means doing something we don't want to do.

Imagine a big rubber band inside of you. When dissonance is created, the rubber band begins to stretch. As long as the dissonance exists, the band stretches tighter and tighter. You've got to take action before it reaches a breaking point and snaps. The motivation to reduce the tension is what causes us to change; we will do everything in our power to get back our mental balance. We like to feel a level of consistency in our day-to-day actions and interactions. This harmony is the glue that holds everything together and helps us cope with the world and all the decisions we have to make. Dissonance causes us to distort our memories or remember what we want to see or how we wanted it to happen. This blurs reality and allows us to cover our errors and mistakes.

The human brain needs to be right. It is hard for us to admit we are wrong. We are programmed to justify that what we are doing is right and to avoid taking responsibility when things go wrong. Finding ways to prove ourselves right (even when we are wrong) is easier than admitting why we are wrong. Even when backed into a corner or shown evidence that proves we are wrong, we tend to stick with our reasoning or point of view. We will find reasons, proof, or social support for why what we did was OK. We will start to believe our lies to ourselves. We cannot be at fault, so we persuade ourselves why we were justified. This allows us to live with our thoughts, to manage our day-to-day activities, and to sleep at night. Have you ever proved to someone that he or she was wrong? Have you ever backed them into a corner? What happened? You made the perfect case, but you never heard from the person again.

THE HUMAN BRAIN

The past experiences that our brain recalls are generally much different from reality. Here is an interesting example. When interviewed about what percentage of the housework that couples do every week, the results get interesting. The wives estimated they do 90 percent of the work, and the husbands estimated they do 40 percent of the work.[2] Hmmm. Obviously those numbers add up to 130 percent. The numbers varied among couples, but they always exceeded 100 percent. The couples were not deliberately lying; this is how their brains recalled their weekly cleaning percentages.

Neuroscientists have made significant progress on how the brain processes information. Our brain can be very biased, especially in politics. People will always see the good in their party and find the bad in the other. During an election, a scientist asked people questions about their candidate and the candidate from the other side while they were administered an MRI. When they were told information about their candidate that caused dissonance, the logical side of their brain would shut down, and they could not recognize their bias.[3]

Did you know that, based on statistics, when you make a decision, you are right 50 percent of the time and wrong 50 percent of the time? Did you see what happened? I just created dissonance in you. You thought to yourself, "No, that can't be right. Maybe that's true for other people, but not me." Or maybe you thought that statistic is wrong. Either way, I stretched your rubber band, created dissonance, and within seconds you found a way that it could not be true about you.

What does this have to do with influencing other people? Everything. As a persuader, you need to help people feel dissonance about where they are now and where they want or need to go. They will usually resist when you prove them wrong. Just paint the picture for them, and let them feel the internal pressure. They have a problem, and as a persuader you are there to help them solve it. Merely help them realize that the path they are on (where they are) will not take them to where they want to go. This will build dissonance and internal pressure that will be highly influential as they persuade themselves.

METHODS OF PROTECTING MENTAL ALIGNMENT

When we feel dissonance, we have to find a way to deal with the psychological tension. When the rubber band stretches, we cannot live with the internal pressure. We will instantly try to find a way to relieve the tension and reduce our dissonance. We have an arsenal of coping mechanisms at our disposal to help us return to cognitive balance. When you see your prospect exhibit one of these behaviors (except modify), you have stretched the rubber band too far. It has snapped. The internal pressure was too much, and the prospect has gone down an easier or different path to find another solution instead of you. The following list outlines different ways people seek to reduce dissonance.

- *Denial:* To eliminate the dissonance, you deny there is a problem, by either ignoring or demeaning the source of the information. You could attack (usually verbally) the source, making it their fault. This is somebody else's fault! You are not to blame.

- *Reframing:* You change your understanding or interpretation of what really happened. This leads you either to adjust your own thinking or to devalue the importance of the whole issue, considering it unimportant altogether.

- *Search:* You are determined to find a flaw in the other side's position, to discredit the source, and to seek social validation or evidence for your own viewpoint. You might attempt to convince the source (if available) of his or her error. You might also try to convince others you did the right thing.

- *Separation:* You separate the beliefs that are in conflict. This compartmentalizes your cognitions, making it easier for you to ignore or even forget the discrepancy. In your mind, what happens in one area of your life (or someone else's) should not affect the other areas of your life. "Everyone else should obey the rules or conform, but the rules do not apply to me."

- *Rationalization:* You find excuses to explain why the inconsistency is acceptable. You change your expectations or try to rationalize what happened. You also find reasons to justify your behavior or your beliefs. You could say this is not a big deal because everyone is doing it.

- *Modify:* You change your existing beliefs to achieve mental alignment. Most of the time, this involves admitting you were wrong or off course and will make changes or adjustments to get back into alignment.

One real-life example–New Year's resolutions—is familiar to all of us.

You told your friend about your resolution to lose weight through diet and exercise. This will be your year, and you enlist your friend to help. Your friend commits to help you and you are off and running. Fast-forward one month and your friend has caught you polishing off a large container of ice cream. She calls you on your commitment, and your rubber band stretches. You feel dissonance. How to do you handle the tension?

- *Denial:* "You're fatter than I am. Why ride me? Remember the time you...."
- *Reframing:* "What I really meant was I will start my diet after I finish this big project."
- *Search:* "I researched exercise on the Internet and found that exercise actually hurts your knees and your health."
- *Separation:* "I meant to diet during summer for the beach. It's winter now, so I have time before I have to start."
- *Rationalization:* "I had a salad for lunch and a meal replacement drink for breakfast, so I'm way below my caloric intake for today."
- *Modify:* "You're right. I am going to start right now. Thanks for saying something."

Consider how each of these reactions could apply if the following experience actually happened in your own life: Your favorite politician, the local mayor, for whom you campaigned and voted, is in trouble. You spent your own time and money convincing family, friends, and neighbors to vote for this candidate. You thought he was a man of values, somebody who could be trusted. Now, after two years in office, he's been caught taking a bribe from a local company. The news creates dissonance inside you. To alleviate the dissonance, you might react in any one or combination of the following ways:

- *Denial:* "This is just the media going after him. He's doing a great job, so the opposing party is trying to smear his good name. This will all blow over when the facts come out. It's all just a big misunderstanding."
- *Reframing:* "The media said 'bribe.' Well, I'm sure he didn't actually spend the money. Maybe it was just a loan. I'm sure his staff knew all about the whole thing. Even if he did take the bribe, who doesn't? Is it that big a deal?"

➤ *Search:* "I've heard about the reporter breaking this story. He's blown things out of proportion before. All the friends I've talked to don't think the story is true. In fact, this reporter has been against the mayor from the time he became a candidate. I'm going to call that reporter right now."

➤ *Separation:* "I voted for him, and he's doing a great job. Inflation is low, unemployment is getting better, and crime has been reduced. He is doing everything he said he would. It doesn't matter what he does on the side. What matters is how he's doing his job. There's no connection between the bribe and his job performance."

➤ *Rationalization:* "Well, his salary is really low for all the work he does. He should be paid more for all grief he has to deal with. It's OK for him to make deals on the side. This is one of the perks of this office. Everyone probably does it. I would probably do the same thing."

➤ *Modification:* "I can't believe I voted for this guy. I feel swindled and taken advantage of. I really mistook him for a man of character. I need to apologize to my family and friends. I cannot support a man who does not have any ethics."

Buyer's remorse is a form of dissonance. When we purchase a product or service, we tend to look for ways to convince ourselves that we made the right decision. If the people around us or other factors make us question our decision, we experience buyer's remorse. On feeling this inconsistency, we'll look for anything—facts, peer validation, expert opinion—to reduce the dissonance in our minds concerning the purchase. Some of us even use selective exposure to minimize the risk of seeing or hearing something that could cause dissonance. Often people won't even tell family or friends about their purchase or decision because they know it will create dissonance.

EVERYDAY EXAMPLES OF DISSONANCE

Action	Belief	Dissonance Reduction
Eat a grape at grocery store	Stealing	Taste for quality
Speeding	Dangerous	Really important meeting
Texting while driving	Against the law	I'm a better driver.
Eating fast food	Unhealthy	I've been eating healthy.

Action	Belief	Dissonance Reduction
Not exercising on vacation	Exercise everyday	Exercise more next week.
Play lottery	Odds = Can't win	Someone has to win.
White lie	Lying is wrong	Protect their feelings

MAINTAINING PSYCHOLOGICAL ALIGNMENT

A study by Knox and Inkster found interesting results at a racetrack. They interviewed people waiting in line to place a bet and then questioned them again after they'd placed their bets. They found that people were much more confident with their decisions after placing their bets than before.[4] Once we make out decision, the horse sounds better, the product looks better, and our decision seems more correct. Not only does everything look better, but the alternatives look worse and indicate that we made the right decision.

Younger, Walker, and Arrowood decided to conduct a similar experiment. They interviewed people who had already placed bets on a variety of different games (bingo, wheel of fortune, etc.), as well as people who were still on their way to place bets. They asked the people whether they felt confident they were going to win. Paralleling the findings of Knox and Inkster's study, the people who had already made their bets felt luckier and more confident (before the results) than those who had not yet placed their wagers.[5]

These studies show that, to reduce dissonance, we often simply convince ourselves that we have made the right decision. Imagine the psychological toll if we have to continually revisit decisions, especially if they were perceived to be wrong. Once we place a bet or purchase a product or service, we feel more confident with ourselves and the choice we have made.

This concept holds true in persuasion and sales. Once prospects pay for your product or service, they will usually feel more confident with their decisions. Have them make the payment or finalize the choice as soon as possible! This will increase their confidence in their decision, and they will look for reasons to justify that decision. The key is to understand that people are so skeptical these days that they are looking for every reason not to do business with you. Once they find a few reasons or benefits that will help them solve their challenge, it is time to seal the deal. Once the deal is done, they will start finding reasons why it was a great deal. You can always fill in the blanks later.

USING DISSONANCE TO CREATE ACTION

Dissonance is a powerful tool in helping others make and keep commitments. In one study, researchers staged thefts to test the reactions of onlookers. At Jones Beach near New York City, the researchers randomly selected an accomplice to place his beach towel and portable radio 5 feet away from them. The ages of the people ranged from 14 to 60 and included both genders. After relaxing there for a while, the accomplice got up and left. After the accomplice had departed, one of the researchers, pretending to be a thief, stole the radio. Hardly anyone reacted to the staged theft. Very few people were willing to put themselves at risk by confronting the thief. In fact, only 20 percent of the nearby people made any attempt to hinder the thief.

The researchers staged the same theft again, only this time with one slight difference in the scenario. The minor alteration brought drastically different results. This time, before leaving, the accomplice asked each person lying nearby, "Excuse me, I'm going up to the boardwalk for a few minutes. Would you watch my things?" Each person consented. This time, with the Law of Dissonance at work, 95 percent of the individuals sought to stop the thief by chasing them, grabbing back the radio, and in some cases, even physically restraining him.

They did another study in the city of New York. They went to a busy restaurant and had a well dressed young woman take a seat. She would exit the restaurant and leave her briefcase. A few minutes later, the thief walked over and took the briefcase, and very few tried to stop him. In the second part of the study, the accomplice would say, "Excuse me. May I leave this here for a few minutes?" All subjects agreed to watch the briefcase. That commitment again dramatically increased the number of people who stepped in to stop the thief.[6]

Most people try to follow through when they promise to do something, especially if it is in writing. This is why corporations sponsor writing contests about social issues or their products. They really don't care about your writing style. They're really looking for consumer endorsement. The writer puts down, in her own words, what she thinks the company wants to hear about its issue or product. Having made a written commitment to supporting and endorsing a product or issue, the consumer will now support the sponsoring company in their cause or will voluntarily buy their product. You increase persuasion by using commitments throughout your presentation.

GETTING YOUR FOOT IN THE DOOR (FITD)

One aspect of the Law of Dissonance is the urge to remain consistent with our answers and our commitments. Even if someone begins with a small request, and then follows it up with a larger request, we still tend to remain consistent in our behavior and answers. This technique of capitalizing on such a principle has been called by several names, including foot-in-the-door (FITD), self-perception theory, or the sequential request. The principle is a means of using a person's self-perception to motivate her to take a desired action. When an individual complies a first time, she perceives herself to be helpful. If she is asked to comply a second time in an even greater way, she is likely to consent. In an effort to maintain consistency with the first impression and with her own self-perception, she agrees to give even more of herself.

The key to using FITD is to get the person to agree to a small initial request. For example, ask someone, "Can I have just thirty seconds of your time?" Most individuals would respond affirmatively. According to self-perception theory, the person would observe his own behavior and, in regard to this interaction, consider himself a helpful person. The second step in the FITD principle is making another, more involved request. "Can I try this on the stain on your carpet?" The person feels he should consent to the second request because he is "that kind of person." He has already seen himself do other behaviors in support of the product or service, so he willingly complies with the second request.

Another study involved testing to see whether introductory psychology students would rise early to take part in a 7:00 a.m. study session on thinking processes. In one group, the students were told that the session would begin promptly at 7:00 a.m. Of these students, only 24 percent agreed to participate. In the second group, the students were first told what the study was and asked to participate. The 7:00 a.m. time was not mentioned until after they had consented to take part. Fifty-six percent of them did. When the opportunity to change their minds was presented to them, however, none of them took advantage of it. Ninety-five percent of students actually followed through and showed up for the 7:00 a.m. session.[7]

In another study, the researchers wanted to test FITD in door-to-door donations. In the first part of the study, participants were asked to sign a petition two weeks before being asked to make a donation. In the second half of the study, participants were asked for the donation the first time.

When they were asked to sign the petition before being asked for a donation, it resulted in more money donated than those who were asked for a donation first.

This FITD technique also worked well for smokers. They were asked to abstain from smoking for 18 hours. They were told to write down all the reasons they accepted the challenge. Then they were asked to stop smoking for six days. The group who wrote down their reasons and rationalized why they accepted the 18-hour challenge accepted the 6-day challenge 82 percent of the time. The other group who did not write down their reasons complied only 26 percent of the time.

If you can get someone to mentally commit to a product or a decision, he is likely to remain committed even after the terms and conditions change. This is why, when stores advertise very low prices on, say, computers, they include in small print, "Quantities Limited." By the time you get to the store, all the bargain computers are sold, but you are mentally committed to buying a new computer. Luckily for you, more expensive models are available. So you go home having spent $500 more on a computer than you originally planned, just because you needed to maintain a consistency between your desire for a new computer and your action of being in the store.

Using FITD Effectively

Here are three key principles in learning how to use this technique:

1. *Small commitments lead to large commitments.* For example, salespeople often focus first on securing an initial order, even if it's a small one. Once this is accomplished, the customer will be more likely to commit to buying from them again.
2. *Written commitments are more powerful than verbal commitments.* We know the power of the written word. When contracts are signed and promises are put into writing, the commitment level increases tenfold.
3. *Public commitments are stronger than private commitments.* Taking a public stand that is witnessed by others compels us to continually endorse that commitment. Otherwise, we risk being seen as inconsistent or dishonest. For example, many weight loss centers have their clients write down and share their goals with as many people as possible, thereby increasing the likelihood of success.

When utilizing this technique, you must first determine exactly what end result you are seeking. This will be the big commitment you ask for. You should then create several small and simple requests that are related to your ultimate request, making sure they can be easily satisfied.

Remember that the first request needs to be "of sufficient size for the foot-in-the-door technique to work,"[8] but, on the other hand, it cannot be so big that it seems inappropriate and/or is not easily and readily accomplished. Present a request that can be easily accepted, and you get a yes.

FOUR STEPS TO USING THE LAW OF DISSONANCE

Step 1: Find Their Cognition

What are your prospects' beliefs about, past experiences with, and attitude or feelings about you, your product, or service? You have to find out their wants and needs before you can create dissonance. How can you gently stretch the rubber band? What is the difference between where they are now and where they want to be?

Step 2: Get a Commitment

Commitments from your prospects should be public, affirmative, and voluntary.

Public

Make your prospect's decision as public as possible. Get a written commitment, and make that written commitment public. Involve family and friends in the proposed action. Engage your customer in a public handshake to seal the deal in front of other employees and customers.

Affirmative

You want to get as many yes answers as possible because yeses develop consistency within the person that will carry over into your major request. This technique makes it easier for prospects to say yes to your final proposal. Even if it is a watered-down, easy request, getting a yes to any request makes it easier to evoke the same response down the road.

Use a series of questions that all meet with yes. Desire increases with each yes, and decreases with each no. Every time we say yes to a benefit, our desire goes up.

Voluntary

When getting commitments, start small and build up to larger commitments. You cannot force commitments. Long-term approval has to feel as though it comes from your prospects' own will, something they want to do or say. They have to volunteer to test-drive the car, write on the contract, or request more information. Making their own commitment makes the action more voluntary and solidifies the commitment.

Step 3: Create Dissonance

Once you have the commitment, you can create the dissonance. You create that dissonance or imbalance by showing your prospects that they have not kept or are not keeping their commitment. For example, "If we don't act now, the homeless children will go to bed hungry." The person's self-image is squeezed from both sides by consistency pressures. The prospect feels great internal pressure to bring her self-image in line with her actions. At the same time, there is pressure to reduce dissonance.

Step 4: Offer a Solution

As a Power Persuader, whenever you create dissonance, you always need to offer a way out. You need to show, prove, or explain how your product or service can reduce the dissonance your prospect feels. For example, "If something happens to you, will your family be able to survive financially?"

Keep your ultimate request in mind. Prepare your whole persuasive presentation around the moment when you will make that major request. Once your prospects accept the solution, they have convinced themselves that they have made the right and only choice. As a result, they feel great about their decision. This makes the dissonance disappear. The decision was their personal choice. They know exactly what to do.

The solution is your call to action.

FINAL NOTE

As diverse human beings, we have to understand that we will all feel different levels of dissonance for the same experience. Some people need so much consistency and predictability in their lives that they will tend to feel a much higher level of dissonance than others. Also, introverts tend to feel more dissonance than extroverts.

BACKFIRE

Dissonance will backfire when you stretch the rubber band too far and it snaps. This happens when your prospect does not believe you, your claim is considered ridiculous, or you don't provide a solution. During persuasion, never back someone into a corner.

CASE STUDY

In a persuasive presentation training session with financial planners, I found that the planners knew how to give interesting facts and use convincing statistics. Their training goal was to become more persuasive and to generate additional business after their presentations. These planners were able to build the value of their product and prove that planning was a great investment, but they were not happy with the number of new clients. Most of these potential clients thought they had plenty of time and tended to wait to invest. What do you think was the primary reason (using the Law of Dissonance) that these prospects used to resist becoming new clients?

These financial planners stretched the rubber band but did not address the denial factor of dissonance. It is human nature to deny the existence of a problem and to put off their decisions. If people feel they can do something later, then the rubber band is no longer stretched, and they will delay their decision. We all know that usually means *no*.

To overcome their prospects' denial, I had the financial planners add a time element to their presentation. Their prospects saw a visual chart indicating that, if they waited or procrastinated, they would lose money. This addressed the denial factor of dissonance, and client acquisition dramatically increased. They were shown how much money they already lost and would lose by waiting to invest. The key is to prevent them from creating a reason why the negative effect of delay does not apply to them.

Additional Resources: Dissonance Application Video (maximuminfluence .com)

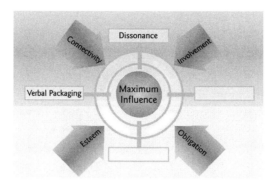

CHAPTER 8

The Law of Verbal Packaging

The Leverage of Language

**Real persuasion comes from putting more of you into everything you say.
Words have an effect. Words loaded with emotion have a powerful effect.**

— JIM ROHN

Have you ever listened to the airlines's instructions before takeoff? The flight attendants are careful with their every word. In the event of a water landing, your seat cushion can be used as a flotation device. Notice that they don't say "life preserver," but rather "flotation device." What they're really saying is, "If we crash into water, grab your seat cushion so you don't drown." Also, there is no barf bag on board; it's a motion discomfort bag. Or, "We are experiencing mechanical difficulties," not, "The plane is broken." They don't clean the plane; they refresh it. Planes aren't late; they're merely delayed. My personal favorite is that they never lost my luggage; they misplaced it.

Once, as a plane I was on was about to take off, one of the engines caught on fire. Smoke billowed past the windows, and fire trucks suddenly filled the runway. The pilot came on the announcement system and described the fire as "slight engine difficulties." "Slight?" What would "serious" be like?

Yes, airlines know the power of word choice in affecting their customers' emotions and point of view.

Over 60 percent of your day is spent in verbal communication, in which you could be persuading, explaining, influencing, motivating, or instructing. You can create movement, excitement, and vision with the words you use. The right words are captivating; the wrong ones are devastating. The right words make things come to life, create energy, and are more persuasive than the wrong words. As Mark Twain said, "The difference between the right word and the wrong word is the difference between lightning and a lightning bug." The bottom line is that the words you use attract or repel your prospects. Numerous studies have shown that a common trait of successful men and women is their skillful use of language.

The Law of Verbal Packaging states that the more skillful you are in the use of language and vocal techniques, the more persuasive you will be. People are persuaded by us based on our words. Words affect our perceptions, our attitudes, our beliefs, and our emotions. The words we use in the persuasion process make all the difference in the world. Language used incorrectly will trigger the wrong response and decrease your ability to persuade. Word skills are also directly related to earning power. Successful people all share a common ability to use language in ways that evoke vivid thoughts, feelings, and actions in their audiences. Carl Jung (the famous psychiatrist) revealed that all words are full of symbols and that each symbol triggers an emotional reaction or feeling. All words have emotional meanings that are different from their definitions in the dictionary. Understanding words and their emotional triggers will enhance your ability to persuade and influence.

THE INHERENT POWER OF WORDS

Words are used to explain events, to share feelings, and to help visualize the future. Words shape our thoughts, feelings, and attitudes toward a subject. They help us decide whether we should run, stay neutral, or take action. Even reading words can affect your thoughts, attitudes, and feelings. For example, read these six words out loud, slowly and with emotion. Notice how each word makes you feel.

Murder … Hate … Depressed … Cancer … War … Despair

Now read the following six words out loud, slowly and with emotion, Notice how each word makes you feel.

Wealth … Success … Happiness … Health … Inspired … Love

How did these words make you feel? Successful persuaders know how to use the right words to create the desired response in their audiences. Speakers with great verbal skills come across as more credible, more competent, and more convincing. Speakers who hesitate, use the wrong words, or lack fluency have less credibility and come across as weak and ineffective.

THE FUNDAMENTALS OF LANGUAGE USAGE

Properly used and packaged, language is a powerful instrument that can be fine-tuned to your advantage. We all know the basics of language, but mastery of the aspects of both language usage and vocal control can affect human behavior. The proper use of verbal packaging makes you adaptable, easier to understand, and more persuasive. This type of language is never offensive and is always concise.

Word Choice

Understand that proper language varies from setting to setting and from event to event. A particular word choice does not work in every circumstance or culture. Word choice can also be critical in defusing situations or in getting people to accept your point of view. Even one word can make the difference between rejection and acceptance. In a study by social psychologist Harold Kelley,[1] students were given a list of qualities describing a guest speaker they were about to hear. Each student read from either one of the following two lists:

1. Cold, industrious, critical, practical, and determined
2. Warm, industrious, critical, practical, and determined

Of course, the students who read the first list had less than positive feelings about the speaker. The interesting thing, though, is that the lists are exactly the same except for the first word! They found that the first word at the front of the list conditioned how the student felt in reading through the rest of the list. It didn't matter that none of the following words were negative. Just reading the word *cold* tainted how the students read the rest of the list.

As mentioned, the airline industry has mastered the power of words. They know that word choice is critical to getting their point across and to reduce stress. In one situation, a flight attendant had run out of steak as an option for dinner entrée. Instead of telling the customers their only option was chicken, the flight attendant said, "You can have a piece of marinated chicken breast, sautéed in mushrooms in a light cream sauce, or a piece of beef." Consequently, people chose the chicken because it sounded better. Think about the words describing the food the next time you read a restaurant menu.

Sales professionals also use words carefully. They know that one wrong word can send their prospect's mind somewhere else and lose them the sale. Here are some examples of language that salespeople use to help diffuse a potentially tense situation:

Words That Repel	Superior Words
Contract	Agreement/paperwork
Sign here	OK the paperwork
Cancellation	Right of rescission
Salesperson	Business consultant
Commission	Fee for services
Cost	Investment
Credit card	Form of payment
Objection	Area of concern
Expensive	Top-of-the-line
Cheaper	More economical
Service charge	Processing fee
Problem	Challenge
Appointment	Time to visit

Words also have a strong bearing on how we remember certain details. In one study, subjects were asked whether they had headaches "frequently" or "occasionally." Those who were interviewed with the word *frequently* reported 2.2 headaches per week, whereas those interviewed with the word *occasionally* reported only 0.7 per week.[2]

In another study, one group of individuals was asked whether they thought the United States should *allow* public speeches against democracy, whereas another group was asked whether they thought the United States should *forbid* public speeches against democracy. Although the questions bear similar implications, notice that the word choice makes them contrary to each other. Still, one might think the answers would be similar because they drive at the same point. Because of the word *forbid*, which caused them to want to hear the speeches, the response to the second question was much higher.

Have you ever noticed the opposite of Verbal Packaging in pharmaceutical commercials? They portray all these wonderful benefits and use a soothing, sophisticated voice to highlight them. Then, at the end of the commercial, they have to run through all the negative side effects: vomiting, headache, diarrhea, and so on. They read through these negatives quickly using a monotone voice! The effect is that negatives are deemphasized, and we, as viewers, are left with an overall positive impression. We never hear that the sleeping pill could cause diarrhea.

Double-Speak: Tame the Sting

The term double-speak means replacing an offensive word with a less offensive word or turning a negative into a positive that creates less sting and appears more attractive. Here are some examples of how double-speak has made its way into the business world:

Negative	Positive
Downsizing	Right-sizing
Demotion	Correct workforce imbalance
Dumb it down	Simplify
Stock market crash	Correction
Stupid idea	With all due respect
Lost money	Negative gross profit
Lying	Misrepresent the facts
Failure	Incomplete success
Bankrupt	Substantial negative net worth
Disinformation	Creative license
Employee theft	Inventory shrinkage
Irregularity	Practically perfect

Package Your Numbers

Often in marketing, or in any persuasive situation, people need to either play up or play down the greatness or smallness of certain numbers. When playing up a number, persuaders use this type of language:

- More than three quarters . . .
- Almost eight out of every ten . . .
- Better than two out of three . . .

When playing down a number, they use this type of language:

- Less than half . . .
- Fewer than two out of three . . .
- Under three quarters . . .

Word Choice in Marketing

Word choice in marketing and advertising is absolutely critical. Even in copywriting, every word matters. When you write copy, an e-mail, or a letter, every word can attract or distract the reader. Use words that capture their curiosity, grab their attention, and trigger emotions.

When advertisers spend millions of dollars each year, you can bet they have tested every word they are going to use. They want their word choices to psychologically lead you to believe their product is the best and that it will change your life. Skilled advertisers can get us to absorb their message unconsciously. They might even package an identical product with different words and phrases to reach a wider segment of the public.

Psychologist Daryl Benn conducted a study on how advertisers use word choice and catch phrases to sell different, but identical in effectiveness, brands of aspirin. Consider the following:

- *Brand A:* Proclaims 100 percent pure, nothing is stronger. Benn notes that governmental tests also showed that no brand was weaker or less effective than any of the others.
- *Brand B:* Advertises "unsurpassed in speed—no other brand works faster." The same governmental tests showed brand B works no faster than any of the others.
- *Brand C:* Declares that it used an ingredient "that doctors recommend." Governmental tests revealed that the special ingredient is nothing more than regular aspirin.[3]

The word choices in these advertisements work because the positive connotations make us assume that each advertised brand is the best. Advertisers know that changing just one word in their ad can dramatically increase the response rate.

Advertisers employ other words known as weasel words. These words sound good but don't allow you to put an exact number on the advertiser's claim. They let you justify and believe what you want. They are called weasel words because weasels are notorious for breaking into the chicken coop and sucking out the inside of the eggs without breaking the shell. The eggs look fine but in reality are hollow and empty, just like these words. Use these words when you don't want to use an exact number or when you are downplaying something potentially negative.

WEASEL WORDS

Helps	Up to	Hopefully
May	Almost	Might
Possibly	About	Claim
Improved	Approximately	Supposedly

Probably the biggest challenge with word choice in marketing comes when billion-dollar corporations want to translate just the right English word into the perfect equivalent in another language. The most famous marketing translation fiasco (or urban legend) was the Chevy Nova. Translated into Spanish, *nova* meant "doesn't go." When American Airlines wanted to advertise its new, leather, first-class seats in the Mexican market, it translated its "Fly in Leather" campaign literally, coming out as "Fly Naked" in Spanish! When Coors put its slogan "Turn It Loose" into Spanish, it read "Suffer from Diarrhea." The Dairy Association's huge success with the "Got Milk?" campaign prompted them to expand advertising into Mexico. It was soon brought to their attention that the Spanish translation read, "Are you lactating?" Scandinavian vacuum manufacturer, Electrolux, used the following in an American campaign: "Nothing sucks like an Electrolux."

The Use of Silence

How often have you noticed a sales rep overselling a product? You are ready to make the purchase. The sales rep feels you need to know everything about the product, and he starts to fill you in on all the details. This causes doubt to creep into your mind and you ended up leaving, telling the salesperson you would think about it. When someone has been persuaded and convinced, there is no reason to say any more. Strike when the iron is hot!

Sometimes the right word is no word. On occasion, we need to remain silent and let the other person talk. We have heard that, in negotiation, that the first one to talk loses. After the persuasion process and the final decision is ready to be made, make your proposal and shut up. The silence is nerve-wracking, but it's a critical time to let your prospect make the decision without your rambling on and on about your product or service.

More communication is not necessarily better persuasion. In fact, the less you talk, the smarter people think you are. The more you say, the more common and less in control you appear. Many individuals try to impress others with what they know by flaunting all their wisdom, but usually this strategy is just a turnoff. Why give them reasons not to buy? Let them tell you what they're looking for. After you've discussed what they care about, after they've made the decision to buy, then and only then should you fill in any remaining blanks with other benefits or features.

Use Vivid Language and Paint the Picture

Complete this visualization exercise with me: Pretend you are standing in a beautiful, sunny kitchen. You reach across the counter and grab a bright, juicy orange. You can feel that it is heavy with sweet, ripe juice. You bring the orange to your nose and can smell the delicious orange aroma. Reaching for a knife, you slice the orange and begin to peel back the skin. The aroma only becomes stronger as you tear the sections apart. One of the sections drips bright, sticky orange juice over your finger. You raise this juicy section to your lips and take a bite. As your teeth sink into the orange, you feel the juice burst out and swish around your teeth and tongue. The juice is incredibly sweet!

Did your mouth water? Almost everyone's does. The extraordinary thing is that if I had simply instructed you to produce saliva, you couldn't have done it. The vivid picturing technique works far better than the command because your mind cannot distinguish between what is imagined and what is real.

A Power Persuader has the ability to paint a picture with words. Your prospects will be able to see, hear, feel, and experience exactly what you are talking about. Your prospects become part of the message and can more fully understand how the product or service will change their lives. You must stimulate your prospects' senses by using words that activate their mind. You present your message through positive emotions because the positive thoughts of the audience will color their perception of what you want them to do.

We can all say, "I walked on the beach." But that's not half as effective as saying:

> **The sun was up and shining brightly on the warm sand. I took off my shoes and felt the soft sand between my toes. The seagulls floated lazily across the ocean sky. The waves soothed my soul as they rhythmically crashed against the shore. I could taste the salt of the breeze on my tongue.**

I think you can feel the difference between the two statements. Words activate all that we do. The words we use can make you physically ill, emotionally drained, hungry, and even salivate. And they can especially increase your desire to buy!

A utilities company, trying to convince customers of the advantages of home insulation, sent auditors to visit homeowners and point out the ways they were wasting energy. The auditors provided the homeowners with suggestions on how they could save money if they were willing to become more energy efficient. In spite of the clear financial benefits over the long term, only 15 percent of the audited homeowners actually went ahead and paid for the repairs. After seeking advice from two psychologists on how they could better sell the advantages of home insulation, the utilities company decided to change its technique by describing the inefficiencies more vividly. With the next audits, homeowners were told that the seemingly tiny cracks here and there were collectively equivalent to a gaping hole the size of a basketball. This time, 61 percent of the homeowners agreed to the improvements![4]

When you find yourself in a situation where you really need people on your side, use words that are going to create strong mental images. Attorney Gerry Spence once said, "Don't say he suffered pain. Tell me what it felt like to have a broken leg with the bone sticking out through the flesh. Tell me how it was! Make me see it! Make me feel it!"[5] Words are more powerful when they have strong emotional connotations. You want your words to be clear and credible, but they will have greater impact if they also strike an emotional chord within your audience.

You can even have fun with derogatory comments. You can just call someone dumb or stupid, but when you can verbally package or vividly describe something, this is what you get:

- Dumber than a box of hair
- He got into the gene pool while the lifeguard wasn't watching.
- If brains were taxed, he'd get a rebate.
- All foam, no beer
- Sharp as a marble
- Too much yardage between the goalposts
- Forgot to pay his brain bill
- Studied for a blood test and failed
- Gates are down, the lights are flashing, but the train isn't coming
- The wheel is spinning, but the hamster's dead

Simple but Powerful Words

We know certain words have more pull than others, but who would have thought that simple words like *let's*, *because*, and *you* would have the power to move mountains? In a study by Langer, Blank, and Chanowitz, researchers found that certain word choices could influence people to act against their own self-interests. The researcher would approach a copier with a long line of students. She would try three different word choices at different times to see how the other students would respond to each request. She didn't change what she was asking, only the word choice. When she said, "Excuse me, I have five pages. May I use the copy machine?" 60 percent complied. When she said, "Excuse me, I have five pages. May I use the copy machine *because* I am in a rush?" 94 percent complied. But when she said, "Excuse me, I have five pages. May I use the copy machine *because* I have to make some copies?" 93 percent complied.[6]

The magic was in the word *because*. Even when she used an obvious reason, for example, I have to make copies, she had a higher compliance. The word *because* is very powerful. It prepares the mind for a reason. Even if the reason is not legitimate, it is still a reason.

On the other hand, the one word that will impede your ability to persuade is *but*. *But* negates everything you said before it. We all know the drill:

"I love you, but . . . ," or, "I want to help, but . . . ." The word *but* puts the brake on persuasion. You can strategically use *but* to negate things, *but* it usually is used in the wrong place. Practice your vocabulary and use the word *and* in your persuasive communication instead of *but*. Another simple change is to use the word *can* instead of *could*. For example, say "Can you carry this for me?" instead of "Could you carry this for me?" Similarly, it is better to use *will* than *would* and better to use *do* than *try*.

Often we need to direct, delegate, or even order others. Usually our assignments are just short sentences, such as, "Can you please do this or that?" You can create unity and alliance and lessen defensiveness when you use let's in place of you, even when it's the other person, not you, who is carrying out the assignment. For example, "Let's be sure and get this out in the mail today, OK?" It's such a simple thing, yet you will find it works wonders. Make a habit of using the word let's, and you will meet with more cooperation.

The Value of the Simple Statement

Simple is better than complex. Because we are unable to recapture or replay our spoken words, we hope that they will be correctly interpreted the first time they are heard. Unfortunately, spoken words can be the most misread and misinterpreted form of communication and therefore can be a great hindrance to effective persuasion. When you're in a persuasive situation, use simple, direct, and concise language, rather than fretting about how eloquent you're sounding. Persuaders normally try to speak to the lowest common denominator. You might feel smarter using big words, but simple words are more persuasive. Complex words will cause people to pretend to understand, but they will not be persuaded.

SIMPLE GUIDELINES TO KEEP YOUR PRESENTATION ON TRACK

- ► Don't use technical language unless you are sure every member of your audience understands the meaning.

- ► Don't use profanity. In general, using profanity damages your credibility.[7] Be sensitive to whatever language your audience might find offensive or politically incorrect.

- ► Speak in everyday language. You want your audience to relate to you and to feel as comfortable with you as possible. Use language that will make you seem familiar and easy to follow.

➤ Keep your language simple and clear.

➤ Keep your sentences short. Use as few words as possible unless you are painting the picture. Present just one idea at a time.

➤ Use words that will engage the audience. Use *you*, *we*, and *us*.

➤ Don't use vague and abstract words. They muddle your meaning and confuse your listener.

➤ Don't talk down to your listener by using pompous and pretentious words.

➤ Use verb-driven language. By using verb-driven language, you will arouse a greater sense of action and motivation. Using action verbs will make your statement more convincing because your audience will engage their emotions, consciously and subconsciously. Verbs that are abstract or overused do not communicate excitement.

Attention-Grabbing Words

With so many words in the English language to pick from, you must be very particular about which ones to use. Some will grab more attention than others. The following 21 words are commonly used to effectively persuade:

1. Discover	8. Wealth	15. Guarantee
2. Guarantee	9. Quick	16. Benefit
3. Now	10. Easy	17. Proven
4. Improve	11. Money	18. Prevent
5. Results	12. Free	19. You/your
6. Save	13. Avoid	20. Transform
7. Health	14. New	21. Eliminate

Among all those on the list, the word *free* always gets attention anytime it is used. Suppose you were in charge of designing and wording the fliers your company is planning to send out in three weeks. Which phrase would you use?

1. Half price!
2. Buy one—get one free!
3. 50 percent off!

Each of the three denotes exactly the same offer, but the second phrase is the most effective. In fact, studies have shown that phrases using the word *free* outsell other phrases stating the exact same thing, only in different terms, by 40 percent![8]

VOCAL TECHNIQUES: KEEP PEOPLE ATTENTIVE AND LISTENING

Voice plays a critical role in influence.[9] How we say the words we choose is just as important as the words themselves. Our voice is a powerful instrument that can motivate the troops or lull them to sleep. There is a huge difference between presenting and persuading, informing and influencing, and communicating and convincing. Your voice is a complete arsenal of persuasive techniques in and of itself. For example, you can say the same thing but convey four different meanings, depending on the tone of your voice. You can say "Thank you" laden with sarcasm, love, hate, or anger just by changing the tone and inflection of your voice.

Peter Blanck, in his research, found that judges communicated their biases and attitudes by the tone of their voice. The juries in California were twice as likely to convict trial defendants when the judges already knew the defendants had a record and prior convictions. The law states that a judge cannot share this private information with the jurors, but, as researchers found, judges can convey their attitude toward defendants when the words and tone of voice in their instructions to the jury lack warmth, patience, and tolerance.[10]

You can change your rate of speech, the volume, pitch, inflection, emphasis, and even the pauses that you use. You can keep your audience's attention, increase their energy, and render them absolutely spellbound because of the power of your voice.

Your voice is who you are. It is your trademark and your calling card. Your voice must exude energy, confidence, and conviction. We tend to judge others by their voice: Is it confident, nervous, relaxed, energized, tired, weak, or strong? If you sound unsure and timid, your ability to persuade will falter. Persuasive voices have good volume, varied emphases, good articulation, and a pleasing pitch.

The good news is you can change many characteristics of your voice. Record your voice and listen to it. What does it project? Your voice must be interesting and easy to listen to in order to help, rather than hinder, your ability to persuade. Does your voice work for you or against you? What about these aspects of your vocal delivery and voice?

Pace

Pace refers to how quickly you speak. Mehrabian and Williams found that people who spoke faster, louder, and more fluently as well as those who varied their vocal frequency were perceived as more persuasive than those who did not.[11] A similar study found speakers with a faster rate were considered more competent.[12]

Speeches delivered at fast speeds are more persuasive than those of slow or moderate speeds because persuaders who speak faster appear more capable and knowledgeable. At these faster rates, the audience is not able to mentally engage in counterarguing.

Pace and speed are also important to keep and capture attention. We can think three times faster than we can speak. We have all had conversations and were able to listen while thinking of other things. When we speak faster, we can keep attention longer. There is less time for our audience's mind to wander. Studies show that we generally like faster speakers and find them more interesting. Persuasive speakers will speak fast enough to excite and energize the mood of the audience and at times will be able to slow their pace down to create a mood of anticipation.

To counteract boredom, use a fast pace most of the time, and vary it from time to time. Slow your pace down when you wish to appear thoughtful or have something important or serious to say, or when you wish to show great respect. Increase your pace when you want to create excitement, influence, and energy.

There was a study done at University of Southern California to discover the persuasiveness of the rate of speech. Those conducting the study approached people in a shopping mall or went door to door. They introduced themselves as being from a local radio station. The experimenters had people listen to an audio on various opinions of the day. There would be an audio at a slow rate (102 wpm) and a different audio at a fast rate (195 wpm). After the subjects listened to the audio, the researchers asked a few questions. The study found that, when the audio was at the fast rate, the speakers were perceived as more knowledgeable and more persuasive.

Vocal Fillers

Fillers can destroy your presentation, hurt your credibility, and annoy your audience. Most people feel they don't have a problem with this, and most of them are wrong. You will be amazed when you record yourself what words you use to fill in space during a presentation. Fillers are not acceptable and need to be eliminated from all speech. Vocal fillers include the common *um*, *er*, and *uh*. Some people have their own ways of filling in that uncomfortable silence between ideas. Some repeat the first two or three words of a sentence until their brain catches up and they decide what they're going to say. Others might say, "Okay?" at the end of every sentence, as if they're checking audience comprehension. Although we all tend to use a few natural fillers, it is always good for you to reduce their number during any conversation.

Pitch

Pitch is the highness or lowness of the speaker's voice. Low is best. In most cultures, deeper voices are generally interpreted as reflecting authority and strength, for both men and women. In addition, a deeper voice is stereotypically considered to be more believable, indicative of an individual's sincerity and trustworthiness. Many speakers practice lowering their voices because of the benefits of a lower pitch. Some speakers even drink hot tea before they speak, a technique that creates a lower sounding voice.

Remembering to employ variety in your speaking is a constant challenge, but it is of paramount importance. The worst thing for persuasion is a memorized speech or a presentation that is read word for word. You can help people remain alert and pay attention while you speak if the pitch of your voice rises and falls. This strategy works for two main reasons. First, the varying pitch will prevent your voice from sounding monotone. Second, the varying inflections can help emphasize a particular point. If you are not an engaging speaker, you will not be persuasive.

WHAT STUDIES IN PITCH CONCLUDE

➤ Low pitch creates more favorable attitudes.[13]

➤ A rise in pitch shows nervousness and indicates that you are hiding something.[14]

➤ An increase in pitch decreases competence.[15]

➤ High-pitched voices are perceived as weak.[16]

Volume

Obviously you're not going to be very persuasive if no one can hear you. You've probably experienced the aggravation of straining and struggling to hear a speaker. Before your presentation, test the room to ensure that you can be heard in all parts of it. Also, test to see whether you're going to need amplification. Certainly, the converse is also true: Be sure the audience does not feel you are yelling or shouting at them. This understandably is just as aggravating for the audience—or even more so—as struggling to hear you. These points are also true for how you sound on the phone or via the Internet.

Raising your voice for impact or dramatic effect is not as effective as lowering it. The technique can work, but you must be very careful about how you use it. Additionally, people who keep a calm and steady voice in emotional moments are considered more credible and competent.

Articulation

Clearly articulate every sentence, phrase, and word. When your speech is clear and coherent, it conveys competence. Sloppy articulation suggests a lack of education and laziness. Consider how lawyers, doctors, supervisors, motivational speakers, and the like must be articulate if they are to survive professionally. Good articulation conveys credibility and experience. Another practical reason to have good articulation is simply that it will make your presentation so much easier to follow. As discussed, people will comply with you more when you are easy to understand.

Downward inflection demonstrates power and control.[17] News broadcasters are trained to inflect their voices downward at the ends of sentences because doing so suggests confidence and authority. Upward inflections tend to suggest a lack of confidence and doubt. Airline pilots are also trained to inflect down to portray more confidence. Imagine a pilot making the following announcement while inflecting his or her voice up at the end: "We're going to have a safe flight today." It sounds more like a question than a statement.

Pauses

Treat your pauses like gold. Well-timed pauses attract attention to a particular part of your presentation, give others time to tune in and process your message, and help you gain poise and confidence if you're rattled. Use intentional pauses for the points you want to drive home. Not only does a pause increase comprehension, but it also helps to highlight important points. Use pauses to create attention, emphasis, and mood.

A carefully planned pause usually comes before the point you want to highlight. It is a common mistake not to hold the pause long enough. Be sure you allow enough of a pause that the full effect will be felt. When you do so, the audience anticipates and listens closely to what you will say next. They can tell something important is about to happen. This strategy is made even more effective when you combine it with pitch strategies: Be sure that, as you come to the pause, your pitch is high, thereby building suspense and giving momentum to what will follow. Inflecting your pitch downward will defeat the purpose, providing a feeling of resolution instead of suspension.

EXAMPLES OF GOVERNMENT VERBAL PACKAGING

Negative	*Repackaged*
Recession	Accelerated negative growth
Garbage man	Sanitation engineer
Poor people	Fiscal underachievers
Shot by police	Legal intervention
Pot hole	Pavement deficiencies
Illegal alien	Undocumented worker
Riot	Civil disorder
Tax increase	Revenue enhancement

BACKFIRE

Don't sound too polished or use words that are complex or difficult to understand. Words that are obviously sugarcoating the blunt truth will backfire on you. Vocal variety is key to persuasive presentations. Verbal packaging will backfire when you sound too polished or use words that are complex or difficult to understand. Also, sugarcoating the blunt truth can backfire on you.

CASE STUDY

A famous politician (a member of congress) was in a very close reelection race. He wanted help to become more charismatic in his speaking. He also wanted to increase his influence, connect better with his audience, and increase donations. He had given a speech that he felt was critical to his reelection and would clarify his position in the race. I watched the video, and he was very articulate as he read his presentation word for word and made sure everyone understood his position. He stood tall at the podium, and he used persuasive words. Why didn't his speech resonate with the audience? Why were donations so low? Using the Law of Verbal Packaging, what would you recommend?

The actual words and phrases in his speech were persuasive. His word choice was perfect. The challenge was the delivery. Reading a speech always takes away your energy and your presence. When you are stuck behind a podium, you connect less with the audience. Because he read his speech, his rate was reduced. This caused his delivery to lose the attention of his audience and reduced his ability to persuade. He was more concerned about the reading of the speech and his articulation than reaching and inspiring his audience. There was no emotion because of the forced delivery.

Additional Resources: Verbal Packaging Triggers Video (maximuminfluence.com)

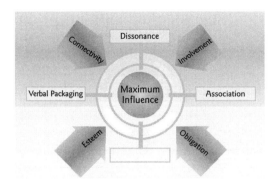

CHAPTER 9

The Law of Association

Create the Environment of Influence

It's not the situation. It's your reaction to the situation.　　—BOB CONKLIN

One association trigger is color and how certain colors make us feel. Add those colors to food, and some interesting things happen. Even if I told you each one of these items tasted great, you would probably have an association trigger that would make you feel a little different. What about when margarine was first introduced and it was white? Would that affect your buying decision or would you want to eat it? Pepsi and Coke both introduced clear colas. Does that sound right to you? Did you hear about the green ketchup that hit the market and failed miserably? Would you ever order Pantagonia tooth fish? Or would you feel better if they renamed it "Chilean Sea Bass?" Do you prefer steak that is fatty or marbled? All these items create different feelings and association triggers. Those triggers are the focus of this chapter.

To maintain order in the world, our brains link objects, gestures, and symbols with our feelings, memories, and life experiences. We mentally associate ourselves with such things as sights, sounds, colors, music, and symbols. These associations create quick subconscious triggers, and the feelings you generate can help or hurt your ability to persuade.

Power Persuaders take advantage of association triggers to evoke positive feelings and thoughts that correspond with the message they are trying to convey. In this sense, you, as a persuader, can actually arouse a certain feeling in your audience by finding the right association key to unlock their door. Associations are not the same for all people; obviously, each person and culture has a particular set of triggers. However, once you understand the general rules, you can find the right associations to match any situation. Why do you think restaurants decorate a certain way, have their lighting just right, and play certain types of music? *The Law of Association defines the mental triggers and anchors that will generate the right feelings, emotions, and thoughts to create a persuasive environment.*

The Law of Association is constantly at work. If an audience likes a picture, a logo, or a musical jingle that appears in an advertisement for a product, they also tend to like the product. The law can work negatively too—you've heard of kill the messenger! A study was done with students waiting their turn for an experiment. One student was given the responsibility of telling a fellow student about an important phone call that he had received. Half of the time the news was good, and half the time it was bad. What the study revealed was that how students revealed good news was very different from how they reported bad news. When the phone call brought great news, the students relayed the news. On the other hand, they separated or disassociated themselves from bad news. The bottom line is that we all know deep down that we like to be associated with good news and separate ourselves from the bad news.[1] Another study revealed that the simple association with the bad news, even when we had no part in it, creates dislike.[2]

Once, when in the employ of an (unnamed) corporation, I had a corporate credit card. The company had a nasty habit of not paying their bills. One day I got a phone call from a collection agency claiming that because my name was on the credit card, I was responsible for making the payments. I informed the representative of the situation, but he was quite persistent. Of course, I was not responsible, but the interesting association was that the representative said his name was Thor (the God of Thunder). The point is that if you want to create the feeling of a tough, persistent, strong person, then Thor is the perfect name. Herbert or Percival is just not as threatening.

Advertisers know we naturally want to be associated with fame, fortune, and success. That is why we follow the lead of celebrities we admire, respect, and like. It's also why we use the products they endorse. It is amazing to see teenagers ignore their parents' warnings about drugs, but when their favorite star or professional athlete says it's not cool, they stop. This is the power of association.

ANCHORS: CAPTURE THE FEELING

Anchoring is a technique that captures the feelings, memories, and emotions of certain events, places, or things. The psychology lies in the use of elements from a previous situation to replay the emotions and feelings of that experience. An anchor can be anything that brings up a thought or feeling and reminds you of something you have previously experienced. It will usually reproduce the exact prior emotion or feeling. You use a certain stimulus to create an association that will bring about a desired response.

An anchor can be produced either externally or internally. Anchors don't have to be conditioned over a period of several years to be established. They can be learned in a single event. The more intense the experience, the stronger the anchor. Phobias are also considered an anchor that was created during an intense emotional experience.

Let's talk about three different sets of anchors: smells, music, and symbols. Other elements (sights and taste) can be used as anchors, but these three are the most powerful stimuli in evoking memories.

Here is an interesting study about anchors. College students had to work on their favorite topic—you guessed it—math problems. Before they started on the problems, half of them were asked to recall 10 books they read in high school. The other half were asked to recall the Ten Commandments from the Bible. After they wrote down the books, they were allowed to solve their math problems. One key condition was that they were able to cheat if they wanted to. The students who recalled the 10 books from high school were more likely to cheat, and the students who recalled the Ten Commandments rarely cheated.[3]

Smells: The Aroma of Persuasion

We all know what the smell of movie popcorn does to us. Smell is directly linked to our emotions.[4] Our sense of smell is so powerful that it can quickly trigger associations with memories and emotions. Our olfactory system is a primitive sense that is wired directly to the center of our brain. By four to six weeks, infants can tell the difference between their own mother's scent and that of a stranger.[5] Almost everyone has experienced situations in which a smell evoked a nostalgic (or not so nostalgic) memory. Think of the smells that take you back to your childhood. For some, it is the smell of fresh baked bread, freshly cut grass, or the neighborhood swimming pool. You can go back 20 years in a second with the sense of smell. Smells require little mental effort to be experienced, and the subconscious reaction happens with little conscious attention.[6]

Fragrances, aromas, and odors trigger memories, feelings, and attitudes in our minds. Smell can enhance or reinforce desired responses as well as trigger positive and negative moods. There are many examples of this. Supermarkets with bakeries fill the air with the warm aroma of breads and coffee. Some children's stores send baby powder through the air ducts. Victoria's Secret uses potpourri scents to augment their customers' feelings of femininity. Pizza stores depend on the smell of freshly baked pies. Car dealers use the new car smell, even on used cars. In the Kajima Corporation in Japan, management uses aromas to increase productivity throughout the day. Their formula is citrus in the morning, for its rousing effects; floral scents in the afternoon, to encourage concentration; and woodland scents before lunch and at the end of the day, to help relax employees.[7] One study showed that people were more than twice as likely to provide a stranger with change for a dollar when they were within smelling range of a Cinnabon store.[8] Real estate agents are famous for having homeowners bake bread before they have interested buyers tour the house. Large amusement parks will pipe in certain scents at certain times of the day to trigger responses and get immediate reaction. The use of smell in these instances is an attempt to link the seller's products and services with a positive attitude, thereby inducing the shopper to buy. In the same way, you can link positive smells with your message to create a positive attitude in your prospects.

Numerous studies have been conducted on the impact of scent and fragrances on association. A study conducted among undergraduate students found that female students wearing perfume were rated as more attractive by male students.[9] Scents were even found to improve scores on job evaluations.[10] Of course, offensive odors can also be used (and have been used) to evoke a negative response. This technique was once used while campaign committees were rating and appraising political slogans. Not surprisingly offensive odors caused the ratings for the slogans to go down.[11] The smell of citrus Windex helped people to be more generous with their money and time toward Habitat for Humanity. Cleaning aromas also help more people be honest and fair and their dealings with others.[12]

ADDITIONAL AROMA RESEARCH

➤ Pleasant ambient aromas increase the amount of time people linger in a store.[13]

➤ Pleasant smells increased attention and reaction time in driving simulations.[14]

➤ Pleasant smells in medical situations increase relaxation and reduce tension before a MRI exam.[15]

➤ Pleasant aromas increase bakery sales by 300 percent.[16]

➤ Pleasant odors lead to better moods, whereas unpleasant odors lead to unpleasant moods.[17]

➤ Pleasant fragrances help in the persuasion process.[18]

Music: Feel the Beat

Music is much like smell in that our brains link music with past attitudes and experiences. Music is closely tied to our emotions. Local gyms play upbeat music to associate it with high energy and good times. In one case, a local convenience store had problems with teenagers loitering outside. The store owners wanted the teenagers' business but not the drugs and fights that seemed to go with it. They decided to play Frank Sinatra songs outside the store and soon found that the teenagers voluntarily stopped loitering.[19] You may still remember the particular song that played during the dance with your high school flame. Music has a powerful pull on us and triggers instant memories.

In department stores, shoppers who are exposed to music shop 18 percent longer and make 17 percent more purchases than shoppers in stores not playing music. There are even rhythms, pitches, and styles of music that are best for different shoppers. Grocery store shoppers respond best to slow tempos. Fast-food restaurants use a higher number of beats per minute. For music to be effective, customers can't really be aware of it. The music should not be overpowering but merely an atmospheric presence.

Because music is so powerful, persuaders need to carefully select the music they're going to use. Advertisers often use a popular song or a catchy jingle. Notice the next time you watch television how many songs you recognize from all the commercials; you will be surprised. Every time the ad is played, the tune reinforces the product's appeal. Music is universal because it has the power to evoke the emotions shared by all of humanity. We know music can soothe the savage beast or create instant energy and excitement.

ADDITIONAL MUSIC RESEARCH

- ► Music has a positive relationship with comprehension and recall.[20]

- ► Sales increase in restaurants and supermarkets with slower music.[21]

- ► When the music tempo increases, so do happiness and animation.[22]

- ► Music changes moods in consumers.[23]

- ► Music does not affect consumers who are purchasing products that involve high mental involvement (i.e., cars, computers, cameras, etc.[24]).

The Might of Symbols

We live in a symbolic world. Symbols bypass our thoughts and our logic, and they affect our perceptions and behaviors. Gold is an example. As one of the world's most precious metals, gold is the very symbol of wealth and success. Countless stories are told of the search for it, even though other precious metals are harder to find and far more precious. Gold, however, just holds a certain symbolism; it denotes success and wealth.

Symbols can also help us understand and feel a message without actually having to undergo the experience. For example, a skull and crossbones on a bottle says it all; we don't have to ingest the poison to know of the fatal experience. The simple symbol of a red stop sign triggers an automatic response. For many, the sight of a police car on the highway will trigger the automatic braking response.

As you read the following list, think of the symbols and pay attention to the feelings, memories, attitudes, and experiences they trigger in your mind:

- ➤ Crucifix
- ➤ Statue of Liberty
- ➤ World Trade Center
- ➤ American flag
- ➤ Swastika
- ➤ Military uniform
- ➤ Olympic symbol
- ➤ Wedding dress
- ➤ Christmas tree

When you are trying to mold attitudes, it is useful to know how symbols shape your audience. Carefully study and research the symbols you want to use before employing them. When used well, they will influence your audience's feelings and behavior to your benefit. Marketing and advertising executives use symbols in a very sophisticated way to increase recognition with consumers. Did you know that most children recognize the arches at McDonald's before they are 20 months old?[25] There are symbols of freedom, symbols of success, and symbols of poverty. Find and use the symbols you need to create the proper association with your prospect.

AFFILIATION: CREATE THE LINK

Another aspect of the Law of Association is the use of affiliation. Persuaders want you to affiliate their company with positive images, feelings, and attitudes. Our surroundings and environment trigger feelings, and we transfer those feelings to those we are with. For example, one frequently used technique is to take someone to lunch. Food can also generate subconscious triggers (if the food and company are good). The studies show that subjects like people better when they are eating. Food gives us good feelings and a better attitude.[26]

The idea is to link something positive in the environment with your message. For example, a good game of golf, a weekend at the beach, NFL tickets, or an exotic cruise would all typically build positive associations and feelings in your prospects. People want to be associated with winners. In fact, a study showed that when a university football team won, more students would wear the college sweatshirts the next week. The bigger the victory, the more college sweatshirts become visible. When you bring positive stimuli into the situation, you will be associated with the pleasant feeling you have created.

ADVERTISING AND MARKETING

Three affiliation techniques are the most often used: advertising, images, and color. Each has a unique role in affiliation.

Advertisers and marketers use affiliation to evoke valuable associations in the minds of their prospects. They know that babies and puppy dogs automatically carry great associations of warmth and comfort in the minds of their audience. Consequently, we see tire commercials with babies and car commercials with puppies, even though cars and tires aren't really warm and cuddly. These warm appeals grab our attention and create positive associations in our mind.

One of the most common examples of advertising affiliation occurs with alcohol advertisements. Instead, advertisers in this industry use young, vibrant people who are in the prime of their lives. The beer companies want you to associate drinking beer with having fun and attracting the opposite sex. Their ads portray images of men and women having fun while surrounded by beer. Their message is, "If you aren't drinking, you aren't having fun." On an intellectual level, we all know that these are just advertisements, but the associations they arouse in us stick in our minds and trigger future purchases.

When companies need to change their image, they usually find a good cause to latch onto. They will typically find a good social or environmental issue to tap into. For example, an ice cream company advertises their support for an environmental movement, or yogurt companies start a campaign to stop breast cancer. You also see patriotic endorsements being employed to create a positive association in your mind. The simple sight of the American flag or such phrases as "Buy American" and "Made in America" can trigger instant positive associations.

Sponsorship is also used in advertising. Companies and organizations sponsor events that they believe will produce a positive association in the eyes of the public. They hope the positive association will transfer to their company. The Olympic Games pull huge sponsorships; companies pay big money to get their names and products associated with the games. What company wouldn't want to be associated with unity, perseverance, determination, success, and winning the gold? The affiliations that companies create for us are very strong and memorable.

Images: How to Get Through Their Guard

It really isn't a secret that we are abundantly influenced by imagery when making everyday decisions. We are much more likely to donate to someone wearing a Santa Claus suit than to someone in street attire. Some are more trusting of a sales rep wearing a gold cross around her neck. The images we see create attitudes within us. It is no random accident that most U.S. presidents have a pet dog in the White House. Consciously and subconsciously, we believe a loving, obedient, trusting dog creates a positive image of its owner. Voters would be more likely to reject a politician who preferred hamsters, snakes, or even a tarantula.

Credit card companies are among the greatest users of imagery and association. Because credit cards give us immediate gratification without our having to face the negative consequences until weeks later, we often think of the perceived positive associations before the negative ones. Consumer researcher Richard Feinberg conducted several studies testing the effects of credit cards on our spending habits. He came across some very interesting results. For example, he found that restaurant patrons gave higher tips when using a credit card as opposed to cash. In another study, consumers increased their spending 29 percent when a store displayed a credit card symbol.

Color Triggers

Countless hours of research indicate that color matters. Notice how fast-food restaurants, schools, and professional sports teams all choose certain colors that represent them. You know, of course, that colors can suggest a mood or attitude, but did you also know that color accounts for 60 percent of the acceptance or rejection of an object or a person?[27] These impressions don't change overnight. We all have automatic color triggers and hidden associations with various colors. Color impacts our thinking, our actions, and our reactions. Armed with this knowledge, we must take into account the association of colors in our persuasion and marketing efforts.

Color is a great persuasive device. Because we don't consciously perceive what is happening, we don't develop a resistance to persuasive color techniques. This process happens at a completely subconscious level. Color is critical in marketing, in advertising, and in product packaging. Colors are not just for appearance; they have significance. The favorite food colors are red, yellow, orange, and brown.[28] These colors trigger automatic responses in our nervous system and stimulate our appetite. Fast-food restaurants decorate with shades of red, yellow, and orange. These hues are known as arousal colors because they stimulate the appetite and encourage you to eat faster. Compare these bright colors to the calming colors found in higher-end restaurants. These restaurants tend to use greens and blues in their design, colors that encourage you to stay and linger.

Colors can also be used to attract our attention. The shades that grab our attention are reds and oranges. Yellow is known as a fast color and is the first color to register in the brain. Yellow causes you to be alert and watchful. These research results explain why fire trucks and fire hydrants are being painted yellow. The challenge is that each color has multiple meanings; one person might draw one conclusion while another person might perceive an entirely different meaning. Red can be exciting to one group and say "unprofitable" to another. To others, it could signal "stop" or "danger." Red can denote boldness, aggressiveness, and extroversion, but it also represents anger, danger, sin, and blood.

An interesting study on the use of color occurred at the U.S. Naval Correctional Center in Seattle, Washington. The entire holding cell was painted pink, except for the floor. Many inmates at this stage of confinement were hostile and violent. The cell was painted pink to see whether the color would have a calming effect on them. Each person was held only 10 to 15 minutes a day in these pink cells. After 156 days of constant use, there were no incidents of erratic behavior among the inmates.[29]

Jail cells are not the only place where pink plays a role. Iowa's Kinnick Stadium has an interesting locker room for the visiting football team. The whole locker room, including the toilet seats, is pink. The walls and floors are all pink, and the visiting teams get very upset. The use of the color has become very controversial. Coach Hayden Fry, who decided to go pink, had read that pink has a calming effect on people. He claims that the color is a big factor in their success.

What about the color of the pills you take? Research has shown that the color of medicine can change its perception or association. When scientists studied the drugs people took and the associations they formed of them based on their colors, they found that most people felt white pills were weak, whereas black ones were strong. In another study, researchers gave blue and pink placebos to medical students, who were told the pills were either stimulants or sedatives. The students taking the pink pills felt more energy, whereas the students taking the blue pills felt drowsy.

Color even enhances the perceived flavor and desirability of the food we eat. For example, orange juice with an enhanced orange hue was preferred over naturally colored orange juice and was thought to be sweeter. This was also true for strawberries, raspberries, and tomatoes. The redder they looked, the more they were preferred.[30]

In one experiment, the flavor of coffee was manipulated by the color of the serving container. Two hundred people were asked to judge coffee served out of four different containers: red, blue, brown, and yellow. All containers held the same brand of coffee, yet the coffee in the yellow container was found to be "too weak." The blue container coffee was labeled "too mild." Seventy-five percent found the coffee in the brown container to be "too strong," and 85 percent found the red container coffee to be "rich and full-bodied."[31]

A similar experiment was also done with women and facial creams. Subjects were given pink and white face creams, which were identical except in color. One hundred percent of the women surveyed said that the pink cream was more effective and milder on sensitive skin.[32]

In another experiment, researchers gave subjects laundry detergent to test for quality. Of course, all the boxes contained exactly the same detergent, but the outsides of the boxes were different colors. The test colors were yellow, blue, and a combination of both. After a two-week testing period, the test groups reported that the detergent in the yellow boxes was "too harsh" and that the detergent in the blue boxes was "too weak." The detergent in the combination yellow and blue boxes was "just right." The findings indicated that the yellow represented strength while the blue represented antiseptic power.[33]

COMMON COLOR ASSOCIATIONS

- ➤ *Red:* Strength, power, anger, danger, aggression, excitement
- ➤ *Blue:* Coolness, truth, loyalty, harmony, devotion, serenity, relaxation

- *Yellow:* Brightness, intelligence, hostility, wisdom, cheerfulness, loudness

- *Green:* Peacefulness, tranquility, youthfulness, prosperity, money, endurance, growth, hopefulness

- *Orange:* Brightness, unpleasantness, sun, warmth, bravery, invigoration, radiation, communication

- *Purple:* Royalty, passion, authority, stateliness, integrity, mysticism, dignity

- *White:* Plainness, purity, coldness, cleanliness, innocence, hygiene

- *Black:* Desperation, wickedness, futility, mysteriousness, death, evilness

- *Gray:* Neutrality, nothingness, indecision, depression, dullness, technology, impersonality

USE ASSOCIATION TO PERSUADE AND INFLUENCE

The Law of Association is a powerful tool in helping you influence and persuade your audience. When used correctly, you will be able to create the desired feelings, emotions, and behavior in your prospects. You will be able to use association to bring about the best experiences and create a persuasive environment. Whatever your subject is drawn to, impressed by, or desirous of, seek to incorporate it into your message, your product, or your service.

BACKFIRE

Be aware of the symbols and associations you use during the influence process. When you create the wrong anchor or trigger the wrong emotion, the Law of Association will backfire. Do your research on their profession, industry, or culture to know their association triggers.

CASE STUDY

· ·

A new all-you-can-eat restaurant opened in California. When you walked into the restaurant, you saw a large scale used for weighing people. This scale did not have any numbers on it, only various payment categories. To find out how much you were going to pay to eat (based on your weight), you had to step on this scale. Depending on what area of the scale the arrow landed on, the scale determined how much money you would pay. What a creative, fun idea! The place was decorated nicely and had great food, but business was not booming. Using the Law of Association, what would you recommend?

The owners were smart enough to take out the actual numbers of the scale but did not understand association triggers. Going to a restaurant, especially an all-you-can-eat restaurant, we want to think that calories don't count. We really don't want to be reminded of our weight or how much we should or should not eat. The scale acted as a bad association trigger, causing people to leave and never return—and sometimes they did not even know why they left; they just subconsciously felt they did not like the restaurant. On the flip side, kids thought it was fun to get on the scale; children can have different association triggers than many adults.

· ·

Additional Resources: How to Resist Persuasion Report (maximuminfluence .com)

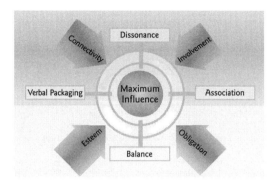

CHAPTER 10

The Law of Balance

Logical Mind Versus Emotional Heart

When dealing with people, remember you are not dealing with creatures of logic, but with creatures of emotion, creatures bristling with prejudice and motivated by pride and vanity. —DALE CARNEGIE

All companies want to be unique and have that competitive edge. They feel as though they have to create the perfect product, but then it fails. Marketing professors claim that 80 percent of all new products fail. Why is this so? The companies did their research, they did their testing, they talked to the consumer, but the product still failed. Could it be that consumers really don't know what they want?

One issue is that companies look at the new product offering logically, but consumers purchase with their emotions. A certain manufacturing company found out that people waste electricity every year staring in their fridge with the door open, even though the trend is to be green and save money. So they developed a solution that was green and would save the consumer on the electric bill. They created a see-through transparent fridge. What a great idea! You can decide what you want before you get it, be green, and save money all at the same time. Logically, it made perfect sense, but emotionally it was a train wreck. Our fridges in many ways are like our medicine cabinets: no one's business. What happens when Aunt Edna comes over, looks in the fridge, and asks it that meatloaf or pudding? The key is to balance the logic with the emotions.

That is the Law of Balance. Logic and emotion must be blended and balanced. Emotions will trigger action, whereas logic will justify the agreement. The proper fusion of emotion and logic will speak to both the conscious and subconscious parts of the mind and increase your ability to persuade.

Emotions create movement and action. They generate energy during the presentation and get prospects to act on the proposal. The challenge with relying exclusively on emotion to persuade your prospect is that, after she has left the persuasive situation, her emotions fade, leaving her with nothing concrete to fall back on. This balance between logic and emotion could be called the twin engines of persuasion and influence.

Power Persuaders know that each audience and individual has a different balance of logic and emotion. Analytical personalities need more logic than emotion. Amiable personalities require more emotion and less logic. Always remember that you need both elements in your message, regardless of their personality types listening. This means you need to shoot the rocket of emotions and always provide the parachute of logic. A Power Persuader will create a proper balance between logic and emotion to create the perfect persuasive situation and message.

We are persuaded by reason, but we are moved by emotion. Several studies conclude that up to 90 percent of the decisions we make are based on emotion, and then we use logic to justify our actions to ourselves and to others.

Note: Emotion will always win over logic, and imagination will always win over reality. Think about talking to children about their fear of the dark or to someone about their snake phobia. You know it is difficult to use logic to persuade them that their thoughts and actions don't make sense. They remain afraid.

This emotional pattern can also be seen in how we buy and even how we convince ourselves of something. Our heads see the numbers and tell us to stick with the modestly priced car, but our hearts see the expensive sports car. Our heads tell us it's ridiculous to buy another pair of shoes because we already have 14 pairs. We may even realize that no one is going to notice or care about the new shoes as much as we will. But our hearts win out, thinking of all the stunning new outfits these shoes will go with. We go home with the new shoebox tucked under our arm. Our heads tell us not to believe everything we hear—that politicians are a bunch of liars—but impassioned speeches win our hearts.

LOGIC: WHAT STIRS AN AUDIENCE?

Are we rational human beings? Do we follow logic? Do we only act only if it feels right? Do we even want the facts? Have you ever tried to persuade an emotional person with logic? What about persuading a logical person with emotion? We generally think we make decisions based on facts, but truly this is not the case. It has been found that, when people agree with a message, they tend to perceive it as being logical or rational. On the other hand, when people disagree with the message, they perceive it as an emotional plea.[1] The truth is that our decision-making process relies on a mixture of emotion and its partner, logic. However, we cannot rely entirely on emotion until our logical side has been engaged.

In one study, college students prepared speeches that were written from either a logical or an emotional standpoint. The speeches were presented, recorded, and then evaluated by other college students to find out whether the speeches were perceived as either emotional or logical. The study found that the speeches with which the evaluator agreed were rated as more logical (even if they were intended to be emotional), whereas those the evaluator did not agree with were considered to be more emotional (even if they were intended to be logical). Whether a speech was considered logical or emotional seemed to depend on the listener. Researchers also concluded that, as a general rule, people seem unable to consistently distinguish between logical and emotional appeals.[2] The logical side of an argument appeals to our reason. Reasoning is the process of drawing a conclusion based on evidence. For an argument to be legitimate, it has to be true and valid, and logical reasoning must be used to back it up.

EVIDENCE AND LOGIC

Concrete evidence should be the cornerstone of a logical presentation. Evidence not only makes an argument ring true in persuasive situations, but it also substantially enhances your credibility. There are four major types of evidence: testimony, statistics, analogies, and examples. You will strengthen your position when you use elements of all four forms, rather than depending on only one. When you provide proof in this manner, you remove doubts that may linger in your audience's mind.

Testimony

Your audience wants to know what the experts have to say about you or your topic. Testimony is the judgment or opinions of others considered experts in the field or area of interest. A testimony can be a quote, an interview, or an endorsement from a credible person. It can be implied by someone's presence (attending your event), picture (on your product), or endorsement (on your website).

Statistics

Statistics are numerical proofs of your claims. For example, "This demographic uses . . . ," or, "four out of five dentists recommend . . . ." Using graphs and charts makes statistics more memorable and makes a greater impression on the listener.

Some people are suspicious of statistical proof, so make sure your statistics are credible and sound. Your audience needs to know where you got them and who did the research. People know you can arrange statistics to say just about anything. Use statistics sparingly and only in conjunction with other forms of evidence. Besides, a roll of statistics can be very boring.

Analogies

Analogies have a great impact in the mind of the receiver. They enable you to make your points quickly and easily in a way that prospects will understand immediately. ("Installing our new home security system is like having a police officer standing guard on your front porch twenty-four hours a day.") Analogies allow you to present a new and foreign idea and compare it with something similar that your prospects can relate to in their own lives. Analogies can also give us a new perspective on an old concept.

Examples

Examples can really make your evidence come alive. We love to relate to examples that bridge the gap between logic and our personal lives. Your prospects understand examples at a deeper level because they are based on common experiences and interpretations of meaning. Examples can be real or hypothetical and can include personal accounts, physical evidence, empirical studies, or published reports.

COMPELLING EVIDENCE

As you prepare your message, understand that humans aren't capable of absorbing all of the information presented. We are bombarded with data all day long, and most of the time we don't absorb it. In fact, we are very selective in what we allow ourselves to absorb and retain. When we hit information overload, we turn our minds off and retain nothing.

A study on the comprehension of persuasive messages produced very revealing results. After watching commercials and other messages, an amazing 97 percent of viewers misunderstood some part of every message they saw. On average, viewers misunderstood about 30 percent of the overall content they viewed.[3] Information is just poured out too fast. The evidence that you choose must be selective, precise, and powerful. You can't afford to bombard your audience with a data dump.

Spend whatever time you need to fully research the types of evidence you want to use to strengthen your arguments. You already know that using the right evidence from the right sources greatly increases the credibility of your message. However, the opposite is also true; poor or irrelevant evidence undermines the credibility of your message. The more confidence the prospect has in a speaker, the less thinking and processing they will do about the message.[4] When compiling evidence, consider the following:

➤ Use evidence supported by an independent expert.
➤ Statistical evidence is more persuasive when combined with case studies.
➤ Document the sources of all testimonials.
➤ Use new information. New facts and research are more convincing.
➤ Acknowledge the other side. A two-way discussion bears more weight than a one-sided lecture.[5]

Evidence works best when it is suited to the audience and their experience. Consider the following presentation points:

➤ Referring to evidence as fact increases its weight.

➤ Evidence that is verifiable is more persuasive.

➤ Evidence that is specific is more persuasive.

➤ Unbiased testimony is more persuasive than a biased one.

➤ Personal experience is more persuasive than no personal experience.

➤ Presenters with low credibility will benefit from the use of evidence.

➤ Evidence is especially important when the audience is unfamiliar with the topic.

➤ Factual evidence is persuasive when the audience consists of highly intelligent people.

➤ Evidence is more persuasive when you provide the sources and their qualifications.[6]

EMOTION: WINNING PEOPLE'S HEARTS

Whereas logic is the language of the conscious mind, emotion is the language of the subconscious mind. We know that emotions are reactions to perceived and imagined stimuli; they are based on one's own personal experiences, not on logic. Emotions often outweigh our logic. Imagine a shark tank with a large 12-foot shark. You were told this type of shark does not hurt people and has never attacked anyone. They want you to take a swim with the shark. You know logically you will be OK; hundreds have done this before. They would never ask you to do it unless they were sure it would be safe, but your emotions take over. All of a sudden your emotions and fear outweigh logic. Your what-ifs and your imagination supersede the concrete knowledge of your ability to be safe and swim with the shark.

When you are persuading someone, emotions provide the springboard for a successful execution of your argument. In fact, I would even say emotions are the energy and very fuel of the persuasion process. Without tapping into your audience's emotions, your message has no strength or energy. Emotion is a power you can harness and use in practically every aspect of persuasion. Logic is important, but emotion helps you catapult an otherwise dull or flat exchange to the next level.

Consider the following advantages of emotion over logic:

- ➤ Emotions engage your listeners and distracts them from your intention to influence.
- ➤ Emotion requires less mental effort than logic. Logic solicits cognitive effort; emotion is automatic.
- ➤ Presentations using emotions are more interesting than logical ones.
- ➤ Emotion-based presentations are easier to recall than logic-based arguments.
- ➤ Emotion leads more quickly to change than logic does.[7]

You must know when to create positive or negative emotions and when to dispel emotions that disrupt persuasion. You have to find ways to tap into your prospects' emotions, such as hope, love, pride, gratitude, and excitement. When you can do this, you can influence anyone. Decide ahead of time what emotional climate you want to create, capture those emotions within yourself, and you'll be surprised how you can transfer those emotions to your audience.

TYPES OF EMOTIONS

Here are some of the major emotions and how they affect persuasion.

Worry

When your prospect is worried or preoccupied with something that is occurring now or that could happen in the future, your ability to persuade declines. Worry is feeling anxious, uneasy, or concerned about something that may happen or that has already happened. Anxiety creates tension—a fear that occupies our thoughts, which if encouraged will grow and continue to dominate our thoughts. I have heard worry referred to as negative goal setting.

You can combat worry in your prospects by easing or modifying their anxiety. Bring them back to reality by having them realize we can't change many things in the past or forecast the future. Stress that most of the things we worry about are the very things that we cannot change or control and that won't likely ever happen in the first place. Help your prospects replace their negative mental images with positive ones.

Worry can also be caused by indecision. Get them to make a series of minor decisions, and their worry will decrease.

Fear

Fear is tension caused by danger, apprehension, pain, or destruction. The possibility of harm can be real or imagined. Fear motivates and moves us away from unpleasant circumstances or potential destruction. Fear persuades us to do many things we might not otherwise do. Out of fear we buy life insurance, medicine, home alarms, and guns. Fear causes people to closely evaluate the situation and increases their perception of risk.[8]

Fear does not work in every situation, however; if we were solely motivated by fear, we would never speed or start smoking. The proper dose of fear is essential in persuasion. If the dose is too small, it will not stimulate action. If the fear is too large, it will trigger resistance, and acceptance will decrease.[9] For fear to stick and to create action and persuasion, it must have the following characteristics:

- ► The image of fear must be unpleasant, such as the threat of pain, destruction, or grief.
- ► It must be imminent. Your prospects must feel not only that the fearful event is likely to happen soon but also that it could victimize them. They must feel vulnerable.
- ► You must provide a solution to the fear. Give your prospects a recommended action to suspend or eliminate the fear.
- ► Your prospects must believe they are capable of doing what is asked of them. Do they have the tools?

Anger

Anger is a secondary emotion. Prospects' anger is usually an indicator that something else is troubling them and that they need or want attention. You can assist in diminishing their anger by determining the key issue that they are upset about. It is also often effective to ask for their help, opinions, or advice. This will usually diffuse the anger or even change their attitude and demeanor completely. In some circumstances, you may want to use anger to make a certain point or to evoke a certain reaction. However, angry people are more likely to blame someone else. In their mind, they are not at fault. When they are sad, they will usually blame the situation.[10]

When people become angry, they tend to rely on intuition or a quick educated guess. Anger triggers nonanalytical information processing. Anger causes us to use mental shortcuts to decide whether the argument is right.[11] An experiment was done that induced anger. The participants who were angry tended to discriminate between weak and strong persuasive arguments more than those in a neutral mood. In other words, those who were angry tended to be more influenced by heuristic cues (intuition) than those in a sad or neutral mood.[12]

MOOD AND HAPPINESS

Moods affect our thinking, our judgment, and our willingness to say yes. When the persons you are trying to persuade are in a good mood, they are more likely to accept your offer. The opposite is also true. If they're not in a good mood, chances are much higher they won't bite. A good mood is a huge advantage to you in persuasion. Great persuaders create the right mood. Great persuaders actually put people in a happy state. When we are feeling happy, we tend to think happy thoughts and to retrieve happy ideas and experiences from memory. Conversely, when we are in a negative mood, we tend to think unhappy thoughts and retrieve negative information from memory. The bottom line is that, when we are in a negative mood, we focus more on the person, but when we are in a positive mood, we focus both on the person and the message.[13] Negative moods usually cause our minds to look for a problem and find something wrong.

There is evidence across the board that mood is a major factor in persuasion. Even simple mood-boosting methods like eating a sweet snack or listening to pleasant music have been shown to make people easier to persuade.[14] An interviewer who is in a good mood tends to assign higher ratings to job applicants.[15] Consumers who are in a good mood will be more aware of positive qualities in products or experiences they encounter.[16] The feeling of happiness interferes with our mental ability to compare and causes us to think less.[17] You are more persuasive when your prospect is in a happy and benevolent mood.[18] Psychology author Harry Overstreet said it: "The best way to get a yes response is to put them in a yes mood."

Although negative emotions can trigger persuasion, they have to be used with caution because too much of a negative emotion will cause the brain to shut down, impeding your ability to persuade. On the flip side, happiness and being in a good mood actually make the persuasion process easier.

POSITIVE MOOD TRIGGERS...

➤ Make us spend more time looking at ads.[19]

➤ Help us have a better attitudes toward advertising.[20]

➤ Improve attitudes toward the brand.[21]

➤ Make us more willing to help those in need.[22]

➤ Increase the chances we will donate to a charity.[23]

➤ Increase our willingness to participate in an experiment.[24]

➤ Increase the likelihood of an attitude change.[25]

A study was done with participants who watched one out of two television programs. One program was upbeat and happy, and the other program was depressing and sad. The participants were then asked to list their thoughts about the commercials they experienced during the program. As you probably already know, those who watched the happy program had more positive thoughts about the commercials than did those exposed to the sad program.[26]

TIP THE SCALE

As a Power Persuader, you need to know how to use the dual engine of balance, which allows you to fly straight and true in any persuasive situation. Become a student of both logic and emotion, develop the ability to articulate logic that rings true with your audience, and learn how to use your human emotion radar. It will help you determine important aspects of your audience, such as what your prospects are feeling, which emotions they are trying to hide, which emotions you should trigger, and how you can use each of these emotions in the persuasive process. As a Power Persuader, you know which emotion to use, when to use it, how to trigger specific emotions, and how to balance the audience's emotion with logic. Engineer your persuasive message with balance.

BACKFIRE

The Law of Balance will backfire when you use the wrong dose of logic and emotion. This is caused by the lack of research, triggering the wrong emotions, or not being able to adapt to the person or situation. Use the Prepersuasion Checklist (Chapter 15) to discover which emotion to use and what type of logic to implement.

CASE STUDY

A large corporation had two departments—the marketing department and the IT department—that were not cooperating and were getting insensitive and hostile toward each other. The conflict got to the point that something had to be done to get these departments to cooperate and finish up a major project before the looming deadline. Each department blamed the other for the delays. The CEO asked everyone to put their differences aside and get the project done, but the request did not help. Thinking about the Law of Balance, what is happening here? What would you do?

The issue was that the communication styles between marketing and IT are as different as night and day. Usually IT tends to be more logical, and marketing tends to be more emotional. Everyone was communicating as they liked to be communicated to. Each department thought the other department was wrong because of the different styles of communication and difference in personalities. Teaching each department how to communicate with the other and to understand the different personalities was the key. Helping them understand how coworkers thought and processed information opened their eyes. Their ability to adjust the balance between emotion and logic unified the departments.

Additional Resources: Psychology of Motivation Audio (maximuminfluence .com)

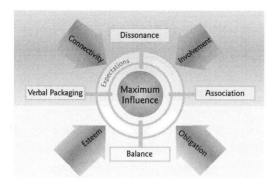

CHAPTER 11

The Law of Expectations

The Impact of Suggestion

What gets measured, gets done. —PETER DRUCKER

We can influence reality. Although I am not recommending you do this, just visualize this happening. Select a coworker and get three or four other people in on the prank. You approach her and say, "Are you sick, you don't look well." She will probably say, "Nope. I'm OK." The next colleague approaches her and says, "You look a little pale. Are you sick?" She responds, "No, I'm ok." The third person approaches her and says, "You look a little green. Are you sick?" She now might say, "Yeah, I am feeling a little under the weather." Finally, the fourth person asks, "Are you OK? Are you sick? Do you need to go home?" Eventually this person will feel sick and go home.

The Law of Expectations uses expectations to influence reality and create results. Individuals tend to make decisions based on how others expect them to behave or perform. As a result, people fulfill those expectations, whether they are positive or negative. Expectations have a powerful impact not only on those we trust and respect but also, interestingly, an impact on strangers. When we know others expect something from us, we will try to satisfy them in order to gain respect, trust, and likability.

You probably know the saying, "What gets measured, gets done." The same is true for expectations. What is expected is what actually happens. People rise to meet your expectations of them. This is a powerful force that can lead to the improvement or destruction of a person. You can express an expectation of doubt, a lack of confidence, and a skepticism, and you will see the results. If you believe in others, show confidence in them, and expect them to succeed, you will see different results. Author John H. Spalding expressed the thought this way: "Those who believe in our ability do more than stimulate us. They create for us an atmosphere in which it becomes easier to succeed."[1] When you create the right expectations, you change people's behavior.

We communicate our expectations in a variety of ways. It may be through our language, our word choice, voice inflections, or body language. Think of when you're introduced to people. Usually, if they introduce themselves by their first name, then you do the same. If they give their first and last name, you do likewise. Whether you realize it or not, you accept cues from others regarding their expectations, and you act accordingly. Similarly, we all unknowingly send out our own cues and expectations. The power is in using the Law of Expectations *consciously*!

Numerous studies have shown how the Law of Expectations dramatically influences people's performance. For example, in one study, girls who were told they would perform poorly on a math test did perform poorly. In another, assembly line workers were told that their job was complex, and they performed less efficiently at the same task than those who were told it was simple. Another case study demonstrated that adults who were given complex mazes solved them faster when told they were based on a grade-school level of difficulty.

By adding the Law of Expectations to your persuasive toolbox, you can change your audience's expectations of you—and their expectation to buy your product, service, or idea—and you will be infinitely more persuasive.

ASSUMPTIONS: EXPECT WITH CONFIDENCE

Consider the profound impact this law can have in your own life. Are the assumptions and expectations you have about yourself (or others) liberating or victimizing? There are countless examples of so-called self-fulfilling prophecies–or the Law of Expectations at work in everyday life. Did you ever notice how people who think they're going to be fired suddenly experience a drop in the quality and enthusiasm for their work? Then what happens? They get fired! Their belief causes them to act a certain way, and those expectations then work to bring about the very thing that at first was only a figment of their imagination.

A study done on a military base where combat soldiers trained. Soldiers of equal aptitude were randomly divided into three groups: high expectancy, regular expectancy, and unspecified expectancy. The three groups were assigned three different types of instructors, and the group that was expected to perform better scored significantly higher on achievement tests, felt more positive, and had better attitudes.[2]

In another study, second-graders listened to statements from their teachers before taking a math test. They heard one of three types of statements: expectation, persuasion, or reinforcement. The expectation statements went something like, "You know your math really well!" Or, "You work really hard at your math." Persuasion statements involved sentences like, "You should be good at math." Or, "You should be getting better math grades." Finally, for the reinforcement statements, teachers said things like, "I'm really happy about your progress." Or, "This is excellent work!" The scores turned out the highest in the expectation category because they created personal assumptions within each student. Those assumptions conditioned the actual external results.[3]

This can also be called implicit priming. In one study in this area, participants were asked to complete a scrambled sentenced in a puzzle. They were shown various groups of words to create these sentences. Some of the participants were shown rude words (e.g., *obnoxious, aggressively, annoyingly, disturb, interrupt, impolitely*). The other group was shown polite type words (e.g., *respect, courteous, considerate, patiently, polite, behaved*). When they went to the next room to complete a second task, they found the experimenter with another student trying to explain a task that the student could not comprehend. The group that was primed with the rude words waited an average of 5.5 minutes before interrupting and the group primed with the polite words waited an average of 9.3 minutes.[4]

Another interesting study demonstrated how numbers can prime your brain. Participants were given the following set of numbers and were told to estimate (not calculate) the answer in 5 seconds.

$$8 \times 7 \times 6 \times 5 \times 4 \times 3 \times 2 \times 1$$

Then other participants were asked to estimate the answer based on the following numbers:

$$1 \times 2 \times 3 \times 4 \times 5 \times 6 \times 7 \times 8$$

Logically, we know the estimation should be the same for both (40,320). One group was primed with the 8 in front of the problem and the other group was primed with the 1 in front of the problem. The average estimation for the first problem was 2,250. The average estimation for the second problem was 512.5 No one even came close to the right answer.

THE EXPECTATIONS OF OTHERS AFFECT BEHAVIOR

The expectations we create for others often become reality. This effect can have interesting consequences when applied in the real world. This section contains multiple examples of how expectations have changed the lives and persuaded the behavior of other individuals.

Honestly assess how you think you make others feel when they're around you. Do you make them feel small and unimportant, or do you inspire them to achieve more? Your actions toward others will tell them how you feel or think about them. How you treat someone and what you expect from them will open or close the doors to persuasion and influence.

School Teachers

Under the umbrella of expectations, teachers can be the greatest asset or the greatest negative influence in a child's life. We know what happens when a teacher labels a student a troublemaker because that tag creates certain expectations for the student's actions. We have seen that the labels slow learner, below-average student, and ADHD become projections for a child's future academic success. This is often called social labeling. People tend to live up to the positive or negative labels bestowed on them.[6]

One interesting experiment revealed how teachers' expectations influenced students. Two Head Start teachers were selected who were as equal as possible in potential and in practice. Then two classes were formed from pupils who had been carefully tested to ensure that they were as similar as possible in background and learning potential. Next, the principal spoke with each teacher alone. He told the first teacher how fortunate she was. "You have a class of high-potential students this year! Just don't stand in their way. They're racers and ready to run." The second teacher was told, "I'm sorry about your students this year. But you can't expect top students every year. Just do the best you can. We'll be understanding, regardless of the results." At the end of the year, the two classes were tested again. The first class scored significantly ahead of the second.[7] The major differentiating factor appeared to be each teacher's expectations.

Littering

We know that children tend to put their trash directly on the floor. In one elementary school, students were given individually wrapped pieces of candy. Of course, most of the wrappers ended up on the floor and not in the garbage can. Over the next two weeks, the teacher frequently commented on how neat and tidy the children were. On a visit to the classroom, the principal remarked to the children that their classroom was one of the neatest and cleanest in the school. Even the custodian wrote a note on the blackboard telling the children how clean and tidy their classroom was. At the end of the two weeks, the children were given individually wrapped pieces of candy again. This time, most of the wrappers ended up in the trash can.[8]

Parental Expectations

One thing you notice with toddlers and small children is that they behave according to the expectations of their parents. When I was single, I noticed that, when children fell down or bumped their heads while running and playing, they looked at their parents so they would know how to react. If the parents showed great concern and pain in their face, the children would start to cry. This happened regardless of whether the child really felt pain or not.

One of the techniques my wife and I tried as new parents was the exact opposite of this approach. We changed the expectation, and the tactic has worked great! When our children hit their heads or get a small scrape, they look up to us, and we laugh. The amazing thing that happens is that they begin to laugh too. They realize it's not a big deal and go off to resume their activities, usually laughing with us. (Of course, I am not talking about broken limbs or any other serious injury.) Children base their actions on the expectations of their parents. You create the expectations in your voice, in your actions, and in your choice of words.

Sales

I love seeing door-to-door salespeople use the Law of Expectations to their advantage. They approach a door, ring the bell, and with a big smile tell the home owner they have a great presentation that the person needs to see. Of course, all the while, they are wiping their feet on the person's doormat in the expectation of being let in the house. You would be surprised how often this technique actually works. You see a salesperson handing the prospect his pen in expectation of signing the contract. Have you ever felt guilty leaving a store or situation where you have not bought something? The store has created the expectation that you would make a purchase.

PRESUPPOSITION: ASSUMING THE SALE

Using expectations, we can create immediate reactions to stimuli so that subjects don't even have to think; they just perform the action. Presuppositions often involve using words and language indicating your assumption that your offer has already been accepted. When blood drive organizers make reminder calls, they may end their conversations with something like, "We'll see you tomorrow at 10:00 a.m., OK?" Then they wait for the person's commitment. They put things this way because studies have shown that when you create a presupposition, attendance rates dramatically increase.

The power of suggestion can also be extremely effective when you engage the emotions in your presentation. For example, by saying, "You're really going to love how this car handles in the mountains," the car salesperson is shifting the focus away from the sale and creating an exciting image in your head. The statement presupposes that you have already agreed to the sale—you wouldn't be driving the car in the mountains unless you were going to buy it. He's acting as though it's a done deal, and the truth is that the more he does this, the more it is! We see this in business. A manager might say thanks in advance or that you will love being on this team.

PRESUPPOSITIONS (ASSUMPTION IN PARENTHESES)

- ➤ "Do you want me to bring lunch to the meeting?" (There will be a meeting.)
- ➤ "When do you want your couch sent?" (You are buying the couch.)
- ➤ "Should I call you Tuesday or Wednesday?" (You want to talk again.)
- ➤ "Your first class will start next Monday." (You're signing up for the class.)

You'd be amazed how often people will just go along with your proposal! They don't even stop and think about their response because now they're already finishing the deal in their mind.

Another way to use presuppositions is to put them in writing. People tend to think that if something's in writing, it must be true. We often go along with something without questioning it just because it's what the directions tell us to do. For example, one stunt involved a stop sign placed on a sidewalk, even though there was no reason to stop there. The sign was in an odd place, and there was no danger of oncoming traffic. Yet almost everyone obediently stopped and waited at the stop sign, just because that is what the sign told them to do! In another stunt, a sign reading "Delaware Closed" actually made people start asking for how long Delaware was going to be closed![9]

THE PLACEBO EFFECT

One type of expectation is the placebo. A placebo is a nonmedicinal substance that is given to patients who are told that they are receiving medicine. The placebo often works because the expectation that the medicine will help is so strong that our brains actually turn the expectation into reality. Various studies show that placebos worked 25–40 percent of the time![10] When patients were told they would get a stimulant (placebo), their blood pressure and heart rhythm were affected. When they were told it was a depressant, it had the opposite effect.[11] When people were told the placebo was a form of alcohol, it caused perceptions of intoxication.[12] In another study, participants thought they had received "improved self-esteem" audios or "memory enhancement" audios felt the changes, and the audios had the stated effects.[13]

Here is fun study done at Harvard. The researchers wanted to find out whether placebos would work on irritable bowel syndrome (IBS) even if the participants were told they would be taking a placebo. It was made clear to the subjects that the pills were not real medicine. In fact, the word *placebo* appeared right on the pill. The subjects were told to take the pills twice a day and that placebos can produce healing effects on the body. What do you know? After three weeks, the placebo group reported improvements of their symptoms and found relief taking the placebo. The study found that 59 percent reported relief by taking the placebo.[14]

THE GET-WHAT-YOU-PAY-FOR EXPECTATION

Why doesn't a generic brand cough medicine seem as effective as the national brand? Why do we think expensive designer jeans fit better than the pair we bought at the Walmart?[15]

Many studies have been done on the perception and impact of price. For example, a study was done to find out the effectiveness of painkillers and electric shock. Researchers gave two sets of shocks to participants. The goal was to find out how much pain they felt. (Psychiatrists love the electric shock.) In this series, each shock was increased to the point that it would get your attention and make your heart skip a beat.

Before the first series, however, participants were given a brochure to read on a new painkiller they would be testing. It was described as the latest thing and "cutting-edge." The brochure said that 92 percent of patients receiving this new painkiller found significant pain relief in 10 minutes and that the medication would last for 8 hours. The price for this new medication would be $2.50 a pill. The other participants saw the same brochure, but the price for this medication was 10¢ a pill.

After the first set of shocks were given to the participants, both groups were given the medication and told to wait after taking the placebo (sugar pill). Then the study and the second round of shocks were started.

The participants were asked how effective was the new painkiller? The study found that 85 percent of the participants said the $2.50 pill group reported that they felt less pain. Only 61 percent in the 10-cent pill group reported they felt less pain.[16]

Expensive wine is another example. Researchers gave test subjects five different wines to taste and then had the subjects rate each of them.

The results were interesting. When the subjects thought the wine was a $10 bottle, it was rated of 2.4 out of 6. When they thought the wine was a $90 bottle (the truth), it was rated 4 out of 6.[17]

TIME EXPECTATIONS

In our modern world, we are bound by time. We have certain expectations about how time works and how long it will take us to accomplish something. Often, time becomes distorted through our perceptions and expectations. Why do some afternoons speed by faster than others? And why do we finish projects a minute before our deadline?

Parkinson's Law states that work expands to fill the time available. So, if a project is given a 3-month deadline, it will take the full 3 months to complete. If that very same project is given a 6-month timeframe, it will still take the full 6 months. The law may sound strange, but it has bearing because the time allotted for completion sets our expectations. Our expectations actually influence how we will work on a project and therefore when it will be completed. Ever notice how there's a sudden burst of activity right before the deadline appears? We all have the tendency to procrastinate, waiting until the deadline to do most of the work. This is why it is often effective to set multiple deadlines for large projects. Projects without deadlines never seem to be accomplished, no matter how good the intentions are. We see the law have a negative effect in business all the time. Even when a deadline is given, if the company expectation is that it is just a formality, employees know that it will be extended, and they act accordingly.

EMBEDDED COMMANDS

An embedded command is a technique used to communicate to the subconscious mind. The aim is to actually bypass the conscious mind and talk directly to the subconscious mind. Embedded commands are commonly used in marketing and advertising as hidden suggestions within written or spoken language, and the conscious mind is unaware of their existence. Embedded commands create expectations without creating inner resistance. For example, Pepsi used to have the slogan, "Have a Pepsi Day." The embedded command was, "Have a Pepsi." Embedded commands can also work in the wrong way. When parents say, "Don't walk in the street," the command children hear is "Walk in the street."

Embedded commands are used to reinforce potential behavior and can help people come to a faster decision.[18] We see them in advertising and sales copy on the Internet. Using embedded commands can increase your marketing efforts by 10–20 percent.[19]

The most effective embedded commands are short and concise; they should be no longer than two to four words. It is much easier to use these commands in persuasive writing because you can visually highlight the command. When using this technique, first determine what exactly you are trying to say to your audience. Then create sentences where the embedded words and phrases will logically and contextually fit. Finally, set the embedded commands apart in some visual way: italics, bold face, underlined, highlighted, or a different color.

Embedded commands are also a powerful tool in marketing. Certain phrases have specific command forms that follow the two–to-four-words rule. Phrases can include word associations, cause-and-effect statements, presuppositions, questions, or hidden suggestions. Essentially, you are looking for phrases that will jump out.

EXAMPLES OF EMBEDDED COMMANDS

- Become really interested.
- Take action now.
- Become wealthy.
- Buy now.
- Use this material.
- How good it feels!
- Going to happen.
- Read each word.
- Follow my lead.
- Act now.

- Change your life.
- You will understand.
- Use this process.
- Learn quickly.
- Use this skill.
- Learn how.
- Improve your results.
- Get it today.
- Adopt this solution.
- Discover.
- Can you imagine?

Studies show that embedded commands can actually change our attitudes or beliefs, even if we are totally unaware.[20] This is how embedded commands have their effect: The conscious mind tends not to analyze or evaluate the material. We can create expectations of behavioral changes with embedded commands and indirect suggestions. The subconscious mind will create an internal reality to match the commands.[21]

GOAL SETTING: CREATING PERSONAL EXPECTATIONS

Many people don't like the idea of goal setting; in fact, just the mere mention of the words makes them cringe. However, goal setting works. The problem is that most people or groups don't go about it in the right way. Without going into the many aspects of goal setting, suffice it to say that goal setting works and is an important aspect of the Law of Expectations.

Goals must have the power to stretch and inspire, and they must be realistic in the mind of the person being persuaded. Helping others or your team set goals increases their future expectations for themselves. Visualizing themselves reaching their goals also makes the achievement of those goals more tangible.

Research shows that goals dictate future performance. Conscious goals influence our overall performance. In one study, there was a large difference in the performance between asking people to do their best and helping them set their goals (or a standard) for their performance.[22] In a classic study, students were given math problems and were told to "do their best," or they were given specific goals. Over a week and a half, the group with the goals performed better than the students who were told to do their best.[23]

It is a general rule of thumb that greater or more difficult goals actually increase performance. The reason is that lofty goals set a higher expectation, and, as explained, expectations strongly influence behavior. In a production plant, workers with little experience were divided into two groups. One group was told to simply observe the experienced workers and try to be able to perform at a skilled level themselves within 12 weeks. The second group received specific weekly goals that were progressively more demanding. Needless to say, the second group fared much better.[24] The goals you set have to be realistic in the mind of your prospect, or the expectations will not be set and will have an adverse effect.

For goal setting to work effectively, individuals or the members of a group have to be able to visualize and see themselves achieving their goal and be committed to its success. The goal cannot be so hard, so complex, or so overwhelming that it does not seem realistic. Recognize minor results, and help them keep their eyes on the big picture.[25] Goals work just as well for groups as they do for individuals.[26]

ENVIRONMENT

Your environment and the expectations of that environment should be persuasive. The Phillip Zimbado's Broken Window Theory suggests that a building with many broken windows will cause people to assume that no one cares about the building or its appearance. This in turn will spur more vandalism and more broken windows. In other words, the environment's condition gives clues that lead people to make certain assumptions, and people then act on those assumptions. The broken windows invite greater damage and crime.[27] Zimbardo did a study illustrating this point. He left a car out on the street in Palo Alto, California. The first week the car blended in with all the other cars, and nothing happened to it. After the first week, he broke one of the windows of the car and left it on the street. Vandalism to the car increased dramatically after the window was broken.[28]

In his book, *The Tipping Point*, Malcolm Gladwell uses an example of the Broken Window Theory as he explains the New York City subway cleanup. The subway system was in dire need of rebuilding—a multibillion-dollar endeavor. With the system about to collapse, the focus was understandably on issues like reducing crime and improving subway reliability. As a consultant hired by the New York Transit Authority, George Kelling urged officials to utilize the Broken Window Theory. Hired to clean up the subways, David Gunn immediately assigned people to start cleaning up all the graffiti. Removing the graffiti seemed to be of such little consequence compared to everything else there was to worry about, but Gunn was insistent. In his own words:

> The graffiti was symbolic of the collapse of the system. When you looked at the process of rebuilding the organization and morale, you had to win the battle against graffiti. Without winning that battle, all the management reforms and physical changes just weren't going to happen. We were about to put out new trains that were worth about ten million bucks apiece, and unless we did something to protect them, we knew just what would happen. They would last one day and then they would be vandalized.[29]

The entire antigraffiti campaign took years, but finally the incidence of graffiti subsided.

In another study, volunteers were asked to participate in an experiment on prison environments. Half of the volunteers posed as prison workers, while the other half posed as prison inmates. The results were astounding. Previously tested to be psychologically sound people, the participants rapidly became more and more hostile, crude, rebellious, and abusive—both those acting as inmates and those as guards! One "prisoner" became so hysterical and emotionally distressed that he had to be released. The study was supposed to last 2 weeks, but was called off after only 6 days![30]

BACKFIRE

Expectations will not work and the subconscious trigger will not respond if the expectations are unrealistic (too high or low), or don't make sense, or if the prospects can't visualize themselves accomplishing your goals. Set realistic expectations that your prospects can see themselves accomplishing.

CASE STUDY

A real estate company bought a nice tract of land on which to develop midrange homes. The backyard fence of many of the homes were next to a railroad track, but trains rarely came by. The real estate agent assigned to market the homes was having a hard time selling the last homes near the tracks. The moment the potential buyers saw the tracks, they lost interest regardless of what the agent said or offered. He tried to reduce the prices, offered free kitchen upgrades, and put a Jacuzzi in the master bedroom. Using the Law of Expectations what would you do to make these homes sell faster?

The visualization and expectation of a railroad in their backyard is more than most consumers can handle. They are programmed to assume the worst: The train will be noisy, shake the house, break my things, keep me up at night, or even scare the kids. Expectations needed adjustment. The key was to have the prospective owners show up 10 minutes before the train arrived. They were briefed about all the extras the home contained and all these items came to over $10,000 in value. They were then asked to sit in the living room as the scheduled train went by. They were told the train came only at 10:20 a.m. and 2:00 p.m. every day. They discovered for themselves that the train was not a big deal. Plus they would get all the extras. Expectations were adjusted, and the homes sold.

Additional Resources: Goal Mastery Form (maximuminfluence.com)

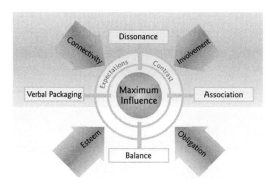

CHAPTER 12

The Law of Contrast

How to Make Price (or Time) a Nonissue

Price is what you pay. Value is what you get. —WARREN BUFFETT

What if you brought your to your mechanic, and he told you that you might need new brakes, a new transmission, a new fan belt, and that the timing sounds off? You go away thinking, "Oh, man! I'm sunk. I might as well just buy a new car." Then, when you come back, he tells you, "All you needed was new brakes." You feel unburdened, having to pay only $300 for what could have been a $3,000 repair job. Now imagine if the mechanic had given you an estimated $300 and the bill ended up being $3,000.

That is the Law of Contrast in action. The perception of value will always trump price. If your prospect gives you the old excuse that your offer is too expensive, then you have blown your presentation. Your goal is to have the value exceed the price or the benefit to exceed the prospect's time commitment.

The Law of Contrast explains how we are affected when we are intro-
duced to two different alternatives or options in succession. We know that
contrasting two alternatives can distort or amplify our perceptions of price,
time, or effort. Generally, if the second item is very different from the first,
we will tend to see them even more differently than they actually are. As a
Power Persuader, you can use this contrast to navigate your audience
toward the object of your persuasion.

Contrast works in many arenas. You can contrast just about anything
and immediately see its effects. For example, imagine you are at a mountain
resort with three pools: a spring-fed (cold) pool, a heated (warm) pool, and
a Jacuzzi (hot). What happens when you are swimming in the warm pool
and jump into the cold pool? On the flip side, what if you jumped from the
warm pool into the hot Jacuzzi? Both times you originated in the warm
pool, but you had two completely different reactions. This is the Law of
Contrast. Any product, service or perception of time can be contrasted to
appear very different or have more value than what it actually has.

The use of contrast is based on our perception of items or events that
happen one right after the other. If you've had a rotten day because you
found out you're losing your job and you come home to a scratch on your
new car, you will have one kind of reaction. On the other hand, if you were
having a great day because you're getting a promotion and then came home
to the scratch on your car, your reaction would be very different. It's the
same scratch, but your perceptions and reactions to it are very different.
Contrast is used for negotiations. When we offer a really low or high bid or
when we ask for $200 and expect only $50, this is contrast. What if you
thought you were going to a 60-minute meeting and it only 30 took minutes? What if a 15-minute meeting lasted 30 minutes?

This is all about human perception. The human mind has to find a
benchmark or comparison to make judgments, especially when we are talking about unfamiliar situations or new products. People need to make com-
parisons with their past experience and knowledge. The brain will always
attempt to contrast your product or service. Is it the best or worst, cheapest
or most expensive? Is your product a safe or risky choice? Is it familiar or
strange?

By presenting your prospects with contrast, you are creating those com-
parisons for them. The mind cannot process everything at once, and so it
develops shortcuts to help in making decisions. Instead of making a com-

pletely internal judgment, we look for boundaries, patterns, and polar opposites. We want to know the difference between our options, so we naturally contrast them. We mentally create a value or price in our mind from highest to lowest. Do you want your prospects to compare your product or service to a second-hand used car or to a Mercedes-Benz? You get to decide where you want them to start their benchmark.

How much is a cup of coffee really worth? When Starbucks launched their coffee stores, they had to deal with the perception of pricing. Why would consumers spend three times more for a cup of coffee? They set up their stores using high-end décor and created an environment with coffee that originated from different parts of the world, almost like a winery. They even changed the names of all the cup sizes. This all changed the perception of price. We see expensive juice or health drinks take on the look of an expensive bottle of wine. We also see software packaging that is 100 times bigger than the software, and size also adjusts the perception of price. If all you get is a single CD or an instant download, the perception of price is much lower than for a new piece of software in a large box.

Airlines also contrast news to you one piece at a time. They will say there is a slight delay, but they add that they should be ready to go in a few minutes. Then, in a later announcement, they state that, although everything is fine, they don't want to take any chances, so they are going to replace the part. They come back on the loudspeaker and say they are close to being finished and will announce when they are ready to go. The next announcement you hear is that they are waiting for final clearance and will be taking off shortly. These small announcements, in relation to each other, keep the passengers calmer and more peaceful than if the airline just flat out announces a two-hour delay.

We also see the contrast technique used at large amusement parks. If we hear ahead of time how long the lines are going to be, we won't stand in them. You look to see how long the wait looks and, perceiving it to be of reasonable length, get in line. When you think you are almost there, you see another section of ropes and people. This happens three more times until finally, 2 hours later, you are at the front of the line. They are also using contrast when we see a sign that says 90-minute wait and we have to wait only 45 minutes.

Time can erode your ability to use the Law of Contrast. The key to this law is that the two contrasting items must be presented one right after the other. This has an effect on group meetings and decision making: If in a meeting you put forth your great idea right after another great idea, it won't have the same impact as it would if it had followed someone else's poor idea. Likewise, if we are talking to a beautiful woman or man at a party and we are then joined by an unattractive person, the beautiful person will seem even more beautiful, and the less attractive person will seem even less attractive.

TYPES OF CONTRAST

Examples of the Law of Contrast fit into different categories. Let's examine the relationship among these categories and examples of each.

Sweetening the Pot: Triple the Value

Sweetening the pot is a technique often used by marketers and on infomercials to make the deal appear sweeter, or valued more than it actually is, that is, making prospects believe they are getting an exceptionally good deal. What can you add on as an incentive? What can you give as a bonus? What do you have that will add value to your product or service? It could be an added feature, a larger discount, free delivery, gift wrapping, batteries, an extended warranty, or free consulting. Whatever it is, use it to create a contrast and increase the perception of heightened value.

Think about the last infomercial you saw on late-night TV. You watch them display and demonstrate the product, and you start to get interested. You begin to think about how this product will really make your life easier. They have not told you the price, but when they finally do, it is much higher than you thought. You are thinking around $99, but the announcer says it is $499. Your heart drops, but you keep watching because you are really getting into this product and how it will change your life forever.

Oh, now wait a minute—they are giving a special deal (Scarcity) today. There is a temporary price reduction. This is your lucky day! Now they are offering it for $297! It's a good deal, but still a little expensive. Wait! They are adding three additional items to the package, for an extra value of $350. You can hardly believe it; you'll get over $800 worth of products for only $297. You're really interested now, and you're just about ready to buy, when it gets even better! If you order now, you can even make three easy payments of $99 for the next three months. You can't believe your luck, so you order right away. You were thinking of spending only about $99, and you wound up spending triple that amount—$297 to be exact. Why? Because of the Law of Contrast, you were going to get over $800 worth of product, and the deal kept getting better.

This law is critical for you to understand when showing others the value of your product. People do not buy unless they feel as though they are getting value for their money. When you sweeten the pot, you add additional items to make the deal more and more valuable.

We can all learn from the high school bake sale: In one study, when the cashier told one group of customers they could purchase one cupcake and two cookies for a total cost of 75¢, 40 percent of customers bought. The cashier then told another group of customers that they could purchase one cupcake for 75¢. However, a few seconds later she added that, because of a special that night, two more cookies would be included as a bonus. By the end of the night, 70 percent of the customers purchased cupcakes and cookies when the three-for-the-price-of-one technique was used, even though it was really exactly the same deal.[1] It's all in the presentation. You have to sweeten the pot!

You see this technique used in supermarkets and in other advertisements when a company plans their packaging strategy to show the contrast between before and after prices. You may see diapers that have the "Save 20 percent" slashed out and replaced with "Save 40 percent." Or maybe their method is, "Buy five, and we'll give you another one free." Or they might have the "16 oz." slashed out and the "New 20 oz." written in for the same price. Whatever the form, it is all just sweetening the pot, the Law of Contrast in action. It isn't the actual price but rather the add-ons that make the deal so much better.

Put yourself in the mall candy store buying a pound of chocolate candy for your sweetheart. The young lady at the counter scoops up the chocolates and places them on the scale. She notices that she does not have enough and starts to add more. The other alternative is that she dumps all the chocolates on the scale and begins to take them away. Which method will make you more satisfied? In the first scenario, you would feel as if you were getting more and that the deal was being sweetened, whereas the second method might make you feel as though you were being robbed.

ADJUSTING VALUE EXAMPLES

- ► *Bonuses:* Three bonuses worth $25 each have more value than one bonus worth $75.

- ► *Product:* Having all your product arrive in one box has less value than receiving three separate shipments.

- ► *Retail:* Keeping the high prices at a grocery store increases the perception of value and savings when the savings are shown on the receipt.

- ► *Cars:* We feel as though we get a better deal on a car when we see the large retail price and then get a rebate.

- ► *Payments:* It is easier to swallow the monthly payments on a large purchase than to see the whole price tag up front.

- ► *Gas:* Getting a 10¢ discount when you pay cash is easier to swallow than a 10¢ surcharge for using your credit card.

- ► *Payroll:* There is higher perceived income when you separate all their benefits on their check versus putting it all in one large sum.

- ► *Negotiation:* Starting as high or low as possible will get you better terms.

Reducing It to the Ridiculous

This technique involves paring down your request to something that seems manageable, easier to comprehend, or easier to monetize. Let's say you are trying to convince someone to purchase a life insurance policy. The client wants a $250,000 policy, and you feel that is not high enough for his needs. To adequately take care of his family, you suggest a $500,000 policy. His perception is that the monthly payment for a $500,000 policy is too high. So you break it down for him, telling him that for an extra 50¢ a day, or the cost of a can of soda, he can insure himself and adequately take care of his family if something were to happen to him. With this contrast, your client can see that the extra 50¢ is worth it to have the extra $250,000 in coverage. You have reframed your request into simple terms to help your prospect see it fitting into his way of life.

Another example: Suppose you are getting resistance from coworkers when you ask them to participate in a new project. You could say you are only looking for their help for, say, 10 minutes a day or 45 minutes a week. This doesn't sound like much of a commitment.

Door-in-the-Face (DITF)

Door-in-the-face (DITF) is one of the most common techniques for implementing the Law of Contrast. Basically, an initially large and almost unreasonable request is made, likely to be declined—hence the door is slammed in your face when the prospect rejects the proposal. Then a second smaller and more reasonable request is made. People accept the second request more readily than if they'd been asked for more the first time because the contrast between the two requests makes the second one seem so much better. The technique is effective because social standards state that each concession must be exchanged with another concession. When you allow a rejection, it is considered a concession. The person you are persuading will then feel obligated to agree with your smaller request. DITF is so effective because society and the Law of Obligation tell us that each concession must be responded to with a concession. When you give them a concession, they will be more inclined to give you a concession.

This has also been called the social responsibility model. When your prospects turn down the initial request, they subconsciously feel guilty for not helping and don't want to let you down again. Sometimes the feelings of guilt drive them to comply with the second request in order to rid themselves of those negative feelings. They also might think they will feel even worse if they don't comply with the second request.[2]

Demonstrating this point, researchers first asked college students to donate blood every two months for three consecutive years. Requiring a long-term commitment of not only time, but also of physical and emotional responsibility, the request was overwhelmingly turned down. The next day, the same students were asked to donate blood just one time, and 49 percent agreed. The control group, consisting of students who were approached only with the second request (will you donate today?) demonstrated only a 31 percent compliance rate.

The door-in-the-face technique is effective is because the contrast between the two requests makes your prospects feel as though they are getting more/or less than if you didn't adjust their perceptions. They feel as though they've made a fair compromise, while you get exactly what you wanted in the first place.

By way of example, pretend your local high school football team is canvassing door to door to ask for donations for their football program. They ask you to donate $100, saying that your next-door neighbor has donated this amount. After some discussion, the football players ask for a $25 dona-tion. You feel relieved and give them $25—and you feel lucky that you got away with giving less than your neighbors. In another study, subjects were solicited for a large donation, and, after they refused, they were asked for a smaller donation. Using DITF increased compliance by 17 percent.[3]

In these examples, the second request seems much more logical and reasonable in comparison to the outrageous first request. We create a per-ceptual contrast whereby we are defining what we think the standard of comparison should be. When the second request comes along, it seems much smaller than the first and, in our case, much smaller than the request would seem if presented alone.

Many times, of course, you don't feel like playing the negotiation game. You might be thinking, "Why doesn't everyone just start with their real final first offer?" The notion sounds good in theory, but it does not work because the other party is expecting to negotiate. Accepting their first offer too fast creates a high emotional toll. They will think they could have done better, even if they got a great deal. You goal is to present the other party with a contrast—a high or low number to establish a starting point to the negotia-tion. The game is about mutual concessions. You give a little, and they are inclined to give a little. If you don't play by the rules of the game, then you can't win the game. You goal is to create as much room as possible when you start the negotiation.

In the negotiation process, the door-in-the-face technique can be a pow-erful tool. Watch a skilled property developer. He may look for quality properties that have been on the market for some months, often because of the seller's high asking price, say, $500,000. To drive down the seller's expec-tation, the property developer employs an agent who, acting anonymously, displays great enthusiasm for the property and then makes a very low aggressive offer—say $350,000—which the seller angrily rejects. The devel-oper then moves in and offers a much more reasonable price—say $430,000—which, after some negotiating, is accepted. Labor negotiators fre-quently employ this tool as well. They begin with extreme demands that they expect to be turned down. Abruptly, they repeat a series of smaller demands, or concessions, which will then be more easily accepted. These smaller demands are the real target of the negotiation.

The door-in-the-face technique can also save you from lots of headache and hassle. You can get people to go from hating you to thanking you for exactly the same thing. For example, when assigning my college students a

10-page final paper makes them tense and vocal. They complain about time, length, font size, and so on. You name it; they'll bring it up. Tired of the complaining, I changed how my approach using the Law of Contrast. I bring up the paper and wait for the moans, but then I tell them this 20-page paper will have to include the following. . . . The uproar starts: "Twenty pages! I won't have time for that!" I then graciously comply and tell them that, if they promise to do a great, concise paper with the proper research, I will make it only 10 pages. The cheers erupt, and everyone is happy. The students see the 10-page paper as a great deal by comparison. Now the students thank me rather than give me grief.

In my university class, students were learning about the different Laws of Persuasion and were asked to write a letter to their parents requesting money, using one of the laws. (This was just an exercise; they were not allowed to send it.) They decided the best way was to use the Law of Contrast. Here is a sample:

Dear Mom and Dad,

I hope this letter finds you both well and happy. I wish I could say that is how I feel. I know you love me, but it is hard to come to you in such an embarrassing situation. Now, I don't want you to worry too much. I can see Mom now, already skimming through this letter to find out exactly what is wrong, so I guess I'll cut right to the chase. I'm really worn out, but I'm getting better. At least I have a place to stay, especially during this cold winter weather.

The last couple of weeks I have been sleeping on the streets, looking for food and shelter. I finally met this nice man who is letting me stay in his room for free. It sure is nice to have a roof over my head. Sometimes I still get wet at night, though, because there's a crack in the wall on my side of the bed. But with five of us sharing the room, we've got some body heat going and that helps out. We hope that between the five of us, we can make rent this month. They sure have been nice letting me stay here, and letting me keep out of sight. It seems there is some type of warrant out for me, and I am unfortunately "on the run," as they say.

I'm afraid I can't tell you exactly where I am; I don't want to endanger you with too much information in case the authorities come to question you. As you may guess, I am in desperate need of a large sum of funding so that I can settle my accounts before another, more ruthless party begins to hunt me down. I was hoping for, but not counting on, your assistance. I know I have done wrong, but I plead for your forgiveness and prayers.

Just kidding! I wanted you to see my problems in the proper perspective. I crashed my car last weekend. No one was hurt. I did have $300 in damage to my car though. I was wondering if you could send me the money so I could get back on my feet.

I love you forever,

Jill

CONTRAST AND INTERESTING PRICING FACTS

- ► Our mind tends to focus on the left-hand digits over the right-hand digits[4] (i.e., dollars, not cents).

- ► Most consumers tend to round down when they see a price[5] (i.e., $9.97 = $9.00).

- ► A study reduced a price of an item by 14¢ (0.89 to 0.75 and 0.93 to 0.79). Most people felt the second set was a greater reduction.[6]

- ► Consumers tend to like and underestimate odd prices over even prices.[7]

- ► Mail order catalogs tried ending prices in 0.88, 0.99, and 0.00. When 0.99 was used, it outsold other endings by 8 percent.[8]

- ► Other researchers found ending the price in 9 increased sales on average by 10 percent.[9]

COMPARISON EFFECT: TAKING THEIR TEMPERATURE

The last form of contrast is the more general Comparison Effect. This is closely related to the door-in-the-face technique except that, instead of presenting an outrageous request up front, the persuader presents prospects with an undesirable form of what they are looking for. Then, when the good (or even mediocre) item is presented, the prospect takes the offer a lot faster. The Comparison Effect focuses on how the prospect is able to compare two options simultaneously and come to the conclusion that the second option really is desirable.

Some real estate companies maintain what they call setup properties. These are run-down properties listed at inflated prices, which are used to benefit the genuine properties in the company's inventory by contrast.

Agents show customers the setup properties first, then they show them the homes they really want to sell, both of them listed at the same price. The second home looks much better in comparison to the dump they see first.

The comparison principle comes into play in our everyday lives. It can even influence how we perceive the physical attractiveness of our partner. A study at Arizona State and Montana State Universities tested to see whether we might think our own spouses or partners were less attractive because of the media bombardment with ads showing very attractive models. In the study, students were first shown pictures of models before rating the attractiveness of members of the opposite sex who were not models. These students rated the nonmodels as significantly less attractive than did students who had not first looked at pictures of models.[10]

An interesting study proved this point. Volunteers went door to door to solicit money for a made-up charity. It was a bowling fund-raiser called "Strike Against Cancer." Everyone was trained to deliver a presentation at the door. They were trained to say, "I'm working as a volunteer coordinator to help organize the charity bowling event." There were three requests: large, moderate, and small.

- ► *Large:* "We're looking for volunteers to help with the event. It takes about ten hours a week. Would you be interested?"
- ► *Moderate:* "We're looking for people to take part in our event. Participants need to raise at least thirty dollars in pledges and come bowl with us. Would you be interested?"
- ► *Small:* "Since you can't participate [volunteer], would you like to sponsor me for the event? Any amount would be fine."

The two things learned from this study was that the larger the first request was, the higher the compliance was for the second request. The second thing learned was that friends were always more compliant than strangers.[11]

Another example of the Comparison Effect uses the same concept with a different product: funeral caskets. Funeral directors exploit the contrast principle to get families of the deceased to spend more money. Directors show the deceased's family the expensive model first, and then they show them a very plain, cheap one. They know that the family members are grieving and will do anything for their loved one. The grieving loved ones are often shocked by the contrast in the two caskets and rebound to the more expensive one. One study revealed that by showing the most expensive item first, it increased the amount of the sale by 45 percent.[12]

Automobile dealers use the contrast principle. They wait until the final price for a new car has been negotiated before suggesting one option after another that might be added on. After committing to $20,000, what is an extra $200 for undercoating (most of us are not even sure what that is), an extended warranty, or a entertainment system? The strategy is to bring up the extras independently of one another. After you've already decided to buy a $1,000 couch, what is $70 for fabric protection? People will always pay more for accessories or add-ons after the purchase has been made.

These principles also apply when you have to compare people. The Law of Contrast is constantly at work, even influencing judgments in job interviews, ideas, or speaking order. If you first interview an outstanding candidate and then immediately afterward you interview someone who is less favorable, you will be inclined to underrate the second person even more than if you had not interviewed the outstanding candidate first. Certainly the reverse is true: If an average candidate follows someone who has interviewed very poorly, you may view that individual as better than average.

We see diet ads that use contrast to convince us to use their products. The before-and-after pictures are intentionally made to look like stark opposites. The before picture is in black and white, with the person slouching, frowning, and pale. The after picture is of the same person in full color with a smile, erect posture, and tan skin. We look at the two pictures, see the comparison, and decide we want to be more like the after picture.

JUST NOTICEABLE DIFFERENCE (JND)

Many times, we can fly under the radar with the contrast principle. The Just Noticeable Difference (JND)[13] is the minimum amount of difference in the intensity of the stimulus that can be detected, that is, the minimal amount of change the brain can handle before it begins to notice. In practical terms, it is, say, how much can you raise the price of a product without anyone noticing. In the area of taste, for example, companies want to offer the best taste for the lowest cost. The quality of the ingredients causes people to notice or not notice the quality of the product.

Many marketers would rather change the packaging and offer less product than resort to charging more. When we don't notice the difference, we think we are getting the same deal. When you raise the price of a product, you don't want anyone to notice. The price of gas going up another 10¢ is not noticed unless it breaks the dollar threshold, that is, $3.00 to $4.00. Is the yogurt cup now 2.9 ounces or 3 ounces? We don't notice because the cup size has not changed; the bottom of the cup is more concave.

HOW TO USE THE LAW OF CONTRAST

Given all the examples in this chapter, you can guess the steps to take when employing this law. But let's simplify the process by looking at a few elements of the Law of Contrast.

Starting High

Make your initial request really big (or really small)—not so high that it is totally unrealistic, but big enough that you know you will get a no. Then follow this initial request with smaller offers that will bring about the result you desired all along.

For example, fund-raising organizations often send letters asking for donations in amounts that are usually pretty high for most people's pocketbooks. Soon after the letter is sent out, the organization places a follow-up telephone call. The person making the call asks whether the letter was received and then makes a request for a smaller donation.

Timing

For contrast to be effective, the two scenarios, options, or offers must be presented one right after another. Researchers Dillard, Hunter, and Burgoon[14] and Fern, Monroe, and Avila[15] agree that the timing between the initial and follow-up requests influences the success of using this technique. Specifically, to increase compliance, the interval between the two requests must be short. If there is too much of a delay between the first and second requests, your prospect may not remember that you are comparing the two items or requests, and your ability to persuade will falter.

Situation

The situation applies to all the Laws of Persuasion, and it certainly applies to the Law of Contrast. You have to think about your situation before you can choose which method to use and to what degree to implement the law. It is easy to see that the attitude and feelings of a funeral attendee will be different from those of a wedding guest.

BACKFIRE

Two major limitations could cause the Law of Contrast to backfire during a persuasion encounter. The first is the insult zone. If your request is so unrealistic that it is not believable or insulting, it will backfire. The second is contrast will always work better when your request is not selfish or all about you; the request should either directly benefit the prospect or benefit society.

CASE STUDY

A client wanted to increase sales of their high-end product. This audiovisual (AV) company had two options for their equipment. Their basic product sold well, but their higher-end (most profitable) product was not doing as well. The company tried sales and consumer intercepts to sell more of their higher-end product. That helped but not as much as they wanted. They felt the higher-priced option was better for the consumer and had a better value. Using the Law of Contrast, what would you recommend?

To make the higher-priced option seem more valuable, I recommended that they offer an even higher-priced option. I told them to create a higher-end product that had more value, more bonuses, and a longer guarantee and that would contrast with the now middle-range product. The middle-priced product would look like a better deal contrasting the new, higher-priced product. By using the Law of Contrast, they reached their sales goal of selling the product they really want to sell.

Additional Resources: Negotiation Power Video (maximuminfluence.com)

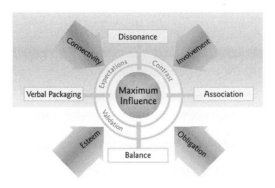

CHAPTER 13

The Law of Social Validation

The Art of Social Pressure

One dog barks at something, and a hundred bark at the bark.

—CHINESE PROVERB

Social validation is all around us. For example, when something strange happens on an airline flight, most look to the flight attendants to see whether they should panic. If there is a strange noise, we look at their reaction; if they stay calm, we tend to stay calm. I was on a flight that hit an air pocket, and the plane dramatically dropped. As the airplane fell, a flight attendant screamed, turned white, hurried to her seat, and buckled up. What do you think happened to the passengers? After seeing this behavior from the flight attendant, they began to tense up and scream. Her behavior caused a social panic.

We are social animals. Look at the explosion of social media. We all have an innate desire to belong to a social group. Many judge their value by their number of social media friends. Because we value this sense of belonging so highly, the more other people who find an idea, trend, or product appealing or correct, the more correct that position becomes in our own minds. *The Law of Social Validation recognizes and builds on our innate desire to be part of the group or part of the majority and that we tend to change our perceptions, opinions, and behaviors in ways that are consistent with group norms.*[1] Even if we don't admit it, or maybe even realize it, we care about what others think. As such, we use others' behavior as a guide in establishing the standard for the products we use, the services we trust, and the decisions we make.

We seek to find out what others are doing as a way of validating our own actions. This is how we decide what constitutes correct, or standard, behavior. We see a behavior as more correct when we see others doing it. The more people do it, the more correct it becomes. Professor Kirk Hansen of the Stanford Business School demonstrated this when he boosted downloads for best-selling files on the Web by personally downloading those files over and over so that the counter was artificially high. He and his team then observed that these boosted downloaded files were downloaded even more frequently. The high number on the counter indicated popularity, and people were most interested in downloading the files that were already ranked the highest. Whether the question is how to react at a sporting event, how we act at a party, or whether we should order dessert at a restaurant, the validation of others gives us our answers and therefore guides our actions.

We all seek validation. We learn early in life that we make fewer mistakes when we follow the social norm. When we are not sure what to do, we seek the social norm by observing what others do. If we don't know the standard, we look around and find it. The Law of Social Validation becomes a way to save time and energy in figuring out what is correct. We use others' behavior to guide our own actions and to validate what we should or should not do. We don't always have to look at the positive and the negative in every situation. This automatic trigger saves us from thinking. We compare what we do against the standard of what everyone else is doing. If we find a discrepancy between what we observe and what we do, we tend to make changes in the direction of the social norm.

GOING WITH THE CROWD

Social validation compels us to change our behaviors, our attitudes, and our actions, even when what we observe doesn't really match our true desire or thoughts. We seek out social norms to help us know what we should be feel-ing, watching, buying, or doing. For the most part, this is not a conscious process. We subconsciously accept many ways of behaving that are deter-mined by our surroundings and the actions of others, such as raising our hands to speak in class, how we behave at a concert, or how we act at work because of the corporate culture. When we become part of a group, our once divergent emotions and feelings tend to converge.[2]

Usually, as long as most people agree with what we are doing or about to do, we feel social validation. For the most part, we are all conformists. We will do what the crowd does. We don't like to admit that about ourselves, but it is true. The bottom line is that people will usually believe what the majority believes or believe what society says they are supposed to believe.[3] Only 5–10 percent of the population engages in behavior contrary to the social norm. When we feel awkward or unsure of how to act in a foreign sit-uation, we look for social cues that will dictate our behavior.[4] This could be at a party, during an orientation, while attending a family reunion, or on one's first day on the job at a new company. When the social information we are seeking is vague, we don't know how to respond and thus continue seek-ing out social clues.

We see this law operating in groups, in organizations, on the web, on an infomercial, and in day-to-day public life. In all of these circumstances, there is a certain standard or norm. In organizations, the years of tradition estab-lish a standard operating procedure. Because we want to fit into these groups and maintain our membership with them, we conform our actions to the norm.

SOCIAL VALIDATION AT WORK

The Law of Social Validation is always happening, everywhere: publicly passing the donation plate to help with a community project; doing the wave at sporting events; going to popular dance clubs when you don't enjoy the surroundings; being afraid to raise your hand in class to ask a question; stacking the top ten most popular books right in the entryway of a book-store; choosing restaurants according to which have the longest lines or the most cars; choosing movies according to which ones everyone is talking about; washing our hands in public restrooms only when somebody else is watching; and restaurants seating their first patrons near the window for everyone else to see. If we are unsure where to eat or what movie to see, what do we do? We check our phones for the restaurants with the best reviews or the movie with the highest ratings.

Sometimes theaters even employ professional audience members to start laughter, clapping, and standing ovations! Those hired by a theater to applaud performances are called claques, the French word for clap. (In fact, French opera houses used professional groups to applaud.) When audience members see others stand and cheer or applaud, they are more inclined to do so. Performers commonly "salt the tip jar" by placing some money in the jar themselves. When people see that others have already made contributions, they assume tipping is the appropriate and acceptable thing to do. Salting the tip jar is a common practice among pianists, bartenders, bus drivers, and the homeless on the street. Even in churches, the practice of salting the collection plate is often employed. People are more inclined to donate if they are passed a plate that already holds some bills.

I once attended a college football game between two fierce crosstown rivals. Emotions were high, and we all wanted our home team to win. One of the fans near me was using a megaphone to taunt the other team and its fans. He only meant it in good fun, but before long before a security guard came up to the man and told him he could not use the megaphone during the game. The guard stood in the middle of the aisle of the sold-out game. The fan said he was just having fun, but the rent-a-cop stressed that it was strictly against the rules. Then the social pressure and validation kicked in. Nearby fans told the security guard that the fan's overzealous actions were OK and that there was no problem. The guard tried to persist, but the crowd only grew louder in their protests. Finally, the rent-a-cop decided it wasn't worth the hassle and left.

Even watching someone else do what's right will give you social validation. For example, one study asked 10,000 high school students to give blood. The study found that students who had been exposed to 38 photos of high school blood-drive scenes were 17 percent more likely to donate blood than the students who had not seen the photos. Seeing others do the right thing prompts us to socially validate the cause and to jump on board.[5] Even at a retail store or swap meet, the more people who are in your store, the easier it is for others to come in.

SOCIAL VALIDATION: THE POWER OF THE GROUP

In a study, participants were asked to identify the longer of two lines displayed on a screen. One line was clearly longer than the other, but some participants had been privately instructed prior to the study to state that the shorter line was longer. The surprising result was that several of the unsuspecting participants actually gave in to social pressure and changed their answers! Over the course of the entire study, 75 percent of the participants gave the incorrect answer at least one time. In a related study, researchers determined that even when the correct answer is obvious, individuals will knowingly give the incorrect answer 37 percent of the time, just to go along with the consensus.[6]

We have often heard the canned laughter on television sitcoms even when nothing really funny is happening. Studies prove that using canned laughter actually influences audience members to laugh longer and more frequently and to give the material higher ratings for its funniness.[7]

Even for the portions of the show that seem to have no humor at all, producers use laugh tracks to get us to laugh along. The sad part is that it actually works! There is evidence that canned laughter is most effective when the joke is really bad.[8] When two audiences watch the same show and one hears a laugh track while the other doesn't, the audience that hears the laugh track always laughs more!

Another study was set up to test whether passersby would stare up into the air if another group of people was already doing so. The researchers arranged groups of one to 15 people to congregate in New York City at 33 West 42nd Street. A camera was set up on the sixth floor to catch the results. Sure enough, the more people in the group who were already gawking and looking into the air, the more people there were who stopped, came over, and looked up themselves![9]

When participants were asked to view a political debate, it was found that the mere presence of a confederate who cheered for one of the candidates influenced the participants' overall positive evaluation of the candidate.[10] Obviously, when receiving information in a social setting, the individual can be skewed to perceive the information the way the group tends to hear it.

We have all seen the signs in the hotels telling us to respect nature by reusing our towels and bed sheets. A study was done using two slogans. The first slogan was, "Help save the environment." The second slogan added a little social validation: "Join your fellow guests in helping save the environment." This small change in the wording, adding the social validation, boosted the amount of towel reuse by almost 10 percent (35 versus 44 percent).[11]

THE OTHER SIDE OF SOCIAL VALIDATION

Bystander Apathy

Numerous studies demonstrate that, when someone is in trouble or in need of help, as the number of bystanders increases, the number of people who actually help decreases. This so-called bystander apathy effect occurs because, in almost any situation, the more people who are present, the more we feel a diffusion of responsibility. Our sense of social pressure is lessened when we feel that any number of people might be more capable of helping than we are. Sometimes we go against our better judgment because we want to be liked, accepted, and found in agreement with social norms. When we are part of a crowd, we "no longer feel individually responsible for our emotions or actions. We can allow ourselves to shout, sing, cry, or strike without temperament imposed by personal accountability."[12]

When we find ourselves in groups, responsibility is diffused. Sometimes we don't know whether we should even involve ourselves in the first place because so many other people can take action. Have you ever been in a situation where, because of the numbers in your group, you didn't really give it your all? For example, maybe on an academic group project you weren't as diligent as you would have been if you had been solely responsible for the assignment. Or maybe you've helped push a stalled car to safety with some other people but didn't really push your hardest. Have you ever seen someone pulled over on the side of the road, but you drove past, along with all the other cars speeding by? When large numbers of people are involved, we tend to assume that someone else will respond and take action, or we might conclude that our help is not really needed.

One case in history stands out as a classic example of bystander apathy. Catherine Genovese, a young woman living in New York City, was murdered one night when returning home from work. The unfortunate truth of the matter was that, in a city like New York, her death was just another of countless murders. Consequently, the incident didn't receive any more coverage than a few short lines in *The New York Times*. Genovese's story would have remained an obscure and incidental case had it not been for the publicity given an additional fact of her killing.

A week later, A. M. Rosenthal, editor of *The New York Times*, went out to lunch with the city police commissioner. Rosenthal asked the commissioner about another homicide in the area. The commissioner, however, mistakenly thinking he was being asked about the Genovese case, revealed a shocking piece of information that the police had uncovered. Genovese's death had not been a silent, hidden, or secretive occurrence. Rather, it had been a loud, drawn-out, public event. As her attacker chased her down and stabbed her three separate times in a 35-minute period, 38 neighbors watched from their apartment windows and didn't even call the police!

Rosenthal promptly assigned a team to investigate this incidence of bystander apathy. Soon after the meeting with the commissioner, *The New York Times* came out with a lengthy, front-page article detailing the incident and the alleged reactions of the neighbors:

> **For more than half an hour, 38 respectable, law-abiding citizens in Queens watched a killer stalk and stab a woman in three separate attacks. Twice the sound of their voices and the sudden glow of their bedroom lights interrupted him and frightened him off. Each time he returned, sought her out, and stabbed her again. Not one person telephoned the police during the assault; one witness called after the woman was dead.[13]**

Everyone was stunned and baffled. How could people witness such a scene and do nothing? Even the very neighbors alluded to in the article didn't know how to explain their inaction. Responses included, "I don't know," "I was afraid," and "I didn't want to get involved." Their explanations didn't really explain anything. Why couldn't one of them have just made a quick, anonymous call to the police? Different branches of the media—newspapers, TV stations, magazines, radio stations—pursued their own studies and investigations to explain the incredible scenario, all of them finally arriving at the same conclusion: The witnesses simply didn't care. They concluded that there was just no other explanation, or so they thought.

Do you really think 38 people did not care enough to make an anonymous phone call? Did the researchers not understand the diffusion of responsibility? The neighbors didn't react, thinking someone else would help or someone else would call the police. Most of us are good people. If each individual neighbor knew it was up to him or her to phone the police for help, the call would have been made.

Bystander apathy happens when an individual's chances of helping decreases when unreceptive bystanders are present in emergency situations. Another experiment conducted in New York highlighted the tendency for bystander apathy to occur. Researchers had participants complete a questionnaire. After a few minutes, smoke began to enter the room from underneath the door. The study found that, when a lone individual observed smoke leaking from under a door, 75 percent of those studied reported the smoke. In groups of three, however, reporting incidences dropped to 38 percent. If in that group two of the people encouraged the third person to do nothing, reporting the smoke dropped to 10 percent. Sometimes the smoke got so thick it was hard to read the questionnaire.[14]

Deindividuation

Social psychologists Festinger, Pepitone, and Newcomb coined the term *deindividuation*.[15] Deindividuation refers to how, when we find ourselves in a group, we become less self-aware and also less concerned with how others will evaluate us.[16] The group becomes the focus because less attention and awareness are paid to individuals. Think of all the people you've heard yell obscenities at sporting events. Do you think they would do that if they were in a small, intimate group watching that same event? Deindividuation means that, in a group, we feel more anonymous and therefore less individually responsible for our actions, often causing us to say or do things that we would not normally feel comfortable with.

One study showed how deindividuation can lead to antisocial behavior.[17] On Halloween, researchers evaluated 1,352 trick-or-treaters—either alone or in groups—who had the chance to steal candy from 27 Seattle homes. The researchers figured that Halloween would be the perfect occasion to conduct such a study because the children would be in costume, making them even more anonymous. When the children came to doors where they were greeted by experimenters, they were told they could choose only one piece of candy. In some cases, the experimenter asked the children their names, while in other cases the children were allowed to remain anonymous. The experimenter would then leave the room, as though they had to go get something. Unseen observers took careful note of how the children responded: When alone, 7.5 percent took more than one piece of candy; when in groups, 20.8 percent took more than one piece! Also interesting was that the children who remained anonymous stole more candy than did the children who gave out their names. Deindividuation prompted many of the trick-or-treaters to go against what was socially acceptable and steal more candy.

Anytime we find ourselves part of a group, we feel some susceptibility to peer pressure and/or the opinions of others in the group. The more connection, similarity, or respect we feel in the group, the more their opinions matter to us, and therefore the more we feel pressured to align our own opinions with the group's. Even when we don't really agree with the group, we will often go along in order to be mentally rewarded instead of punished, or liked instead of scorned. This behavior occurs whether it is part of corporate culture, the norm, or just the assumption that everyone else is correct.

SOCIAL VALIDATION AND MARKETING

The more a brand is advertised, the more popular and familiar it is perceived to be. We as consumers somehow infer that something is popular simply because it is advertised. When people are buying gifts for others, social proof is one of the most effective techniques that a salesclerk can use.[18]

Many salespeople find great success in telling clients that a product is their best-selling or most popular because social validation increases their credibility of the product. When customers feel that something is a hot trend, they spend more money to acquire it, even if there is no proof other than the salesperson's word. So it is with advertising: Asserting that a product is in super high demand or that it is the most popular or fastest selling seems to provide proof enough. Perceiving that a product is popular is often all consumers need to go out and purchase it.

The creation and use of social validation are rampant: Clubs make themselves look like the place to be by allowing huge waiting lines to congregate outside their facilities, even when the place is practically empty inside. Salespeople often recount the countless others who are using the product or service. You also already know that referrals are your greatest source of social validation. Sales and motivation consultant Cavett Robert said it best: "Since 95 percent of the people are imitators and only 5 percent initiators, people are persuaded more by the actions of others than by any proof we can offer."[19]

MAKING SOCIAL VALIDATION WORK

The power of social validation can be used to your benefit in any persuasive situation. When your product or service is socially validated, people are likely to use it or switch to it. People are always looking around and comparing themselves to see whether they line up with everyone else. If they feel a discrepancy between where they are and where everyone else is, they will most likely conform to the group standard.

HOW CAN YOU INCREASE SOCIAL VALIDATION? IS YOUR PRODUCT/SERVICE...

- ► Best-selling?
- ► Number one?
- ► Top 10?
- ► Fastest growing?

- ► Most popular?
- ► The newest trend?
- ► Standard issue?
- ► Number of views.

Consider the following ways you can enhance the effects of social validation to your benefit:

- ► The larger the group, the better. The larger the group is, the more people will conform. Social theory shows us that, when a group grows, so does conformity to that group.
- ► The greater the similarity, the better. The more a person can identify with the group, the more that person will be influenced to change their behavior and/or opinions. Social validation is more powerful when we observe people we consider to be just like us.[20] People prefer the validation or experiences of so-called ordinary people when they are considering purchases or making buying decisions.[21]
- ► The clearer the principle of social validation is, the better. Find the best use of social validation. Is it part of a trend, used by the elite, or the industry standard? Who uses it? Do you have testimonials from other clients or users?

ARE YOU CREDIBLE IN THE EYES OF YOUR PROSPECT?

Credibility is an important aspect of social validation. You could be the smartest person or the most qualified in your field, but, if that is not the perception, you have no credibility. You can transfer (borrow) credibility from others. Make sure you associate yourself or your product with people or companies that your prospect would respect, emulate, or admire. The research shows the customer testimonials will always positively affect the persuasiveness of advertising.[22]

You have to be careful when explaining and exhibiting your credibility. If you launch into a laundry list of your accomplishments or of your education and titles, you might be perceived as self-centered. Take advantage of less direct or less self-proclaiming ways to show your audience how competent you are. For example, you can hang your degrees on the wall or have someone else offer his recommendation of you.

HOW TO INCREASE CREDIBILITY

- ➤ Be prepared.
- ➤ Maintain a professional appearance.
- ➤ Use referrals.
- ➤ Get an introduction.
- ➤ Use credible facts or statistics.
- ➤ Reveal your qualifications.
- ➤ Have professional external surroundings.
- ➤ Get more testimonials.

BACKFIRE

Social validation will not work if there is no credibility or your statement is not believable. When you use a testimonial that feels too good to be true, this technique will backfire. Learn to borrow credibility from others using testimonials, endorsements, and referrals.

CASE STUDY

. . . .

I was helping a client make her Web pages more persuasive. Everything was in order. The offer was great offer, and the site had the right look. She used the right colors, and her site provided a great solution to what people were looking for. It just was not pulling as much as she wanted. The traffic was high, the look was professional, but she wasn't getting enough sales. Using the Law of Social Validation what would you recommend?

I told her no one will believe her personal success story as much as they would other people's success stories. She had something to gain. It was her product, her website, and her profit. A neutral party would increase her credibility and social validation. We increased the number of testimonials she had on her website, and that doubled her sales. Social validation is borrowing credibility and trust from other people. The bottom line is that people will always believe others before they believe you.

. . . .

Additional Resources: The 5 C's of Trust Audio (maximuminfluence.com)

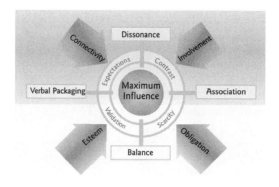

CHAPTER 14

The Law of Scarcity

Get Anyone to Take Immediate Action

Without a sense of urgency, desire loses its value. —JIM ROHN

You have seen the stories. You probably have experienced the tension. That Friday after Thanksgiving—Black Friday! People are not going to sleep because there is a limited supply and they need to make sure they are at the store in time to get the deal of a lifetime. We hear countless stories of fights, arguments, and people becoming hysterical in the lines waiting for the deals. Are these human beings? Do these people live with us in our communities? Sometimes I'm not so sure. When people feel that there is a limited number and there is only so much to go around, you see a different side of humanity. If they sense for one second that you will take away what they deserve or want, look out. This is scarcity in action. When items are limited, when items are scarce, when you cut in line—unimaginable things will happen.

eBay also drives us makes crazy with scarcity. I find an item I like and put in a reasonable offer. I promise myself that I won't bid any higher, but I always get caught. The outbid notice arrives, and I can't believe somebody outbid me. The scarcity starts having its effect. What if I can't find this item again? What if it is more expensive in the future? The other bidders obviously think this item is worth more than I do. Then I find myself wanting it even more—whatever it is—and I bid far more than I originally intended. The thrill of winning usually outweighs the pain of the increased price.

WHY SCARCITY DRIVES US WILD

The Law of Scarcity states that the more scarce an item becomes, the more the item increases in value, and the greater the urge is to own it. Scarcity drives people to action, making us act quickly for fear of missing out on an opportunity. The law plays a large role in the persuasion process. Opportunities are always more valuable and exciting when they are scarce and less available. We want to be the ones to own the rare items or to get the last one on the shelf.

Whenever choice is limited or threatened, we humans need to get a piece of the limited commodity, making us want it and crave it all the more. Scarcity increases the value of any product or service. Potentially losing something before we've even had an opportunity to possess it drives people to action. We don't want to miss out on anything we could own. We want to get around any restriction. We feel uptight and want back our freedom, leading to tension and unrest. The Law of Scarcity pertains not only to physical products, but also to time, information, price, and knowledge.

This law is the most abused and overused of all the Laws of Persuasion. It is always being misused. How often can a furniture store go out of business? Do you really believe the salesperson when you hear it is the last one in your size? Or how many times have you been told to act now because the sale ends today? The law works, but only when used correctly.

The Threat of Potential Loss

Anytime people feel their freedom—to choose, think, or act—is being restricted, they will attempt to restore that freedom.[1] Facing this restriction, we ironically are psychologically driven to latch onto the very thing that we fear will be restricted. Suddenly, that restricted item is even more important to us. Researchers call this tendency psychological reactance.[2] This is an intense motivational state. Reactance causes us to be emotional, single-minded, and even irrational when we feel a threat to our ability to make a choice or to our personal freedom. We react by attempting to restore our freedom. We hate feeling restricted, so we are highly motivated to resolve anything that creates that feeling. It is due to reactance that we act and that we want it now.

Psychological reactance develops during our childhood. A study involving a group of male toddlers illustrates the power of the Law of Scarcity, even in very small children. In the study, the toddlers were brought into a room that held two equally exciting and appealing toys. A clear barrier was set up so that one of the toys sat next to it, whereas the other sat behind it. The barrier wasn't very tall, so some of the toddlers could simply reach over the top and grab for the toy. For others, though, the barrier was too high to reach over, so they could reach the toy only if they went around and behind the barrier. The researchers wanted to see whether the obstructed toy, being scarcer, would draw more attention and be more desirable. The boys who could easily reach over the top showed no preference toward the obstructed or the unobstructed toy; the unobstructed toy was approached just as frequently and just as quickly. For the boys who could not reach over the top, however, the obstructed toy was clearly the more desirable of the two. In fact, the boys made contact with it three times faster than with the unobstructed toy![3] Even toddlers felt an urge to defy restriction of choice!

The Law of Scarcity works because it makes people feel as though they will lose their opportunity to act and choose if they don't do so immediately. The threat of such a loss creates urgency in our decision making. Have you ever noticed how people tend to be more motivated when faced with potentially losing something than when they might take steps of their own accord and gain something of equal value? Studies have verified that this is a common and consistent phenomenon.[4] For example, if homeowners were told *either* how much money they would lose if they didn't improve their insulation *or* how much money they would save, which message would create a greater feeling of urgency to act? They are more likely to act if they are told about their potential loss.[5]

YOU CAN'T HAVE IT

The mental trigger of potential loss causes such great anxiety in people that they act to prevent the loss, even though they might not be completely interested in the product itself. Imagine making a decision where you have all week to make up your mind and you have the reassurance that when you return tomorrow, the item will still be available at the same good price. You could take days, weeks, or months to make that decision.

However, when scarcity enters the picture and you feel that the availability of the product, the timing, or even the price is bound to change without notice, the mental trigger of scarcity is pulled. You are driven to acquire something to alleviate the threat of potential loss. What we can't have is always more desirable and exciting than what we already possess. As the adage goes, "The grass is always greener on the other side of the fence." Any parent knows the result of telling a child she can't have or do something. The child will immediately drop everything and want the one thing she can't have. The forbidden nature of the relationship between Romeo and Juliet, for example, made it even stronger and more appealing to them. Parents need to be cautioned about forbidding their child's friends and lovers because the Law of Scarcity will come back to haunt them.

The manner in which an object becomes scarce also contributes to making it more desirable. In a interesting study, researchers gave subjects a cookie jar containing 10 cookies. Then, taking the jar back, the subjects were given a new jar containing only two cookies. One group of subjects was told that their cookies had been given away to other participants because of the demand for their study. Another group was told that their cookies were taken away because the experimenter had made a mistake and had given them the wrong cookie jar. The cookies that had become scarce through social demand were rated considerably higher than the cookies that had become scarce through the experimenter's oversight. In addition, they were the most highly rated of all the cookies used in the study![6]

There was an extreme water crisis in Orange County, California (where I was born and grew up). The drought was announced as dire because of the lack of rainfall and a reconstruction of a major water main. The authorities told everyone to please conserve water and prepare for the worst. They said it could come down to water rationing in the future or not being able to water their lawns. What do you think happened? Water consumption dramatically increased! Water was now perceived as scarce. With potential water rationing in the future, everyone was watering their lawns, filling their pools, and using it before it could be taken away.[7]

THE LAW OF SCARCITY IN MARKETING

Psychologist Anthony Pratkanis is recorded as saying, "As consumers we have a rule of thumb: If it is rare or scarce, it must be valuable and good."

Even if it is not the day after Thanksgiving, department stores understand the Law of Scarcity. Fights break out at department stores when people go after those scarce items, which are offered at bargain prices for a limited time only. The lower prices are bait—a loss leader for the store—but certain to generate a buying frenzy that is contagious. Blinded by scarcity, consumers will buy anything and everything, whether they need it or not. For example, you see patrons buying three DVD players. You ask them, "Why three?" They don't know. All they know is that the store said supplies were limited, the sale was only for today, and each shopper was limited to three. So they bought three DVD players.

Some stores have the limited-number thing down to perfection. Often when we go shopping, we are only casually interested, telling the salesperson, "Just looking, thanks." We glance over the packaging and examine the sale sign. Then the salesperson plays the numbers game. Approaching us, she says, "It's a great model, isn't it? Especially at this price! Unfortunately, I just sold our last model." We suddenly feel disappointed. Now that it's no longer available, we feel that we really want it, even though we had been only mildly interested. We ask whether there might be another one in the back or at another location. "Well, let me see what I can do. If I can get another one for you at this price, will you take it?"

Odd, we don't even realize this is happening. The technique works like a charm. We are asked to commit to a product when it seems as though it will soon be totally unavailable and therefore seems incredibly desirable. Threatened with potentially losing a great deal, we agree. Then, of course, the salesperson comes back with the great news. The product will be shipped to the store in three days. In the meantime, all you have to do is sign the sales contract.

We also see the Law of Scarcity frequently employed by cable shopping networks. They make both time and quantity scarce resources. A little clock is always running in the corner of the screen, along with a sales counter.

Sometimes the counter runs down with every sale. So the host says, "We have only a limited number of these imported widgets, and when they're all gone, we will never sell them again." This will be the last time they will be available. You only have a few minutes to purchase this precious item, and the clock lets you know how little time you have left to make this buy of a lifetime. You will also hear, "Not available in stores."

Creating a Demand: Can You Say, "Limited Supply"?

An owner of a successful beef-importing company decided to conduct a study among his people. The staff members were assigned to call the company's customers and ask them to purchase beef in one of three ways. One group of customers just heard the usual presentation before giving their orders. Another group was given the usual presentation, but they were also presented with evidence that imported beef was expected to be in short supply in the coming months. A third group was told about the beef's upcoming scarcity, but they were also told that this news was not available to the general public and that the information provided was exclusive to the company. Not surprisingly, the sudden demand for beef created by these phone calls exceeded the supply on hand, and the company had to scramble to fill the orders. Customers alerted to the coming scarcity of the beef bought double the amount of those receiving only the standard sales pitch, and those learning both of the coming scarcity and that this was secret information bought six times the amount as those hearing only the standard sales pitch![8]

As mentioned, some popular night clubs continue to have waiting lines outside because long lines seem to make the clubs more desirable and fashionable. These night clubs do not eliminate the waiting line by increasing their prices because removing the lines would eliminate the scarcity factor, and demand would collapse. This also happens when you are buying airline travel online. Next to the special price is the notice that only four seats are left at that special price.

How about when you take your child to be photographed? The photographer takes 10 shots and then sends you proofs for all of them. You're told to select the shots you like best and how many copies of each you'd like. Then you're told the files will be deleted if you don't purchase. Of course, you feel like you'd better get all the prints you want now, or you won't be able to later!

Creating Allure

When a woman wants to come across as more attractive to the man of her choice, she can set things up so that she will just happen to meet him while on a date with another successful, handsome man. She then will appear to be more desirable than if she were merely to meet him alone at a club or bar. She creates allure.

Or if you were selling real estate, you would be smart to have several interested people along for the tour of the property because the interest of one client will heighten the interest of another. Instead of your potential buyer thinking, "Okay, I'm going to try to wheel and deal here," he will think, "I'd better jump on this, or the other guy's going to get it before I do!"

Court judges have to deal with their jurors being influenced by scarce or secret information. Attorneys often strategically introduce information that the jury really isn't supposed to evaluate. When this happens, the judge can either declare a mistrial (rare) or tell the jury to ignore the information. In most cases, when the jury is told to ignore the information, doing so heightens its validity in the minds of the jury members. In a study on this issue done by the University of Chicago Law School, a mock jury was to decide the amount of damages in an injury lawsuit. When the professor made it known that the defendant had been insured against the loss, the damages went up 13 percent. When the judge told the jury they had to ignore the new information, the amount went up 40 percent. The censored information was actually embraced even more, jumping the damage payment by $13,000![9]

DAY-TO-DAY SCARCITY TECHNIQUES

- ➤ Country clubs that create exclusive membership requirements
- ➤ Disney DVDs that are offered for sale once every decade
- ➤ Airlines that hold your seat for only 24 hours, informing you that "These seats could sell out"
- ➤ Collectors who specialize in hard-to-find antiques
- ➤ Special by-invitation-only sales
- ➤ Going-out-of-business sales
- ➤ Offers that are not available in stores

- ➤ Exclusive, one-time offers
- ➤ Qualifying for a loan
- ➤ A limited number of spots on a committee
- ➤ A waiting list for new customers
- ➤ Selecting only 10 people for a new training program

HOW TO USE THE LAW OF SCARCITY

Scarcity helps us make decisions. Most of us fear making a decision, so we naturally put it off to allow ourselves time to think and ponder. As a persuader, however, be aware that when your prospects put off the decision, chances are they won't ever make one. You could have the perfect product for them—something they really need right now. If you let them go, however, they will probably not come back later and tell you, "Okay, I finally decided. Let's do it." Creating scarcity helps your prospects make their decision. It also eliminates the amount of time you waste tracking down prospects who are still undecided about your product or service. You can create legitimate scarcity with your product or service without violating your morals.

In sales, this urgency is called the takeaway close. If you take away your prospects' opportunity to get involved with your product or service, they naturally want it more. This strategy also works well when you want to see whether your prospect is really interested in what you are providing. If you are stuck and not sure how much time you want to spend with a prospect, or if the prospect is just looking and not willing to make a decision, do a takeaway. Anyone who is truly interested in your product will perk up and become more interested. If not, the prospect will walk away. Either way, you have saved yourself time and energy.

When you want to increase the impact of your scarcity and adapt it to different personalities, make sure you buffer your scarcity with some type of reward. For example, "This offer ends today [scarcity], but when you enroll today, I will give you in an extra six months of support [reward]."

To create scarcity, be sure you have at least one of these elements firmly in place:

➤ *Deadlines:* Give your prospects a deadline or a point of no return. We all operate on deadlines in our personal lives and in our businesses. Deadlines cause us to take action. If there is no immediate reason to take action now, we won't. Many people don't pay their bills until they have to. Judging by the lines outside the post office at midnight on April 15, most of us don't pay our taxes until the last possible second. No deadline—no consequence means no action.

➤ *Limited Space, Numbers, or Access:* If your prospects feel like they are competing for a limited resource, they will be much more motivated to take action. When people fear they're going to miss out on a great deal, they feel an urgency to act. Think of shoppers at closeout sales. They've got to speed over there and check things out before all the products are picked over. Otherwise, with the store's limited supplies, they'll miss the deal forever! This limit can also include access to information. Our response to banned or secret information is a greater desire to receive that information and a more favorable outlook toward it than we had before the ban was set in place.[10]

➤ *Potential Loss:* Prospects must recognize that they might be limited in their actions if they don't take advantage of your offer. People will always overvalue something you restrict. Create a state of emotion in which your prospect will fear the loss or negative consequence for not taking action. This is an overwhelming feeling they won't be able to ignore. Motivated by restriction, your prospect becomes an emotionally motivated buyer. They will not be denied. The more you deny them, the more energy you give to your cause. You have denied their right to something, so they'll do anything to have it.

➤ *Restrict Freedom:* We want what we can't have. When we are told a product is or will soon be unavailable, we want it even more. Our desire goes up, and so does the urgency to act. Create a scenario where you tell your prospects that the offer is good for only so long. Tell them they have to act now to take advantage of the opportunity, or they will lose out. This technique works so well because we have all walked away from offers like this before, and they weren't there when we returned. Walk through clearance stores, and you will see "Sold" signs on many of the items. These signs create urgency because somebody else has found a deal, and so should you.

SCARCITY LIST

- Unique features
- One of a kind
- Secret information
- Joining an exclusive group
- Selection for a team
- Special discount
- Time constraints

- Limited supply
- Impending event
- Might miss out
- Exclusive or hard-to-find product
- Cutting-edge
- New information
- Limit—4

Three critical elements are needed to create legitimate scarcity:

1. *Believability:* There has to be a good reason for the scarcity. Does it make sense? Is it perceived as legitimate? Is the scarcity clearly understood?
2. *Choice:* When influenced or threatened the wrong way, prospects may resist or do the opposite of what you want.[11] They must feel that they have a choice, not backed into a corner.
3. *Alternatives:* Did they need or want it? Is there an easy alternative? When they come back, will it still be available?

BACKFIRE

If your prospects feel backed into a corner or have no immediate need, this law will not work. If they don't believe you or if the scarcity sounds invented, the Law of Scarcity will backfire. When you threaten freedom, it could backfire on you and have the opposite effect.

CASE STUDY

A martial arts studio was concerned with their ability to persuade call-ins to come into their studio to see the benefits of their service. They would advertise a specific class that was their most profitable.

Potential clients would call in, and the staff would answer all their questions, let them know of all the times, and tell them that there was plenty of room in all the classes. In reality, the classes would fill up. Everyone was told they were welcome to the studio and that they could come by at anytime to see their options. Only a small percentage of these call-ins would actually show up at the studio. Using the Law of Scarcity, how would you help them increase their business?

They created urgency by saying, "Let's see if you your son/daughter qualifies for that class. Our classes tend to fill up, and there is a qualification process, and it is first-come-first-served. We keep it small and limit the numbers for personalized, individual attention." The people who called in would show up, and the studio's enrollment increased.

. . . .

Additional Resources: Increase Your Scarcity Questions (maximuminfluence .com)

CHAPTER 15

The Inside Secrets of Maximum Influence

Your Prepersuasion Checklist

Before anything else, getting ready is the secret to success. —HENRY FORD

A medium-sized business was looking to do business with an employee-leasing company. The business announced that they had narrowed the choice down to two companies and wanted to hear both present their products. The representative from the first employee-leasing company was not prepared, and the presentation did not go as planned. Monitoring the presentation, I could see his nervousness began to shoot through the roof. The manager stopped his presentation midsentence and bluntly stated, "I already know all this. Can you please just answer a few questions for me?" The sales rep started to answer each question as though it were a threat. Things went downhill from there. The representative started to run through all the features and benefits of his company's program and how they would help. This actually generated more questions.

The manager asked the rep what percentage of the payroll this would cost his company. The rep looked surprised and spit out a number. The manager said, "That number seems high." The rep spit out a smaller number. The manager said, "Can you do better than that?" The rep came up with an even smaller number. After 10 minutes, the number fell by 30 percent. The poor representative was negotiating with himself, and, as I found out later, the final number was barely profitable for his company. The manager later revealed that he was happy with the first number but wanted to see where the negotiation would go. In the game of business, you are either going to pay with your preparation time or pay with lost income or lost opportunities.

To be an effective persuader, you cannot use the same techniques for all people all the time. You have to customize your message to fit the demographics, interests, and values of your audience. This chapter reveals what I call the Prepersuasion Checklist. It will help you to effectively adapt your persuasive techniques to your target audience. The foundation of the Prepersuasion Checklist is rooted in a solid understanding of human psychology, in the ways to handle resistance, and in the methods of effectively structuring a persuasive presentation. This is the knowledge necessary to make the Prepersuasion Checklist work in any persuasive situation.

All battles are first won in the mind. You have to be mentally ready to persuade. I know you are busy, but preparation is great time management and an incredible boost to your confidence and productivity. Prepare yourself by knowing as much about your audience as possible. The persuasion process can be thought of as presentation engineering. You have to draw up the blueprint for your persuasive techniques instead of flying by the seat of your pants. Preparation is like programming your GPS before you drive. You need to know where you are going, what route you should take, and what the driving conditions will be. Prepersuasion operates the same way. Feeling competent and prepared increases your motivation, reduces fear, and enhances your ability to influence. Just remember the three D's: discover, design, and deliver:

- ➤ *Discover* what your prospects want and need to hear.
- ➤ *Design* and structure a powerful persuasive presentation.
- ➤ *Deliver* the message with passion, compassion, and purpose.

We all have our own "personal programming." As a Power Persuader, you must unlock your prospects' programming code. Most of this code is hidden from the untrained eye, so you'll have to know what to look for. Consider how code is used in software programs or phone apps. Underlying each program is code that causes the program to work (or not work) and that makes each program look and act differently. These programs all have hidden code that is difficult to find and understand. Similarly, each of us has code that is apparent and some code that is not apparent. Our code is the sum of our beliefs, experiences, motivations, thoughts, attitudes, values and personality. The key for you as a Power Persuader is to decode the situation or the prospect, so that you can know how to most effectively persuade and adapt to your audience.

Finding and interpreting code comes with knowledge and experience, and the more awareness and more understanding you have, the easier it becomes to find and crack the code.

The following items make up the Prepersuasion Checklist:

1. *Change:* Get inside a closed mind.
2. *Monitoring the Acceptance Level:* Where does your audience stand?
3. *Your Listening Skills:* Crack the code.
4. *Meta Programs:* Your persuasion radar.
5. *Persuasive Presentations:* Structure to win.

CHANGE: GET INSIDE A CLOSED MIND

Life is change; persuasion is change. As a Power Persuader, you must be able to create and motivate change. Understanding human nature is knowing that most people will resist change and burrow into their comfort zones. We tend to follow the path of least resistance. However, change is the only thing that can lift us up from where we currently lie. Oliver Wendell Holmes said, "Man's mind, stretched to a new idea, never goes back to its original dimensions." We all want to become better persons and to be stretched to accomplish more, but we are stuck in our daily patterns.

As you go through the Prepersuasion Checklist, find out how resistant to change your audience is likely to be. Will persuading them be like breaking through a brick wall or a cardboard box? Are they ready and willing to make changes because of their circumstances and surroundings? Are they already trying to change? Some of your prospects will oppose you and blatantly resist your persuasive message. This is great news: They are listening, and their resistance is a sign of involvement. If the audience gives no feedback, they are not involved in your message.

Many people won't change or resist change because there is not enough pain. They like the warmth of their comfort zone. They know they should change, but the unknown pain of changing is greater than the known pain of their current situation. To get change to stick, you must make sure three things occur, whether within yourself or within your audience. First, there must be a commitment to change, and they have to conclude they have no other option. Second, your prospects must be willing to pay the price, persisting even when they feel weak. Third, you have to know where the change is taking them. How is this going to affect their lives? What are the end results?

The biggest obstacles to change are lack of motivation, lack of knowledge, and fear. As a persuader, you need to create a vision for your audience, one that shows them what they will be like in the future. When you can get people to see themselves in the future and witness where that change will take them, they will be more willing to embrace change. Understand that people will resist change unless sufficient reinforcement and tools are provided to assist them. Without having this knowledge, their attitudes won't change, and if their attitudes won't change, then neither will their actions.

MONITORING THE ACCEPTANCE LEVEL: WHERE DOES YOUR AUDIENCE STAND?

An important part of the Prepersuasion Checklist is determining the audience's current acceptance level for the subject you want to present. Ask yourself the following questions when making this determination:

- *Knowledge:* What does my audience know about the issue?
- *Interest:* How interested is the audience in my subject?
- *Background:* What are the common demographics of my audience?
- *Support:* How much support (or lack of support) already exists for my views?
- *Beliefs:* What are my audience's common beliefs?

Understanding the types of audiences will also help you determine their acceptance level. Following are some categories of audiences and how to deal with each of them.

The Hostile Audience

This group disagrees with you and may even actively work against you. For a hostile audience, use these techniques:

- Find common beliefs and establish a common ground.
- Use appropriate humor to break the ice.
- Don't start the presentation with an attack on their position.
- You are trying to persuade on only one point; don't talk about anything else that could trigger disagreement.
- Because of your differences, they will question your credibility. Increase your credibility with studies from experts or anything that will support your claim.
- They will try to find reasons not to like you; don't give them any.
- Don't tell them you are going to try to persuade them.
- Express that you are looking for a win-win outcome/situation.
- If possible, meet with the audience more than once before challenging them on areas of disagreement.
- Show them you've done your homework.
- Respect their feelings, values, and integrity.
- Use logical reasoning as clearly and as carefully as possible.
- Use the Law of Connectivity and the Law of Balance.

The Neutral or Indifferent Audience

This audience understands your position but doesn't care about the outcome. The key to dealing with this group is creating motivation and energy—be dynamic. To persuade the indifferent audience:

- Spell out the benefits to them or the things around them.
- Point out the downside of not accepting your proposal. Identify why they should care.
- Grab their attention by using a story. Make them care by showing them how the topic affects them.
- Get them to feel connected to your issues.
- Avoid complex arguments.
- Use concrete examples with familiar situations or events.
- Use the Law of Involvement and the Law of Social Validation.

The Uninformed Audience

An uninformed audience lacks the information they need to be convinced. To persuade them, you should use the following techniques:

- ► Encourage them to ask questions throughout the presentation.
- ► Keep the facts simple and straightforward.
- ► Find out why they are uninformed.
- ► Use examples and simple statistics.
- ► Quote experts the audience respects.
- ► Stress your credibility, such as degrees, special expertise, and experience.
- ► Make your message interesting in order to keep their attention.
- ► Use the Law of Dissonance and the Law of Scarcity.

The Supportive Audience

A supportive audience already agrees with you. You may think that persuading the audience is easy, but remember that your goal is to get them to take action, not just to agree with you. The following techniques should be used with a supportive audience:

- ► Increase energy and passion and motivate with inspiration.
- ► Prepare them for future attacks by inoculating them against other arguments.
- ► Get them to take action and to support your cause.
- ► Let them know what needs to be done.
- ► Use testimonials to intensify the commitment.
- ► Use the Law of Esteem and the Law of Expectation.

Most audiences are a mix of all four of these types. Find out the dominant audience type that will be present, and tailor your remarks accordingly.

The Persuasion Pitfall

Understand your audience and what Laws of Persuasion you are going to use on them. Sometimes and in some situations, certain persuasive laws or techniques are not appropriate. You cannot treat every person or every audience the same way. If you take persuasion too far, you will run into what I call the Persuasion Pitfall. People are persuaded and influenced until they feel cheated, misled, or taken advantage of, and then they never tell you about their feelings or do business with you again.

In sales and marketing, we have a tendency to push the envelope a little too hard when trying to persuade others. This could be in a personal one-on-one encounter with a stranger or during a visit to the local furniture store. Persuaders who do not possess the ability to read others or who do not have the skills necessary to persuade typically fall victim to the Persuasion Pitfall. They will take persuasion a little too far, using extreme pressure or trying to sell you a product you don't need or want. When you use persuasion and influence the wrong way, people lose all trust in you and never will be persuaded by you again. When overpersuading, you do or say something that sets off silent alarms in your prospects' minds. It could be a sensation of uneasiness or a bad feeling toward you, your store, or your product.

This pitfall also includes selling a product that does not meet their expectations. The challenge with this pitfall is that most people will say nothing to you about your product or about you overpersuading. They simply will never return your call, return to your website, or go into your store again. They will never want to associate with you. Or if you are a friend or member of the family, they will never trust or listen to your point of view again. This pitfall is a silent killer because most persuaders don't even realize they made the mistake. You have probably had this happen to you many times, at a car dealership, in retail stores, and on the phone. You have to have a sixth sense in persuasion and know how hard you can push.

We hate to feel manipulated or pressured. We have all been burned or taken advantage of, and when we see signs of such behavior, we start to run. Many uneducated persuaders can be offensive, condescending, obnoxious, and insulting. Some people will need to have space, some will have to talk to a spouse, and still others will have to come back later before making a decision. You have to sense and know, by means of knowledge and experience and nonverbal cues, how many tools of persuasion you can use without falling into this pitfall. You have to sense your limits before you cross the line.

YOUR LISTENING SKILLS: CRACK THE CODE

Fortune 500 companies commonly require listening training, even though many employees think it's a waste of time. The truth is that poor listening skills account for the majority of communication problems. Studies show that poor listening skills are responsible for 60 percent of all misunderstandings.[1] Dale Carnegie asserted many years ago that listening is one of the most crucial human relations skills. Listening is how we find out people's code, preferences, desires, wants, and needs. It is how we learn to customize our message to our prospects. Of all the skills one can master, listening is probably the one that will pay you back the most. There is a positive relationship between effective listening and being able to adapt to your audience and persuade them.[2]

Good listening is not just looking at someone and nodding your head in agreement. You have to acknowledge what is being said and let the other person know that you understand. The more you can acknowledge what is being said, the greater your ability will be to persuade and influence. Why? Because the person speaking with you will feel important and understood (Law of Esteem). Why is listening so difficult for most of us? Why is it that when two people get together and talk, they both walk away with two completely different views about the conversation?

TOP FIVE CHALLENGES TO LISTENING EFFECTIVELY

1. *Prejudging speakers on their delivery and personal appearance.* We often judge people by how they look or speak instead of listening to what they say. Some people are so put off by personal appearance, regional accents, speech defects, and mannerisms that they don't even try to listen to the message.

2. *Thinking about your response.* Instead of thinking about what the other person is saying, we often think about what we want to say next or where we want the conversation to go. We are mentally planning our own agenda and game plan. In effect, we patiently wait our turn to talk, but we never have give–and-take between the two parties.

3. *Not concentrating.* We talk at a rate of 120–150 words per minute, but we can think 400–800 words per minute. This allows us time to think between words we speak. We can pretend to listen while really thinking of something else.

4. *Jumping to conclusions.* Sometimes we assume we know exactly what the other person is going to say next, and we begin forming reac-

tions based on those assumptions. We start putting words into the other speaker's mouth because we are so sure of what they mean.

5. *Lack of training.* Some people just honestly and truly don't know how to listen effectively, even if they want to. If they haven't ever had any training or guidance in how to listen effectively, they may not be accustomed to or even realize the mental effort or level of involvement required to do so.

When you know how to listen, you'll always know what someone is thinking and what they want from you. Follow these proven keys for effective listening, and you'll always be able to get below the surface of your audience:

1. *Give them your undivided attention.* They are the most important people in the world to you at this time; make them feel that way. Don't get distracted by your surroundings. Stop talking or looking at your phone, and concentrate on them.

2. *Look them directly in the face while they are talking.* Lean forward to indicate interest and concern. Listen calmly as if you have all the time in the world.

3. *Show sincere interest in them.* There is no need to talk. Just nod your head and agree with verbal sounds like "uh-huh." Don't interrupt and listen for main points.

4. *Keep the conversation going by asking questions.* Prompt more information from them by repeating their phrases.

5. *Use silence to encourage them to talk.* You have heard that silence is golden. Being silent encourages your prospects to talk about themselves and reveal truths that will help you in the persuasion process. Using silence shows you are interested in your audience and stimulates interest in the conversation.

6. *Pause before replying or continuing.* Wait three to five seconds and reply thoughtfully. Don't leap in, even if you know the answer. When you pause, it shows the other person you consider what they are saying is valuable.

When you apply your listening skills, you will be able to glean golden nuggets of information from your audience. Because you must adapt your message to the persons you are talking to, there is nothing more crucial than listening.

META PROGRAMS: YOUR PERSUASION RADAR

The more we understand meta programs and personality types, the better we will be able to customize our persuasive presentations. A meta program is the way we lean most of the time in terms of how we act and react to most stimuli. We all hate to be put into a box and categorized, but the reality is that (most of the time) we are predictable. Certainly, people can never be 100 percent predictable, but you will be amazed at how predictable we actually are. I could write a whole book on personality types and meta programs, but let's discuss the fundamentals.

Meta programs are essentially looking glasses through which we view the world. A perfect meta-program example is the classic, "Is the glass half full or half empty?" Meta programs dictate our personality and therefore how we behave and how we like to be influenced. For instance, do you tend to be more of an active or a passive person? Do you focus more internally or externally about the world around you? Is your orientation more focused on the past, the future, or the present? Two people may interpret the exact experience from totally different angles.

Each meta program will dictate how you customize your message. When you analyze the meta programs, ask yourself the following questions:

➤ Is your audience mostly logical or emotional?

Logical
- ➤ Use their heads.
- ➤ Go with what makes sense.
- ➤ Are persuaded by facts, figures, and statistics.
- ➤ Rely on past history.
- ➤ Use their five senses.

Emotional
- ➤ Use their heart.
- ➤ Go with what feels right.
- ➤ Are persuaded by emotions.
- ➤ Rely on intuition.
- ➤ Use their sixth sense.

➤ Is your audience introverted or extroverted?

Extroverts

- ➤ Love to communicate.
- ➤ Are talkative.
- ➤ Involve others.
- ➤ Tend to be public people.
- ➤ Want face-to-face contact.

Introverts

- ➤ Keep feelings inside.
- ➤ Listen more than they talk.
- ➤ Like to work solo.
- ➤ Tend to be private.
- ➤ Use memos and e-mails.

➤ Is your audience motivated more by inspiration than desperation?

Desperation

- ➤ Try to get away from problems.
- ➤ Are stuck in the past, don't want to repeat prior mistakes.
- ➤ Avoid pain.
- ➤ Want to get away from something.

Inspiration

- ➤ Work toward a solution.
- ➤ See a better future.
- ➤ Are motivated by pleasure.
- ➤ Want to move forward (have a vision).

➤ Is your audience assertive or amiable?

Assertive

- ➤ Consider results more important than relationships.
- ➤ Make decisions quickly.
- ➤ Want to be in control.
- ➤ Are task oriented.
- ➤ Don't waste time.
- ➤ Are independent.

Amiable

➤ Consider relationships more important than results.

➤ Are friendly and loyal.

➤ Like to build relationships.

➤ Are great listeners.

➤ Avoid contention.

➤ Are nonassertive and agreeable.

Note: When it comes to persuasion, meta programs and personality types create a feeling of comfort and safety for us. Styles that differ from our own create tension and defensiveness. Power Persuaders can match all meta programs.

PERSUASIVE PRESENTATIONS: STRUCTURE TO WIN

Why should we be concerned with the structure of a persuasive presentation? The top predictor of professional success is how much you enjoy public speaking and how good you are at it.[3] Studies also show that the ability to give presentations was ranked as the most critical skill needed to move up in today's business environment.[4] Persuasive messages require several pieces. Just as Plato stated that every message should have a structure like an animal (head, body, and feet), so must our presentations follow an understandable pattern.

If you make up your presentation as it comes into your head, it will be a detriment to long-term persuasion. If the audience can't follow your facts, stories, or the substance of your message, their brains will not accept your message.

At one time or another, you have probably been in a classroom when the teacher has completely lost you. You had no idea where the topic was going or where it had been. When this happens in your prospects, your mind stalls, and the influence process stops. Confusion is a state of mind that creates tension. We hate to be confused, and a confused mind says no. When we create this mental confusion, we are shooting ourselves in the foot. Most uneducated one-note persuaders follow Harry Truman's advice: "If you can't convince 'em, confuse 'em."

As you prepare your persuasive message, remember to focus on one defined issue, not on 10 different ones. Stay focused, and steer clear of sensitive issues that aren't on your original agenda. In other words, don't inadvertently offend your audience on one issue when your focus is on another.

Your persuasive message should be structured as follows

1. *Create interest.* You have to generate interest in your chosen topic. Your audience needs a reason to listen: Why should they care? What's in it for them? How can you help them? A message that starts with a really good reason to listen will grab the attention of the audience, enabling you to continue with the message. Without this attention, you have no hope of getting your message across.

2. *State the problem.* You must clearly define the problem you are trying to solve. The best pattern for a persuasive presentation is to find a problem and relate how it affects the audience. In this way, you show them a problem they have and why it is of concern to them. Why is this a problem to your audience? How can you create dissonance?

3. *Offer evidence.* This is the support you give to your argument. Evidence validates your claims and offers proof that your argument is correct. It allows your audience to rely on other sources besides you. Evidence can include examples, statistics, testimonies, analogies, and any other supporting material used to enhance the integrity and congruency of your message.

4. *Present a solution.* You have gained your audience's interest and provided evidence in support of your message; now you must solve their problem. You present the argument you want them to believe and satisfy the need you have identified or created. You revealed the problem, and now you are providing the solution. How can your product meet their needs and wants and help them achieve their goals?

5. *Call to action.* A persuasive message is not true persuasion if your audience does not know exactly what they need to do. Be specific and precise. To complete the solution to their problem, they must take action. This is the climax, the peak of your logic and emotion. The prescribed actions must be feasible. Make your call to action as easy as possible.

Using this type of structure facilitates people's acceptance of your message and clarifies what you want them to do. We all have a logical side to our minds, which results in our need for order and arrangement. If we don't sense some sort of structure, we tend to become confused. If you can't be clear, concise, and orderly, your prospect will find someone else who is.

To create a good structure for your argument and to reach your audience, it may be helpful to consider the following set of questions.

Questions in Regard to Yourself and Your Message

- What do I want to accomplish?
- What will make my message clear to my audience?
- What will increase my credibility and trust?
- What Laws of Persuasion am I going to use?
- What do I want my prospects to do?

Questions in Regard to your Audience

- Who is listening to my message? (Audience demographics)
- What is their initial mindset? (What are they thinking and feeling now?)
- When will the call to action work? (What do you want them to do, and when do you want them to do it?)
- Why should they care? (What's in it for them?)
- In what areas of their lives does this affect them? (Health, money, relationships, etc.)
- How will they benefit? (What will they gain?)

These questions will help you create effective persuasive presentations in each of the key areas: interest, problem, evidence, solution, and action. The remainder of this chapter will present a variety of techniques that will be helpful in structuring your arguments.

CREATING YOUR CALL TO ACTION

The call to action is the most important part of your presentation. This is where your audience understands exactly what you want them to do. It's where you define yourself as a persuader instead of a presenter. This conclusion should not come as a shock to your audience. Throughout your presentation, you should have gently led them to the same conclusion that you are now giving them. You should have already prompted them to want to do what you are about to tell them to do.

Some people hate this part of persuasion because they are asking their prospects to do something. This should be the best part of the call to action; this is the reason for giving the presentation in the first place. If you become tense and uneasy, so will your prospect. The whole presentation should be structured to make the call to action smooth and seamless.

You should create your call to action before creating the rest of the presentation. Your entire presentation should be built around the call to action. Create the call to action beforehand. From the outset of your message, you must be eager to get to this point. Be positive and enthusiastic. In your preparation, make sure your conclusion is obvious and that the audience is not left on their own to make sense of and understand your message. You need to tell them what to believe; draw the conclusion for them. Make the call to action easy for them to follow and simple for them to do. There should be no doubt in your prospects' minds about exactly what you want them to do.

There is a story of an old man who goes to a dentist because a tooth is killing him. He has been putting it off for months, and finally he has to get the tooth taken care of. Once there, the dentist agrees that the tooth needs to come out. The man asks the dentist how much it will cost. The dentist replies that it will be about $150. The old man yelps and yells, "That much to pull out a tooth?" Then the man asks how long the procedure will take. The dentist replies that it will take about five minutes. "All that money for five minutes of work? That's highway robbery!" the old man protests. "How can you live with yourself charging people that kind of money?" The dentist smiles and says, "If it's the time you are worried about, I can take as long as you want."

When planning and preparing your call to action, remember that the process does not have to be long and painful. Be short, brief, and to the point. Your call to action should be no longer that 5 percent of your total presentation.

Offer Choices

A strange psychological phenomenon occurs when people are drawing conclusions. If someone tells us exactly what to do, our tendency is to reject that dictated choice because we feel it is our only option. The solution is to offer your prospects a few options so that they can make the choice for themselves. People feel the need to have freedom and make their own choices. If forced to choose something against their will, they experience psychological resistance and feel a need to restore their freedom.

We all need options. Once when I was camping with my family, I saw excited tourists, who wanted to take pictures, surround a young moose in a small lake. This moose felt trapped and charged at the people in an attempt to escape. This type of reaction can also present itself in your persuasive efforts. If you don't offer options to your audience, they could try to charge and escape.

The strategy is that you can guide your prospects' options. As a Power Persuader, you give them only options that will satisfy your situation. We have all done this with children: Do you want to finish your dinner or go to bed early? In sales, they call this strategy the alternative close. For example, "Do you want regular or deluxe?" "Do you want it in blue or green?" "Do you want to meet Monday afternoon or Tuesday evening?" The person has options, but both options meet the persuader's goals.

Even if it is just something simple, people need to have options. For example, I heard of an elderly woman who desperately needed to take her medication, or she would die. Her doctor, nurse, son, and husband all tried to get her to take her medication but to no avail. The doctor insisted she take her medication first thing when she arose in the morning, but she just wouldn't do it. Distraught, the family took her to a new doctor. This doctor immediately took in the situation and talked to the patient. He explained the benefits of taking the drugs and how it could help her. Then he gave her an option: "You need to take this once a day. Would you like to take it with your breakfast or your dinner?" The patient thought for a second and said she would like to take it with her dinner. After she made that decision, she no longer gave people a hard time about taking her medication. The key is that both options achieved the same goal.

If you absolutely have to limit your audience's choice to one thing, you must explain to them why there are limitations on their options. If the audience understands why a limit has been put on their freedom, they are more likely to accept it without feeling trapped.

On the flip side, try not to give your prospects more than two or three choices. If you give too many alternatives, your audience will be less likely to choose any of them. Structured choices give the audience the impression of control. As a result, they increase cooperation and commitment.

A study was done on a Saturday at a high-end grocery store. Researchers set up a tasting booth with different flavors of jam. During the study, the booth had either six flavors or 24 flavors. They invited the store patrons to try the jam. The shoppers were allowed to taste as many jams as they wanted. They were also given a dollar-off coupon to purchase this type of jam. Remember that when we get overwhelmed or confused, our mind shuts down, and we don't know what to do. This study revealed that when shoppers had 24 choices, only 3 percent of them bought jam. When they had only six choices, 30 percent bought the jam after the taste test. That is 10 times more purchases with fewer choices.[5]

Offering choices is also called binds. Each option offered gives the persuader what he or she wants without appearing to restrict prospects' freedom. When you use the word *or*, the very opposite is implied, so try to structure your choices with the word *or*. For example, "Would you like to make an appointment now, or should we meet next week?" "Do you have five minutes now, or should we do it tomorrow morning?"

Once the call to action has taken place, your audience needs to remember, retain, and respond to your message. They have to keep doing what you want them to do. Have your points been memorable, easy to understand, and simple to follow? Your message will boil down not to what you say and do but to what the other person remembers.

INOCULATION: DEFEND AGAINST THE ATTACK

Great persuaders know how to presolve objections. Why wait for prospects to go down the wrong road and hit a brick wall or mentally go off course when you can handle the objection up front? This persuasion method is called inoculation, a term that comes from the medical field: Injecting a weak dose of a virus into a patient inoculates or prevents the patient from getting the disease. The body's immune system fights off this weak form of the disease and then is prepared when the full disease attacks.

Likewise, when you are presenting and you know that an opposing viewpoint is standing in the wings, you have to inoculate the audience with a weakened form of that argument. If you know someone is going to attack your viewpoint, prepare your audience in advance. Give them the ammunition (the antibodies) they need to fight off the attack.

The idea is to address the issues that your opponent will bring up and then directly refute them. But the inoculation must be a weak form of the opposing virus. If inoculated with the strong strain of a disease, a person could become sick or even die. The dose must be weak enough to prepare the body for the stronger virus, but not so strong that it overpowers the body. Likewise, in persuasion, don't make the dose too strong. You don't want to give your prospects all the ammunition from the other side of the persuasive message. On the other hand, if you don't prepare your audience for what they are about to hear, the sting of your opponent's words, logic, or testimony might be too much for them to handle, and they could switch sides.

We are surrounded by countless examples of inoculation, many of which are used in the courtroom. The attorney stands up and says, "The prosecution will call my client mean, evil, a terrible husband, and a poor member of society, but this is not true, as I will show you over the next couple of weeks." So, when the prosecutor stands up and states anything close to what the defense attorney has claimed she will, the jury is prepared; She is acting exactly how the defense said she would, and the jurors have a way to ignore or even discount the prosecutor's arguments.

Society needs to understand the importance of inoculation with regard to smoking, gangs, drugs, teenage pregnancy, and others issues that we know our children will face. Who should be the first contact with your children: you or the drug dealer? When you inoculate people, they can mentally prepare arguments supporting their stance. This reinforcement prevents them from switching teams. The more prepared they are, the more they'll hold fast to their attitudes and beliefs. The more deeply this reinforcement is ingrained, the more difficult it will become for them to be swayed.

When do you use inoculation? The correct answer depends on the composition and attitude of your audience. If they already agree with your position, you need to present only one side. If they disagree with you, you need to present both sides. If an opposing speaker is going to follow you, you definitely need to inoculate the audience. Giving both sides of the argument works better with audience members who already know something about the opposition's strength. Be careful if you use inoculation with highly emotional issue like politics or religion. When topics are highly controversial, the effectiveness of inoculation drops.[6]

Inoculation increases your credibility and your ability to persuade. You are not afraid of the truth and have done your research. You prepare your audience in advance about the negative things someone could say about you or your product. You will win a great deal of respect and trust when you answer someone's questions before they even ask them.

When you know your audience, not only can you prepare them for pending attacks, but you can also answer questions in advance with inoculation. This places a solution in your listeners' minds. Suppose you are persuading prospects about the need to use your product, and you know that the competition will describe your product as the most expensive one on the market. Inoculate. Tell your prospects upfront that this is the highest-quality, longest lasting, most expensive product on the market. Let them know why it is the best and the most expensive. Your product has won most of the industry's awards, lasts the longest, and gives the most value for the money. These arguments, strategically planted in the minds of your prospects, will enable them to access these facts when the competition demeans the price or your product.

A study was done with a group of people who were about to be persuaded. The intention was to change their attitude about a certain topic. One group was told they were going to be exposed to a message that would attempt to persuade them, and the other group did not receive the same type of warning. The results showed that the group that was warned up front were actually persuaded less than the group that did not receive the warning. Hence, the group that was told they were going to be persuaded developed resistance before the message even started.[7] This is why you never start your presentation with, "Today I am going to persuade you...."

Long-Term Inoculation: The Booster Shot

Inoculation is not a one-time shot. It must be continued with boosters. Remember that a medical booster shot is an extra dose of an earlier vaccination. The studies show that time does erode inoculations and that they do lose their effectiveness over time.[8]

When your goal is long-term influence, you need to provide periodic booster shots to make sure that your prospect can counteract any arguments from the other side. One study revealed that when you can add boosters to your message, they will reinforce and extend the persuasiveness of your original message.[9] The more you can reinforce those attitudes—the more you can inoculate against future attacks—the more their attitude change will stick.[10] What can you use as boosters shots? Any time you can introduce new research or third-party validation, it will increase the effectiveness of your inoculation. Other options include reciprocity, role-plays, additional information, or anything that would enhance your credibility.[11]

PREPARATION IS THE KEY TO INFLUENCE

Prepersuasion is everything. Prepare your mind, know your audience, know their code, and structure a winning persuasive argument accordingly. Know who, what, when, where, and why about your message and your audience. Power Persuaders know that information and structure are the seeds for perfect persuasion.

Additional Resources: Persuasive Presentations Audio (maximuminfluence .com)

Epilogue

When you follow the laws, techniques, and strategies outlined in this book, your life will change forever. Get ready to find yourself in the driver's seat of life. You will find yourself in a winning situation—all the time—no matter what your challenges are. Look forward to finding yourself among the 3 percent who can control their destiny. You will be able to get what you want, when you want it, and win friends for life. You will be included among those elite few who can help and teach others to control their futures. You will never worry about income or employment again.

NEXT STEPS

1. Feel Influential

There is an essential truth to the old phrase—fake it until you make it. Studies show that if you feel influential, if you feel you will succeed in your ability to influence others—you become that way. One study revealed the more influential you felt, the greater your ability to influence. When you feel influential and feel you can persuade others, it leads to increased happiness, feeling in control and that life has more purpose.[1] The bottom line is when you think and feel that you are influential, you become more influential.

2. Grow Influential

Make up your mind you want to win the race before you start. You can come up with all the excuses you want, but none of them will bring you success or happiness. You can learn and grow every day, but you will never completely master this critical life skill. The more tools you learn, the more successful you are going to be. If you have not achieved your success or your income goals, keep working on your ability to influence. Some of the skills I outlined in this book will come naturally to you. Some of the laws will need a little practice. Others will be completely foreign to you and require concentrated effort. Continue to learn and apply these techniques, and they will become second nature to you. I recommend that you consciously apply one new Law of Persuasion a week, and soon these laws will become part of you.

3. Become Influential

Once you have a concrete knowledge of the 12 Laws of Persuasion, you can take your Persuasion IQ to the next level by mastering charisma. Yes, charisma can be learned. We have all met someone who, after just a few seconds, we felt an instant connection or bond with them. When you can develop charisma, when you can connect with anyone, when others feel comfortable around you, then you can magnify your ability to influence. People will pay more attention to you, and they will want you to influence them. (Measure your charisma at www.charismaiq.com.)

FINAL THOUGHT

Always treat yourself like a do-it-yourself project. Discover that there is a direct correlation between your personal development program and your income. Find a product, service, idea, or cause that you can believe in. When you know you can help someone with your product or service, you have a moral and ethical obligation to persuade that person to get involved with what you are offering. If you don't, an unethical person with an inferior product and better persuasion skills is going to take their money. I believe in you and your ability to improve yourself. I believe in your ability to improve the lives around you and to make the world a better place.

Persuade with power.

Notes

INTRODUCTION

1. Carnegie Foundation, 2005.
2. F. Roselli, J. J. Skelly, and D. M. Mackie, "Processing Rational and Emotional Messages: The Cognitive and Affective Mediation of Persuasion," *Journal of Experimental Applied Social Psychology* 163 (1995).

CHAPTER 1

1. Jay Conger, "The Necessary Art of Persuasion," *Harvard Business Review,* May–June 1998.
2. "The Road Best Traveled," *Success*, March 1988: 28.

CHAPTER 2

1. Joseph LeDoux, *The Emotional Brain: The Mysterious Underpinnings of Emotional Life* (New York: Simon & Schuster, 1998), pp. 29–39.
2. Julie Sedivy and Greg Carlson, *Sold on Language: How Advertisers Talk to You and What This Says About You,* 1st ed. (Hoboken, NJ.: Wiley, 2011), p. 63.

CHAPTER 3

1. A. H. Eagley, R. D. Ashmore, M. G. Makhijani, and L. C. Longo, "What Is Beautiful Is Good, But . . . : A Meta-Analytical Review of Research on the Physical Attractiveness Stereotype," *Psychological Bulletin* (1990): 109–128.
2. J. Horai, N. Naccari, and E. Fatoullah, "The Effects of Expertise and Physical Attractiveness upon Opinion, Agreement and Liking," *Sociometry* (1974), 37: 601–606.

3. M. Snyder and M. Rothbart, "Communicator Attractiveness and Opinion Change," *Canadian Journal of Behavioral Science* (1971), 3: 377–387.

4. R. A. Kulka and J. R. Kessler, "Is Justice Really Blind? The Effect of Litigant Physical Attractiveness on Judicial Judgment," *Journal of Applied Social Psychology* (1978): 336–381.

5. J. Rich, "Effects of Children's Physical Attractiveness on Teachers' Evaluations," *Journal of Educational Psychology* (1975): 599–609.

6. M. G. Efran and E. W. J. Patterson, "The Politics of Appearance," unpublished manuscript, University of Toronto, 1976.

7. M. L. Knapp and J. A. Hall, *Nonverbal Communication in Human Interaction*, 3rd ed. (New York: Holt, Rinehart & Winston, 1992).

8. G. H. Smith and R. Engel, "Influence of a Female Model on Perceived Characteristics of an Automobile," *Proceedings of the 76th Annual Convention of the American Psychological Association* (1968): 681–682.

9. V. Swami, A. Furnham, T. Chamorro-Premuzic, K. Akbar, N. Gordon, T. Harris, J. Finch, and M. J. Tovee, "More Than Just Skin Deep? Personality Information Influences Men's Ratings of the Attractiveness of Women's Body Sizes," *The Journal of Social Psychology* (2010) 150, 6: 628–674.

10. G. W. Lewandowski, A. Aron, and J. Gee, "Personality Goes a Long Way: The Malleability of Opposite-Sex Physical Attractiveness," *Personal Relationships* (2007), 14: 571–585.

11. D. Mack and D. Rainey, "Female Applicants' Grooming and Personnel Selection," *Journal of Social Behavior and Personality* (1990): 399–407.

12. P. Suedfeld, S. Bocher, and C. Matas, "Petitioner's Attire and Petition Signing by Peace Demonstrators: A Field Experiment," *Journal of Applied Social Psychology* (1971): 278–283.

13. H. Russell Bernard and Peter Killworth, "The Search for Social Physics," *Connections* (1997) 20, 1: 16–34.

14. J. C. McCroskey, V. P. Richmond, and J. A. Daly, "The Development of a Measure of Perceived Homophily in Interpersonal Communication," *Human Communication Research* (1975): 323–332.

15. Bernard Asbell, with Karen Wynn, *What They Know About You* (New York: Random House, 1991), pp. 28–33.

16. D. J. O'Keefe, *Persuasion: Theory and Research* (Newbury Park, California: Sage, 1990).

17. McGrath, J. E. "A View of Group Composition Through a Group-Theoretic Lens." In D. E. Gruenfeld (Ed.), *Research on Managing Teams and Groups: Composition*, pp. 255–272 (Greenwich, Conn.: JAI Press, 1998).

18. Justin Kruger, "Lake Wobegon Be Gone! The 'Below-Average Effect' and the Egocentric Nature of Comparative Ability Judgments," *Journal of Personality and Social Psychology* (1999): 77, 2: 221–232.

19. "Damaging Shortage of People Skills (Survey: Two-Thirds of UK Companies Not Committed to Developing People Management Skills," *Personnel Today* (June 18, 2002): 9.

20. L. Zunin and N. Zunin, *Contact: The First Four Minutes* (New York: Ballantine Books, 1986).

21. W. P. Hampes, "The Relationship Between Humor and Trust," *Humor: International Journal of Humor Research* (1999): 12: 253–259.

22. C. P. Duncan and J. E. Nelson, "Effects of Humor in a Radio Advertising Experiment," *Journal of Advertising* (1985): 14: 33–40.

23. Albert Mehrabian, *Silent Messages* (Belmont, Calif.: Wadsworth, 1971).

24. T. G. Hegstrom, "Message Impact: What Percentage Is Nonverbal?" *Western Journal of Speech Communication* (1979): 134–142.

25. P. D. Blanck and R. Rosenthal, "Nonverbal Behavior in the Courtroom." In R. S. Feldman (Ed.), *Applications of Nonverbal Behavioral Theories and Research*, pp. 89–118 (Hillsdale, N.J.: Erlbaum, 1992).

26. J. K. Burgoon, T. Birk, and M. Pfau, "Nonverbal Behaviors, Persuasion, and Credibility," *Human Communication Research* (1990), 17: 140–169.

27. John S. Carton, Emily A. Kessler and Christina L. Pape, "Nonverbal Decoding Skills and Relationship Well-Being in Adults," *Journal of Nonverbal Behavior* (1999), 23, 1: 91–100.

28. J. Kellerman, J. Lewis, and J. D. Laird, "Looking and Loving: The Effects of Mutual Gaze on Feelings of Romantic Love," *Journal of Research and Personality* (1989): 23.

29. J. D. Robinson, J. Seiter, and L. Acharya, "I Just Put My Head Down and Society Does the Rest: An Examination of Influence Strategies Among Beggar," paper presented to the Western Speech Communication Association, Boise, Idaho (1992).

30. J. K. Burgoon, D. B. Buller, and W. G. Woodall, *Nonverbal Communication: The Unspoken Dialogue* (New York: Harper & Row, 1989).

31. J. K. Burgoon, J. B. Walther, and E. J. Baesler, "Interpretations, Evaluations, and Consequences of Interpersonal Touch," *Human Communication Research* (1992), 19: 237–263.

32. J. D. Fisher, M. Rytting, and R. Heslin, "Hands Touching Hands: Affective and Evaluative Effects of an Interpersonal Touch," *Sociometry* (1976), 39: 416–421.

33. J. Hornick, "Tactile Stimulation and Consumer Response," *Journal of Consumer Research* (1992): 449–458.

34. Ibid.

35. N. Gueguen and J. Fischer-Lokou, "Another Evaluation of Touch and Helping Behaviour," *Psychological Reports* (2003), 92: 62–64.

36. P. M. Hall and D. A. Hall, "The Handshake as Interaction," *Semiotica* (1983), 45: 249–264.

37. Ibid.

38. W, F. Chaplin, J. B. Phillips, J. D. Brown, N. R. Clanton, and J. L. Stein, J. L., "Handshaking, Gender, Personality and First Impressions," *Journal of Personality and Social Psychology* (2000), 79: 110–117.

39. Ibid.

40. Adapted from Adam D. Galinsky (Northwestern University), William W. Maddux (professor, INSEAD), and Gillian Ku (professor, London Business School), "The View from the Other Side of the Table." Available at http://www.worldtradelaw.net/articles/laceyaccession.pdf

41. William W. Maddux, Elizabeth Mullen, Adam D. Galinsky, "Chameleons Bake Bigger Pies and Take Bigger Pieces: Strategic Behavioral Mimicry Facilitates Negotiation Outcomes, *Journal of Experimental Social Psychology* (2008), 44, 2: 461–468.

42. Ibid.

CHAPTER 4

1. David Sears, J. Freedman, and L. Peplau, *Social Psychology* (Englewood Cliffs, N.J.: Prentice Hall, 1985), p. 154.

2. A. C. Elms, "Influence of Fantasy Ability on Attitude Change Through Role Playing," *Journal of Personality and Social Psychology* (1966), 4: 36–43.

3. A. Pratkanis and E. Aronson, *Age of Propaganda* (New York: W. H. Freeman, 1992), pp. 123–124.

4. Les Giblin, *How to Have Confidence and Power in Dealing with People* (Englewood Cliffs, N.J.: Prentice Hall, 1956), p. 120.

5. W. L. Gregory, R. B. Cialdini, and K. M. Carpenter, "Mediators of Likelihood Estimates and Compliance: Does Imagining Make It So?" *Journal of Personality and Social Psychology* (1982): 89–99.

6. G. Wells and R. Petty, "The Effects of Overt Head Movements on Persuasion," *Basic and Applied Social Psychology* (1980) 1, 3: 219–230.

7. Ibid.

8. P. Underhill, *Why We Buy: The Science of Shopping* (New York: Simon & Schuster, 1999), p. 37.

9. Ibid.

10. Ibid.

11. Luke 10:30–37.

12. J. Darley and D. Batson, "From Jerusalem to Jericho: A Study of Situational and Situational and Dispositional Variables in Helping Behavior," *Journal of Personality and Social Psychology* (1973), 27: 100–119.

13. S. Lindstedt, "Tops Supermarket in Western New York Entice Shoppers with Free Food Samples," *Buffalo News*, May 24, 1999: B3.

14. S. Godin and M. Gladwell, *Unleashing the Idea Virus* (New York: Hyperion, 2001).

15. J. Middendorf and A. Kalish, "The 'Change-Up' in Lectures," *National Teaching and Learning Forum* (1996) 5, 2: 1–5.

16. P. Y. Martin, J. Laing, R. Martin, and M. Mitchell, M., "Caffeine, Cognition, and Persuasion: Evidence for Caffeine Increasing the Systematic Processing of Persuasive Messages," *Journal of Applied Social Psychology* (2005), 35: 160–182. DOI: 10.1111/j.1559-1816.2005.tb02098.x

17. N. Rackham, *Account Strategies for Major Sales* (New York: McGraw-Hill, 1989), p. 143.

18. E. Loftus, "Reconstructing Memory: The Incredible Eyewitness," *Psychology Today* (1974) 8: 116.

19. L. Wrightsman, M. Nietzel, and W. Fortune, *Psychology and the Legal System* (Pacific Grove, Calif.: Brooks/Cole, 1994), p. 147.

20. L. Wrightsman, M. Nietzel, and W. Fortune, *Psychology and the Legal System* (Pacific Grove, California: Brooks/Cole Publishing, 1994), p. 147.

21. Kurt Mortensen, *Persuasion IQ: The 10 Skills You Need to Get Exactly What You Want* (New York: AMACOM, 2008).

22. R. F. Baumeister and B. J. Bushman, *Social Psychology and Human Nature* (Belmont, Calif.: Thompson Wadsworth, 2008).

23. S. Greist-Bousquet and N. Schiffman, "The Effect of Task Interruption and Closure on Perceived Duration," *Bulletin of the Psychonomic Society* (1992), 30, 1: 9–11.

24. D. Peoples, *Presentations Plus* (New York: Wiley, 1988), p. 66.

25. The 3M Meeting Management Team, *How to Run Better Business Meetings* (New York: McGraw-Hill, 1987), pp. 114–115.

CHAPTER 5

1. J. Maxwell and J. Dornan, *Becoming a Person of Influence* (Nashville: Thomas Nelson, 1997), p. 50.

2. Maxwell Maltz, *Psycho-Cybernetics* (Los Angeles: Wilshire, 1960).

3. M. R. Leary and R. F. Baumeister, "The Nature and Function of Self-Esteem: Sociometer Theory." In M. P. Zanna (Ed.), *Advances in Experimental Social Psychology*, Vol. 32, pp. 1–62 (San Diego: Academic Press, 2000).

4. C. L. Pickett, W. L. Gardner, and M. Knowles, "Getting a Cue: The Need to Belong and Enhanced Sensitivity to Social Cues," *Personality and Social Psychology Bulletin* (2004), 30: 1095–1107.

5. Maxwell and Dornan, p. 43.

6. Science newsletter, April 16, 1949.

7. J. D. Watt, "The Impact of Frequency of Ingratiation on the Performance Evaluation of Bank Personnel," *Journal of Psychology* (1993), 127, 2: 171–177.

8. S. J. Wayne and R. C. Liden, "Effects of Impression Management on Performance Ratings: A Longitudinal Study," *Academy of Management Journal* (1995), 38, 1: 232–260.

9. R. J. Deluga, "Supervisor Trust Building, Leader-Member Exchange and Organizational Citizenship Behaviour," *Journal of Occupational and Organizational Psychology* (1994), 67: 315–326.

10. Peter Doskoch, "Get Expert Advice on How to Suck Up to Your boss," December 01, 1996. Available at http://www.psychologytoday.com/articles/199612/brownnosing-101

11. J. Pandey, "Sociocultural Perspectives on Ingratiation." In B. Maher (Ed.), *Progress in Experimental Personality Research*, Vol. 14, pp. 205–229 (New York: Academic Press, 1986).

12. Randall A. Gordon, "Impact of Ingratiation on Judgements and Evaluations: A Meta-Analytic Investigation," Interpersonal Relations and Group Processes, University of Minnesota.

13. R. C. Liden and T. R. Mitchell, "Ingratiatory Behaviors in Organizational Settings," *Academy of Management Review* (1988), 13: 572–587.

14. Gordon.

15. John S. Seiter and Eric Dutson, "The Effect of Compliments on Tipping Behavior in Hairstyling Salons," *Journal of Applied Social Psychology* (2007), 37, 9.

CHAPTER 6

1. B. M. Depaulo, A. Nadler, and J. D. Fisher, *New Directions in Helping. Volume 2: Help Seeking* (New York: Academic Press, 1984).

2. K. Gergen, P. Ellsworth, C. Maslach, and M. Seipel, "Obligation, Donor Resources, and Reactions to Aid in Three Cultures," *Journal of Personality and Social Psychology* (1975): 390–400.

3. P. R. Kunz and M. Wolcott, "Seasons Greetings: From My Status to Yours," *Social Science Research* (1976): 269–278.

4. Dennis Regan, "Effects of a Favor on Liking and Compliance," *Journal of Experimental Social Psychology* (1971): 627–639.

5. Advertising Specialty Institute, "About the Industry." Available at http://www.asicentral.com/asp/open/aboutasi/promoindustry/index.aspx

6. Sharon Lindstedt, Sharon, "Top Supermarkets in Western New York Entice Shoppers with Free Food Samples," *Buffalo News*, May 24, 1999: B3.

7. M. S. Greenburg, "A Theory of Indebtedness," *Social Exchange: Advances in Theory and Research* (1980), 3: 26.

8. Bob Stone, *Successful Direct Marketing Methods* (Lincolnwood, Ill.: NTC Business Books, 1994), p. 92.

9. N. Weinstein and R. Ryan, "When Helping Helps: Autonomous Motivation for Prosocial Behavior and Its Influence on Well-Being for the Helper and Recipient," *Journal of Personality and Social Psychology* (2010), 98, 2: 222–244.

10. S. M. Horan and M. Booth-Butterfield, "Investing in Affection: An Investigation of Affection Exchange Theory and Relational Qualities," *Communication Quarterly* (2010), 58, 4, 394–413.

11. David Strohmetz, Bruce Rind, Reed Fisher, and Michael Lynn, "Sweetening the Till: The Use of Candy to Increase Restaurant Tipping," *Journal of Applied Social Psychology* (2002), 32, 2: 300–309.

12. E. S. Uehara, "Reciprocity Reconsidered: Gouldner's 'Moral Norm of Reciprocity' and Social Support," *Journal of Social and Personal Relationship* (1995), 2: 483–502.

13. J. M. Chertkoff and M. Conley, "Opening Offer and Frequency of Concession as Bargaining Strategies, *Journal of Personality and Social Psychology* (1967), 7: 185–193.

14. S. Oskamp, "Effects of Programmed Strategies on Cooperation in the Prisoner's Dilemma and Other Mixed-Motive Games," *Journal of Conflict Resolution* (1971), 15, 2: 225–259.

15. S. S. Komorita and James K. Esser, "Frequency of Reciprocated Concessions in Bargaining," *Journal of Personality and Social Psychology* (1975), 32, 4: 699–705.

16. J. M. Burger, M. Horita, L. Kinoshita, K. Roberts, and C. Vera, "The Effects of Time on the Norm of Reciprocity," *Basic and Applied Social Psychology* (1997), 19, 91–100.

18. Robert A. Baron, Donn Byrne, Nyla R. Branscombe, *Social Psychology*, 11th ed. (Saddle River, New Jersey: Prentice Hall, 2006).

18. Komorita and Esser.

CHAPTER 7

1. Paul B. Allwood and the Minnesota Food Safety Planning group, Division of Environmental Health, "Hand Washing Among Public Restroom Users at the Minnesota State Fair," Minnesota Department of Health, 2006. Available at http://www.health.state.mn.us/handhygiene/stats/fairstudy.html

2. Michael Ross and Flore Sicoly, "Egocentric Biases in Availability and Attribution," *Journal of Personality and Social Psychology* (1979), 37, 3: 322–336.

3. Drew Westen, Pavel S. Blagov, Keith Harenski, Clint Kilts, and Stephan Hamann, "Neural Bases of Motivated Reasoning: An fMRI Study of Emotional Constraints on Partisan Political Judgment in the 2004 U.S. Presidential Election," *Journal of Cognitve Neuroscience* (2006), 18, 11: 1947–1958.

4. R. E. Knox and J. A. Inkster, "Postdecision Dissonance at Posttime," *Journal of Personality and Social Psychology* (1968), 18: 319–323.

5. J. C. Younger, L. Walker, and A. S. Arrowood, "Postdecision Dissonance at the Fair," *Personality and Social Psychology Bulletin* (1977), 3: 284–287.

6. Thomas Moriarty, "Crime, Commitment, and the Responsive Bystander: Two Field Experiments," *Journal of Personality and Social Psychology* (1975), 31, 2: 370–376.

7. R. B. Cialdini, J. T. Cacioppo, R. Bassett, and J. A. Miller, "Low-Ball Procedure for Producing Compliance: Commitment Then Cost," *Journal of Personality and Social Psychology* (1978): 463–476.

8. C. Seligman, M. Bush, and K. Kirsch, "Relationship Between Compliance in the Foot-in-the-Door Paradigm and Size of First Request," *Journal of Personality and Social Psychology* (1976), 33: 517–520.

CHAPTER 8

1. H. H. Kelley, "The Warm-Cold Variable in First Impressions of Persons," *Journal of Personality* (1950), 18: 431–439.

2. E. Loftus, "Reconstructing Memory: The Incredible Eyewitness," *Psychology Today* (1974), 8, 1: 116.

3. A. Pratkanis and E. Aronson, *Age of Propaganda* (New York: W. H. Freeman, 1992), p. 43.

4. Pratkanis and Aronson, p. 128.

5. Gerry Spence, *How to Argue and Win Every Time* (New York: St. Martin's Press, 1995), pp. 130–131.

6. E. Langer, A. Blank, and B. Chanowitz, "The Mindlessness of Ostensibly Thoughtful Action: The Role of 'Placebic' Information in Interpersonal Interaction," *Journal of Personality and Social Psychology* (1978): 635–642.

7. R. N. Bostrom, J. R. Baseheart, and C. M. Rossiter, "The Effects of Three Types of Profane Language in Persuasive Messages," *Journal of Communication* (1973): 461–475.

8. Bob Stone, *Successful Direct Marketing Methods* (Lincolnwood, Ill.: NTC Business Books, 1994), p. 4.

9. Stephen M. Smith and David R. Shaffer, "Speed of Speech and Persuasion," *Personality and Social Psychology Bulletin* (1995), 21, 10: 1051–1060.

10. E. Fern, K. Monroe, and R. Avila, "Effectiveness of Multiple Requests Strategies: A Synthesis of Research Results," *Journal of Marketing Research* (1986), 23: 144–152.

11. A. Mehrabian and M. Williams, "Nonverbal Concomitants of Perceived and Intended Persuasiveness," *Journal of Personality and Social Psychology* (1969), 13: 37–58.

12. B. L. Smith, B. L. Brown, W. J. Strong, and A. C. Rencher, "Effects of Speech Rate on Personality Perception," *Language and Speech* (1975), 18: 145–152.

13. Amitava Chattopadhyay, Darren W. Dahl, Robin J. B. Ritchie, and Kimary N. Shahin, "Hearing Voices: The Impact of Announcer Speech Characteristics on Consumer Response to Broadcast Advertising," *Journal of Consumer Psychology* (2003), 13, 3: 198–204.

14. Priscilla LaBarbera and James MacLachlan, "Time-Compressed Speech in Radio Advertising," *Journal of Marketing* (1979), 43: 30–36.

15. Bruce L. Brown, William J. Strong, and Alvin C. Rencher, "Perceptions of Personality from Speech: Effects of Manipulations of Acoustical Parameters," *Journal of the Acoustical Society of America* (1973), 54: 29–35.

16. William Apple, Lynn A. Streeter, and Robert M. Krauss, "Effects of Pitch and Speech Rate on Personal Attributions," *Journal of Personality and Social Psychology* (1979), 37: 715–727.

17. LaBarbera and MacLachlan.

CHAPTER 9

1. S. Rosen and A. Tesser, "On Reluctance to Communicate Undesirable Information: The MUM Effect," *Sociometry* (1970), 33: 253–263.

2. M. Manis, S. D. Cornell, and J. C. Moore, "Transmission of Attitude-Relevant Information Through a Communication Chain," *Journal of Personality and Social Psychology* (1974), 30: 81–94.

3. Nina Mazar, On Amir, and Dan Ariely, "The Dishonesty of Honest People: A Theory of Self-Concept Maintenance," *Journal of Marketing Research* (2008), 45, 6: 633–644.

4. Rachel S. Herz and Trygg Engen, "Odor Memory: Review and Analysis," *Psychonomic Bulletin & Review* (1996), 3: 300–313.

5. M. Schleidt and B. Hold, "Human Odour and Identity." In W. Breipohl (Ed.), *Olfaction and Endocrine Regulation*, pp. 181–194 (London: IRL Press, 1982).

6. Howard Ehrlichman and Jack N. Halpem, "Affect and Memory: Effects of Pleasant and Unpleasant Odors on Retrieval of Happy and Unhappy Memories," *Journal of Personality and Social Psychology* (1988), 55: 769–779.

7. Des Dearlove, "A Breath of Lemon-Scented Air," *The London Times*, April 3, 1997.

8. Matt Crenson, "Scent of Cookies Brings Out Best in Shoppers," *Las Vegas Review Journal*, October 14, 1996.

9. Robert A. Baron, "Sweet Smell of Success: The Impact of Pleasant Artificial Scents on Evaluations of Job Applicants," *Journal of Applied Psychology* (1983), 68: 709–713.

10. Baron.

11. G. H. S. Razran, "Conditioned Response Changes in Rating and Appraising Sociopolitical Slogans," *Psychological Bulletin* (1940), 37: 481.

12. Rachel Herz, "Smell Manipulation: The Subliminal Power of Scent," *Smell Life*, January 6, 2011.

13. Susan C. Knasko, "Ambient Odor and Shopping Behavior," *Chemical Senses* (1989), 14, 94: 718.

14. Robert Baron and Michael Kalsher, "Driving Behavior Pleasant Fragrances Increased Attention and Reaction Times of Drivers in a Driving Simulation," *Environment and Behavior* (1998), 30, 4: 535–552; S. J. Jellinek, "Aromachology: A Status Review," *Cosmetics and Toiletries* (1994), 109, 10: 1–28.

15. Alan R. Hirsch, "Nostalgia: A Neuropsychiatric Understanding," presented at the annual meeting of the Association for Consumer Research Conference, Chicago, Illinois, October 1991; S. E. Gay, "The Effect of Ambient Olfactory Stimuli on the Evaluation of a Common Consumer Product," presented at the Thirteenth Annual Meeting of the Association for Chemoreception Sciences (April 1991).

16. Howard Ehrlichman and Linda Bastone, "The Use of Odour in the Study of Emotion." In Charles S. Van Toller and George H. Dodd (Eds.), *Fragrance: The Psychology and Biology of Perfume*, pp. 143–159 (New York: Elsevier Applied Science Publishers/Elsevier Science Publishers, 1992).

17. K. G. DeBono, "Pleasant Scents and Persuasion: An Information Processing Approach," *Journal of Applied Social Psychology* (1992), 22: 910–919.

18. Robert A. Baron and Jill Thomley, "A Whiff of Reality Positive Affect as a Potential Mediator of the Effects of Pleasant Fragrances on Task Performance and Helping," *Environment and Behavior* (1994), 26.

19. David W. Stewart and David H. Furse, *Effective Television Advertising* (Lexington, Mass.: Lexington Books, 1986).

20. Ronald E. Milliman, "Using Background Music to Affect the Behavior of Supermarket Shoppers," *Journal of Marketing* (1982), 46: 86–91; Ronald E. Milliman, "The Influence of Background Music on the Behavior of Restaurant Patrons," *Journal of Consumer Research* (1986), 13: 286–289.

21. Herbert Zettl, *Sight, Sound, and Motion: Applied Media Aesthetics* (Belmont, California: Wadsworth Publishing, 1973); Deryck Cooke, *The Language of Music* (London: Oxford University Press, 1962).

22. Gordon C. Bruner II, "Music, Mood, and Marketing," *Journal of Marketing* (1990), 54, 4: 94.

23. Ibid.

24. David Leonhardt, with Kathleen Kerwin, "Hey Kid, Buy This!" *BusinessWeek*, June 30, 1997.

25. G. H. S. Razran, "Conditioned Response Changes in Rating and Appraising Sociopolitical Slogans," *Psychological Bulletin* (1940), 37: 481.

26. K. Fehrman and C. Fehrman, *Color: The Secret Influence* (Englewood Cliffs, N.J.: Prentice Hall, 2000), p. 141.

27. Ibid.

28. Ibid.

29. Ibid.

30. Ibid.

31. Ibid.

32. Ibid.

33. Ibid.

CHAPTER 10

1. Arthur Lefford, "The Influence of Emotional Subject Matter on Logical Reading," *Journal of General Psychology* (1946) 34: 127–151.

2. Randall Reuchelle, "An Experimental Study of Audience Recognition of Emotional and Intellectual Appeals in Persuasion," *Speech Monographs* (1958) 25, 1: 49–57.

3. Gerard Tellis, *Advertising and Sales Promotion Strategy* (Reading, Massachusetts: Addison-Wesley, 1998), p. 138.

4. L. Z. Tiedens and S. Linton, "Judgment Under Emotional Certainty and Uncertainty: The Effects of Specific Emotions on Information Processing," *Journal of Personality and Social Psychology* (2001), 81: 973–988.

5. Charles Larson, *Persuasion* (Belmont, Calif.: Wadsworth, 1995), pp. 222–225.

6. J. C. McCroskey, "A Summary of Experimental Research on the Effects of Evidence in Persuasive Communication," *Quarterly Journal of Speech* (1969), 55: 169–176.

7. David Leonhardt, with Kathleen Kerwin, "Hey Kid, Buy This!" *BusinessWeek*, June 30, 1997.

8. J. S. Lerner and D. Keltner, "Fear, Anger, and Risk," *Journal of Personality and Social Psychology* (2001), 81, 146–159.

9. L. Janis and S. Feshbach, "Effects of Fear-Arousing Communications," *Journal of Abnormal and Social Psychology* (1953): 78–92.

10. D. Keltner, P. C. Ellsworth, and K. Edwards, "Beyond Simple Pessimism: Effects of Sadness and Anger on Social Perception," *Journal of Personality and Social Psychology* (1993), 64: 740–752.

11. Rodolfo Mendoza-Denton, *Are We Born Racist?* (Boston: Beacon Press, 2010).

12. Wesley G. Moons and Diane M. Mackie, "Thinking Straight While Seeing Red: The Influence of Anger on Information Processing," *Personality and Social Psychology* (2007), 33: 706. Originally published online April 17, 2007. Available at http://psp.sagepub.com/content/33/5/706

13. Richard E. Petty, David W. Schumann, Steven A. Richman, and Alan J. Strathman, "Positive Mood and Persuasion: Different Roles for Affect Under High and Low Elaboration Conditions," *Journal of Personality and Social Psychology* (1993), 64: 5–20.

14. I. L. Janis, D. Kaye, and P. Kirschner, "Facilitating Effects of 'Eating While Reading' on Responsiveness to Persuasive Communications," *Journal of Personality and Social Psychology* (1965), 1: 17–27.

15. R. A. Baron, "Interviewers' Moods and Reactions to Job Applicants: The Influence of Affective States on Applied Social Judgments," *Journal of Applied Social Psychology* (1987), 16: 16–28.

16. Gerald Zaltman, "How Customers Think: Essential Insights into the Mind of the Market," *Harvard Business School Press Book* (February 21, 2003): 186.

17. D. M. Mackie and L. T. Worth, "Cognitive Deficits and the Mediation of Positive Affect in Persuasion," *Journal of Personality and Social Psychology* (1989), 57: 27–40.

18. Janis, Kaye, and Kirschner.

19. Thomas J. Olney, Morris B. Holbrook, and Rajeev Batra, "Consumer Responses to Advertising: The Effects of Ad Content, Emotions, and Attitude toward the Ad on Viewing Time," *Journal of Consumer Research* (1991), 17: 440–453.

20. David Aaker, Douglas M. Stayman, and Michael R. Hagerty, "Warmth in Advertising: Measurement, Impact, and Sequence Effects," *Journal of Consumer Research* (1986), 12, 4: 365–381.

21. S. P. Brown, P. M. Homer, and J. J. Inman, "A Meta-Analysis of Relationships Between Ad-Evoked Feelings and Advertising Responses," *Journal of Marketing Research* (1998), 35: 114–126.

22. A. M. Isen, "Positive Affect, Cognitive Processes, and Social Behavior." In L. Berkowitz (Ed.), *Advances in Experimental Social Psychology*, pp. 20, 203–253 (San Diego, California: Academic Press, 1987).

23. Ibid.

24. Ibid.

25. T. Biggers and B. Pryor, "Attitude Change: A Function of the Emotion-Eliciting Qualities of the Environment," *Personality and Social Psychology Bulletin* (1982), 8: 94–99.

26. M. Mathur and A. Chattopadhyay, "The Impact of Moods Generated by Television Programs on Responses to Advertising," *Psychology and Marketing* (1991), 8: 59–77.

CHAPTER 11

1. John Maxwell and Jim Dornan, *Becoming a Person of Influence* (Nashville: Thomas Nelson Publishers, 1997), p. 64.

2. Dov Eden and Abraham B. Shani, "Pygmalion Goes to Boot Camp: Expectancy, Leadership, and Trainee Performance," *Journal of Applied Psychology* (1982), 67, 2: 194–199.

3. R. L. Miller, P. Brickman, and D. Bolen, "Attribution vs. Persuasion as a Means for Modifying Behavior," *Journal of Personality and Social Psychology* 3 (1975): 430–441.

4. John A. Bargh, Mark Chen, and Lara Burrows, "Automaticity of Social Behavior: Direct Effects of Trait Construct and Stereotype Activation on Action," *Journal of Personality and Social Psychology* (1996), 71, 2: 230–244.

5. Amos Tversky and Daniel Kahneman, "Judgment Under Uncertainty: Heuristics and Biases," Science (1974), 185: 1124–1131; "Rational Choice and the Framing of Decisions," *Journal of Business* (1986), 59: S251–S278.

6. R. E. Kraut, "Effects of Social Labeling on Giving to Charity," *Journal of Experimental Social Psychology* 9 (1973): 551–562.

7. Kenneth Erickson, *The Power of Praise* (St. Louis, Missouri: Concordia, 1984), p. 56.

8. R. L. Miller, P. Brickman, and D. Bolen, "Attribution vs. Persuasion as a Means for Modifying Behavior," *Journal of Personality and Social Psychology* (1975), 3: 430–441.

9. Roger Dawson, *The Secrets of Power Persuasion* (Englewood Cliffs, N.J.: Prentice Hall, 1992), p. 29.

10. Wilson Bryan, *The Age of Manipulation* (Lanham, Md.: Madison Books, 1989), p. 189.

11. I. Kirsch, "Specifying Non-Specifics: Psychological Mechanism of the Placebo Effect." In A. Harrington, *The Placebo Effect: An Interdisciplinary Exploration*, pp. 166–186 (Cambridge, Mass.: Harvard University Press, 1997).

12. D. J. O'Boyle, A. S. Binns, and J. J. Sumner, "On the Efficacy of Alcohol Placebos in Inducing Feelings of Intoxication," *Psychopharmacology* (Berl) (1994), 115, 1–2: 229–236.

13. Anthony G. Greenwald, Eric R. Spangenberg, Anthony R. Pratkanis, and Jay Eskenazi, "Double-Blind Tests of Subliminal Self-Help Audiotapes," *Psychological Science* (1991), 2, 2: 119–122.

14. T. J. Kaptchuk, E. Friedlander, J. M. Kelley, M. N. Sanchez, E. Kokkotou, J. P. Singer, M. Kowalczykowski, F. G. Miller, I. Kirsch, and A. J. Lembo, "Placebos Without Deception: A Randomized Controlled Trial in Irritable Bowel Syndrome," *PLoS One* (2010), 5.

15. James Montier, "Placebos, Booze, and Glamour Stocks," Societa Generale Cross Asset Research, March 10, 2008. Available at http://www.designs.valueinvestorinsight.com/bonus/bonuscontent/docs/Montier_Cheapness_Bias.pdf

16. R. L. Waber, B. Shiv, and D. Ariely, "Commercial Features of Placebo and Therapeutic Efficacy," *Journal of the American Medical Association* (2008), 299, 9: 1016–1017.

17. Hilke Plassmann, John O'Doherty, Baba Shiv, and Antonio Rangel, "Marketing Actions Can Modulate Neural Representations of Experienced Pleasantness," *Proceedings of the National Academy of Sciences of the United States of America* (2008), 105, 3: 1050–1054.

18. "How Embedded Commands Influence Reader Awareness," Bintang. Available at http://bintang-n.blogspot.com/2010/08/how-embedded-commands.html. According to Johnson (1988), embedded commands can reinforce potential behavior and help.

19. Kenrick Cleveland, "How Embedded Commands Influence Reader Awareness," February 3, 2011. Available at http://www.aladdinelston.com/embedded-commands-influence-awareness/

20. Milton Erickson, Ernest Rossi, and Sheila Rossi, *Hypnotic Realities* (New York: Irvington Publishers, 1976).

21. Milton Erickson and Ernest Rossi, *Hypnotherapy: An Exploratory Casebook* (New York: Irvington, 1979).

22. C. A. Mace, *Incentives: Some Experimental Studies* (London: Industrial Health Research Board, Report No. 72, 1935).

23. D. Pratt, *Curriculum Design and Development* (New York: Harcourt Brace Jovanovich, 1980).

24. Mortimer R. Feinberg, *Effective Psychology for Managers* (Englewood Cliffs, N.J., 1986).

25. G. P. Latham, E. A. Locke, and N. E. Fassina, "The High Performance Cycle: Standing the Test of Time." In S. Sonnentag (Ed.), *The Psychological Management of Individual Performance: A Handbook in the Psychology of Management in Organizations*, pp. 201–228 (Chichester, United Kingdom: Wiley, 2002).

26. Ad Kleingeld, Heleen van Mierlo, and Lidia Arends, "The Effect of Goal Setting on Group Performance: A Meta-Analysis," *Journal of Applied Psychology* (2011), 96, 6: 1289–1304.

27. George Kelling and Catherine Coles, *Fixing Broken Windows* (New York: Touchstone, 1996).

28. Raj Raghunathan, "When the Going Gets Tough, the Atheists Go Praying: Atheism Is a Luxury of the Well-to-Do and the Comfortable," *Sapient Nature*, April 5, 2011.

29. Malcolm Gladwell, *The Tipping Point* (New York: Little Brown, 2000), p. 142.

30. P. Zimbardo, C. Banks, and C. Haney, "Interpersonal Dynamics in a Simulated Prison," *International Journal of Criminology and Penology* (1973): 73.

CHAPTER 12

1. J. M. Burger, "Increasing Compliance by Improving the Deal: The That's-Not-All Technique," *Journal of Personality and Social Psychology* (1986): 277–283.

2. D. J. O'Keefe and M. Figge, "A Guilt-Based Explanation of the Door-in-the-Face Influence Strategy," *Human Communication Research* (1997), 24: 64–81.

3. J. Dillard, J. Hunter, and M. Burgoon, "Sequential-Request Persuasive Strategies: Meta-Analysis of Foot-in-the-Door and Door-in-the-Face," *Human Communication Research* (1984), 10: 461–488.

4. Robert M. Schindler and Thomas Kibarian, "Increased Consumer Sales Response Through Use of 99 Ending Prices," *Journal of Retailing* (1993), 72, 2: 187–199.

5. Robert M. Schindler and Lori S. Warren, "Effect of Odd Pricing on Choice of Items on a Menu," *Advanced Consumer Research* (1988), 15: 348–353.

6. Kent B. Monroe, *Pricing: Making Profitable Decisions* (New York: McGraw-Hill, 1973).

7. Robert M. Schindler and Alan R. Wiman, "The Effect of Odd Pricing on Price Recall," *Journal of Business Research* (1989), 19, 3: 165–177.

8. Schindler and Kibarian.

9. Robert C. Blattberg and Kenneth J. Wisniewski. "How Retail Price Promotions Work: Empirical Results," University of Chicago, working paper 43, 1987.

10. D. Kenrick and S. Gutierres, "Contrast Effects in Judgments of Attractiveness: When Beauty Becomes a Social Problem," *Journal of Personality and Social Psychology* (1980): 131–140.

11. M. M. Turner, R. Tamborini, M. S. Limon, and C. Zuckerman-Hyman, Communication monographs, "The Moderators and Mediators of Door-in-the-

Face Requests: Is It a Negotiation or a Helping Experience?" *Communication Monographs* (2007), 74, 3: 333–356.

12. J. Freedman and S. Fraser, "Compliance Without Pressure: The Foot-in-the-Door Technique," *Journal of Personality and Social Psychology* (1966): 195–203.

13. John Mowen, *Consumer Behavior* (New York: Macmillan, 1993), pp. 81–84.

14. Dillard and Burgoon.

15. E. Fern, K. Monroe, and R. Avila, "Effectiveness of Multiple Requests Strategies: A Synthesis of Research Results," *Journal of Marketing Research* (1986), 23: 144–152.

CHAPTER 13

1. Sharon Brehm, Saul Kassin, and Steven Fein, *Social Psychology* (New York: Houghton Mifflin, 1999), p. 213.

2. M. Sherif, *The Psychology of Social Norms* (New York: Harper, 1936).

3. R. B. Cialdini, C. A. Kallgren, and R. R. Reno, "A Focus Theory of Normative Conduct," *Advances in Experimental Social Psychology* (1991), 24: 201–234.

4. A. Tesser, J. Campbell, and S. Mickler, "The Role of Social Pressure, Attention to the Stimulus, and Self-Doubt in Conformity," *European Journal of Social Psychology* (1983): 217–233.

5. I. Sarason, G. Sarason, E. Pierce, B. Sherin, and M. Sayers, "A Social Learning Approach to Increasing Blood Donations," *Journal of Applied Social Psychology* (1991): 21.

6. S. Asch, "Forming Impression of Personality," *Journal of Abnormal and Social Psychology* (1946): 258–290.

7. R. Fuller and A. Sheehy-Skeffington, "Effects of Group Laughter on Responses to Humorous Materials: A Replication and Extension," *Psychological Reports* (1974): 531–534.

8. T. Nosanchuk and J. Lightstone, "Canned Laughter and Public and Private Conformity," *Journal of Personality and Social Psychology* (1974): 153–156.

9. S. Milgram, L. Bickman, and L. Berkowitz, "Note on the Drawing Power of Crowds of Different Size," *Journal of Personality and Social Psychology* (1969): 79–82.

10. S. Fein, G. R. Goethals, S. M. Kassin, and J. Cross, "Social Influence and Presidential Debates" (manuscript under review), American Psychological Association, Toronto, Canada (1993).

11. N. J. Goldstein, R. B. Cialdini, and V. Griskevicius, "A Room with a Viewpoint: Using Social Norms to Motivate Environmental Conservation in Hotels," *Journal of Consumer Research* (2008), 35: 472–482.

12. Douglas Rushkoff, *Coercion: Why We Listen to What They Say* (New York: Riverhead Books, 1999), p. 123.

13. M. Gansberg, "37 Who Saw Murder Didn't Call the Police," *New York Times*, March 27, 1964, p. 1.

14. B. Latané and S. Nida, "Ten Years of Research on Group Size and Helping," *Psychological Bulletin* (1981), 89: 308–324. DOI:10.1037/0033-2909.89.2.308

15. L. Festinger, A. Pepitone, and T. Newcomb, "Some Consequences of Deindividuation in a Group," *Journal of Abnormal Social Psychology* (1952): 382–389.

16. E. Diener, "Deindividuation: The Absence of Self-Awareness and Self-Regulation in Group Members." In P. B. Paulus (Ed.), *The Psychology of Group Influence* (Hillsdale, New Jersey: Erlbaum, 1980), pp. 209–242.

17. Ibid.

18. M. Cody, J. Seiter, and Y. Montague-Miller, *Men and Woman in the Marketplace: Gender Power and Communication in Human Relationships* (Hillsdale, N.J.: Erlbaum, 1995), pp. 305–329.

19. Cavett Robert, *Personal Development Course* (Englewood Cliffs, N.J.: Prentice Hall, 1966).

20. Festinger, Pepitone, and Newcomb.

21. L. Westphal, "Use Testimonials and Be More Effective," *Direct Marketing* (2000), 62: 35–37.

22. J. D. Mittelstaedt, P. C. Riesz, and W. J. Burns, "Why Are Endorsements Effective? Sorting Among Theories of Product and Endorser Effects," *Journal of Current Issues and Research in Advertising* (2000), 22: 55–65.

CHAPTER 14

1. S. Brehm and J. Brehm, *Psychological Reactance: A Theory of Freedom and Control* (New York: Academic Press, 1981).

2. F. Rhodewalt and J. Davison, "Reactance and the Coronary-Prone Behavior Pattern: The Role of Self-Attribution in Response to Reduced Behavioral Freedom," *Journal of Personality and Social Psychology* (1983): 44.

3. J. Brehm and M. Weintraub, "Physical Barriers and Psychological Reactance: Two-Year-Olds' Response to Threats to Freedom," *Journal of Personality and Social Psychology* 35 (1977): 830–836.

4. A. Tversky and D. Kahneman, "The Framing of Decisions and the Psychology of Choice," *Science* (1981): 453–458.

5. M. Gonzales, E. Aronson, and M. Costanzo, "Increasing the Effectiveness of Energy Auditors: A Field Experiment," *Journal of Applied Social Psychology* (1988): 1046–1066.

6. S. Worchel, J. Lee, and A. Adewole, "Effects of Supply and Demand on Ratings of Object Value," *Journal of Personality and Social Psychology* (1975): 906–914.

7. Adam Townsend, Eric Carpenter, and Vik Jolly, "Officials: Save Water," *Orange County Register*, March 29, 2007: A1.

8. A. Knishinsky, "The Effects of Scarcity of Material and Exclusivity of Information on Industrial Buyer Perceiver Risk in Provoking a Purchase Decision," unpublished doctoral dissertation, Arizona State University, 1982.

9. D. Broeder, "The University of Chicago Jury Project," *Nebraska Law Review* (1959): 744–760.

10. S. Worchel, S, E. Arnold, and M. Baker, "The Effect of Censorship on Attitude Change: The Influence of Censor and Communicator Characteristics," *Journal of Applied Social Psychology* (1975) 5: 222–239.

11. Gisla Grabitz-Gniech, "Some Restrictive Conditions for the Occurrence of Psychological Reactance," *Journal of Personality and Social Psychology* (1971), 19, 2: 188–196.

CHAPTER 15

1. Murray Raphel, "Listening Correctly Can Increase Your Sales," *Direct Marketing* (1982), 41, 11: 113.

2. S. B. Castleberry and C. D. Shepherd, "Effective Interpersonal Listening and Personal Selling," *Journal of Personal Selling & Sales Management* (1993), 13: 35–49.

3. Tony Alessandra, *Charisma: Seven Keys to Developing the Magnetism that Leads to Success* (Business Plus, 2000).

4. *American Salesman* (1991), 36, 8: 16(5).

5. S. S. Iyengar and M. R. Lepper, "When Choice Is Demotivating: Can One Desire Too Much of a Good Thing?" *Journal of Personality and Social Psychology* (2000), 79: 995–1005.

6. D. J. O'Keefe, *Persuasion: Theory and Research* (Newbury Park, Calif.: Sage, 1990).

7. H. Fukada, "Psychological Processes Mediating Persuasion-Inhibiting Effect of Forewarning in Fear-Arousing Communication," *Psychol Rep.* (1986), 58, 1: 87–90.

8. M. Pfau, "The Inoculation Model of Resistance to Influence." In F. J Boster and G. Barnet (Eds.), *Progress of Communication Sciences*, vol. 13, pp. 133–171 (Norwood, N.J.: Ablex, 1997).

9. W. J. McGuire, "Resistance to Persuasion Conferred by Active and Passive Prior Refutation of Same and Alternative Counterarguments," *Journal of Abnormal Psychology* (1961), 63: 326–332.

10. M. Pfau, D. Roskos-Ewoldsen, M. Wood, S. Yin, J. Cho, K.-H. Lu, and L. Shen, "Attitude Accessibility as an Alternative Explanation for How Inoculation Confers Resistance," *Communication Monographs* (2003), 70, 1: 39–51.

11. Ibid.

EPILOGUE

1. M. Bourgeois, K. Sommer, and S. Bruno, "What Do We Get Out of Influencing Others?" *Social Influence* (2009), 4, 2: 96–121.

Index

About the Author

Kurt Mortensen is one of nation's leading authorities on negotiation, charisma, and influence. Through extensive research, consumer interviews, and personal experience, Kurt has developed the most comprehensive training to master the skills and techniques necessary to maximize your influence and increase your success. Kurt has the ability for interpreting scientific studies and social psychology into practical applications. He reveals how easy it is to apply influence in every situation. Kurt shows how valuable influence can be in business, for entrepreneurs, and to increase income.

Kurt has written four books that have been translated into more than 20 languages. Kurt teaches that we all persuade for a living and that professional success and personal relationships depend on the ability to persuade, influence, and motivate. Kurt is also the author of *Laws of Charisma* and *Persuasion IQ*. He is also the creator of Millionaire Psychology, Persuasive Presentations, Power Negotiation, and Psychology of Objections.

Kurt is an extraordinary speaker and entertainer for public and corporate events. He is known to educate, inspire, and entertain audiences worldwide for nearly 20 years. He has trained audiences about sales techniques, influence triggers, advanced leadership, and persuasive presentation skills. His keynotes and seminars help companies and entrepreneurs maximize their influence. His concepts increase sales, enhance marketing, and turn managers into leaders. If your group needs a motivational speaker who is informative, inspirational, and life-changing, contact Kurt Mortensen today.